For EAL/ESL/E2L

Mathematics

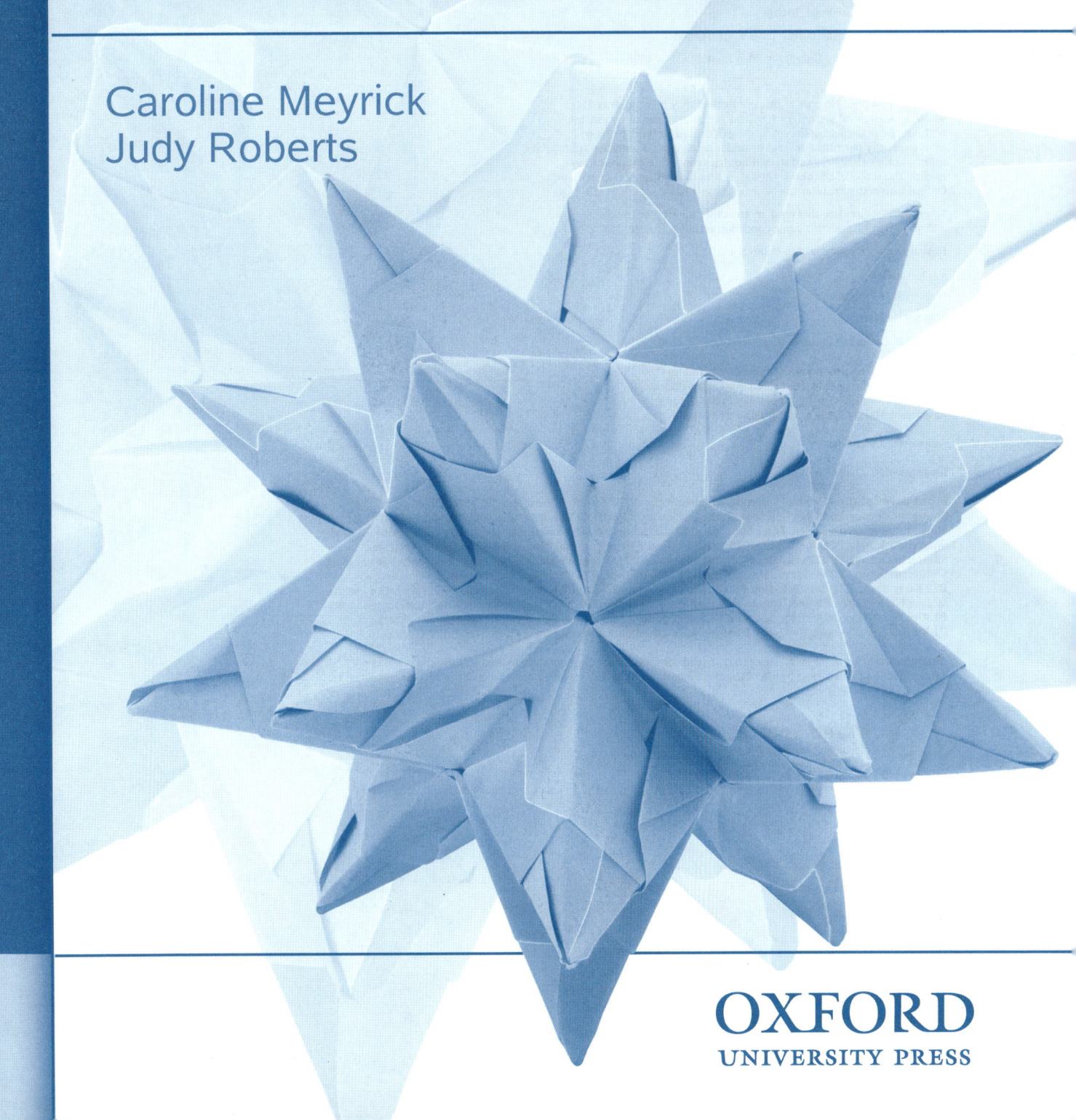

Caroline Meyrick
Judy Roberts

OXFORD CONTENT AND LANGUAGE SUPPORT

OXFORD
UNIVERSITY PRESS

OXFORD
UNIVERSITY PRESS

Great Clarendon Street, Oxford OX2 6DP

Oxford University Press is a department of the University of Oxford.
It furthers the University's objective of excellence in research, scholarship,
and education by publishing worldwide in

Oxford   New York

Auckland Cape Town Dar es Salaam Hong Kong Karachi
Kuala Lumpur Madrid Melbourne Mexico City Nairobi
New Delhi Shanghai Taipei Toronto

With offices in

Argentina Austria Brazil Chile Czech Republic France Greece
Guatemala Hungary Italy Japan South Korea Poland Portugal
Singapore Switzerland Thailand Turkey Ukraine Vietnam

Oxford is a registered trade mark of Oxford University Press
in the UK and in certain other countries

© Oxford University Press 2010

The moral rights of the author have been asserted

Database right Oxford University Press (maker)

First published 2010

All rights reserved. No part of this publication may be reproduced,
stored in a retrieval system, or transmitted, in any form or by any means,
without the prior permission in writing of Oxford University Press,
or as expressly permitted by law, or under terms agreed with the appropriate
reprographics rights organization. Enquiries concerning reproduction
outside the scope of the above should be sent to the Rights Department,
Oxford University Press, at the address above

You must not circulate this book in any other binding or cover
and you must impose this same condition on any acquirer

British Library Cataloguing in Publication Data

Data available

ISBN 9780199135295

10 9 8 7 6 5 4 3 2 1

Printed in Great Britain by Bell and Bain Ltd, Glasgow

Paper used in the production of this book is a natural,
recyclable product made from wood grown in sustainable
forests. The manufacturing process conforms to the
environmental regulations of the country of origin.

Acknowledgements

Illustrations © Garry Parsons.

Front cover photo Mateusz Papiernik/Dreamstime.com; **P5a** Oddphoto/Shutterstock.com; **P5b-c** ZTS/Shutterstock.com; **P5d** Oleg Golovnev/Shutterstock.com; **P5e** STILLFX/Shutterstock.com; **P6a** Nigel Paul Monckton/Shutterstock.com; **P6b** photo online/Shutterstock.com; **P6c** macumazahn/Shutterstock.com; **P6d** ravl/Shutterstock.com; **P7a** photo online/Shutterstock.com; **P7b** macumazahn/Shutterstock.com; **P9a** jocicalek/Shutterstock.com; **P9b** Bragin Alexey/Shutterstock.com; **P9c** Georgios Kollidas/Shutterstock.com; **P9d** Sean MacD/Shutterstock.com; **P23** Iofoto/Shutterstock.com; **P73** Rare Book & Manuscript Library/Columbia University; **P77** Barry Barnes/Shutterstock.com; **P80** The Print Collector/Alamy; **P84** Maxwell/Fotolia; **P95** Mary Evans Picture Library/Photolibrary; **P130a** Georgios Kollidas/Shutterstock.com; **P130b** Nigel Paul Monckton/Shutterstock.com; **P130c** Oleg Golovnev/Shutterstock.com; **P130d** ZTS/Shutterstock.com; **P130e** photo online/Shutterstock.com; **P130f** Oddphoto/Shutterstock.com; **P130g** macumazahn/Shutterstock.com; **P130h** ZTS/Shutterstock.com.

Although we have made every effort to trace and contact all copyright holders before publication this has not been possible in all cases. If notified, the publisher will rectify any errors or omissions at the earliest opportunity.

Mixed Sources
Product group from well-managed
forests and other controlled sources
www.fsc.org Cert no. TT-COC-002769
© 1996 Forest Stewardship Council
FSC

Contents

	About this book	4
1	Starting the course	5
2	Studying mathematics	11
3	Number	17
	Consolidation exercises	29
4	Algebra	35
	Consolidation exercises	48
5	Geometry	53
	Consolidation exercises	67
6	Pythagoras' theorem and trigonometry	72
	Consolidation exercises	81
7	Graphs	86
	Consolidation exercises	96
8	Statistics	100
	Consolidation exercises	111
9	Probability	115
	Consolidation exercises	124
10	Assessment	128
	Glossary	139
	Answers	148
	Index	158

About this book

This new series is designed with students in mind whose first language is not English. The books include content and workbook style activities, with the intention that these activities are done in the students' own notebooks. They can be used alongside regular textbooks, or outside class as independent work.

This book is not intended as a replacement for a textbook. It is not aligned to any particular course or country, just to those who are learning their mathematics in English for the first time. Much of the mathematics may be familiar, but the language and presentation will be very different to that which the student has met before.

The structure of each chapter follows the same pattern, making it easy for learners to navigate their way through each topic. Each chapter opens with some Lead In questions. The students are then guided through the material which is presented in a variety of ways to suit different learning styles. Talking points are suggested in each chapter to highlight areas where speaking and listening skills can be worked on in small groups within the subject context. By the end of each chapter the students should be able to answer the Lead In questions with confidence, knowing that they have completed a thorough revision of the topic. The chapters have been written to clarify points in mathematics and English. The exercises are short, often multi-choice, as they are meant to check the students' understanding. At the end of each chapter there are some more conventional exercises to give extra practice if the student needs it.

To facilitate the learning of key terms and concepts these are highlighted in boxes which stand outside the main body of the text. Further key vocabulary is highlighted in bold throughout each chapter. Many of the terms recur so the students have the opportunity to see how they are used in different contexts, and also to assimilate their meanings.
The extensive glossary provides an important resource for the acquisition of the terms and concepts introduced in the book, allowing students to check their understanding.

We hope you enjoy using this book.

CM and JR

1 Starting the course

In this chapter you will answer...

- What do you use to measure an angle accurately?
- What do you use a drawing compass (pair of compasses) for?
- What do you use a scientific calculator for?
- Should you draw a graph with a pen or a pencil?

1.1 Equipment used in mathematics lessons

When you start a new course or syllabus in a new language it can be difficult to understand the names of the pieces of equipment, or instruments, that you need to use.

Here is a list of useful equipment for this course. You should make sure that you have these items.

KEY WORD

Syllabus the scheme of work for your course or examinations

KEY WORD

Diagram a plan or picture drawn to help you to understand a mathematical problem

Name	What is it?	
Pencil		You should use a pencil to draw diagrams and to write down your working. HB and B pencils are good as they are clear and easy to erase.
Pencil sharpener		You should keep your pencil sharp so that your diagrams and working are easy to understand.
Rubber/eraser		Everyone makes mistakes. They are an important part of learning mathematics.
Pen		Some examinations must be completed in pen.
Highlighter		You can use a highlighter to mark key points. They can be useful when you are revising for an exam.

5

Name	What is it?	
Ruler		You can use a ruler to draw accurate lines or to measure lengths. Standard rulers are 15 cm or 30 cm long.
Protractor		You can use a protractor (semi-circle or full circle) to measure and draw angles.
Drawing compass/pair of compasses		You can use a drawing compass to draw circles or arcs of circles and to construct other shapes and angles.
Set square		You can use a set square to draw right angles or other set angles.

> **KEY WORD**
>
> **Ruler** a straight-edged tool used to measure and draw straight lines

> **KEY WORD**
>
> **Protractor** a circular or half-circular tool for measuring and drawing angles

Exercise

1 Choose from the following words to complete the sentences.

> eraser   drawing compass   set square
> ruler   protractor   pencil

a To draw a straight line, I need to use a .... and ....

b A .... is used for drawing circles.

c "Did you use a .... when you drew this graph?"

d Diagrams should be drawn in .... You can use a/an .... if you make a mistake.

e To measure an angle, I need to use a ....

f When you measure a line, you use a ....

g I measured the angle with a .... but it was not as accurate as the ....

6

1.1.1 How to use a protractor

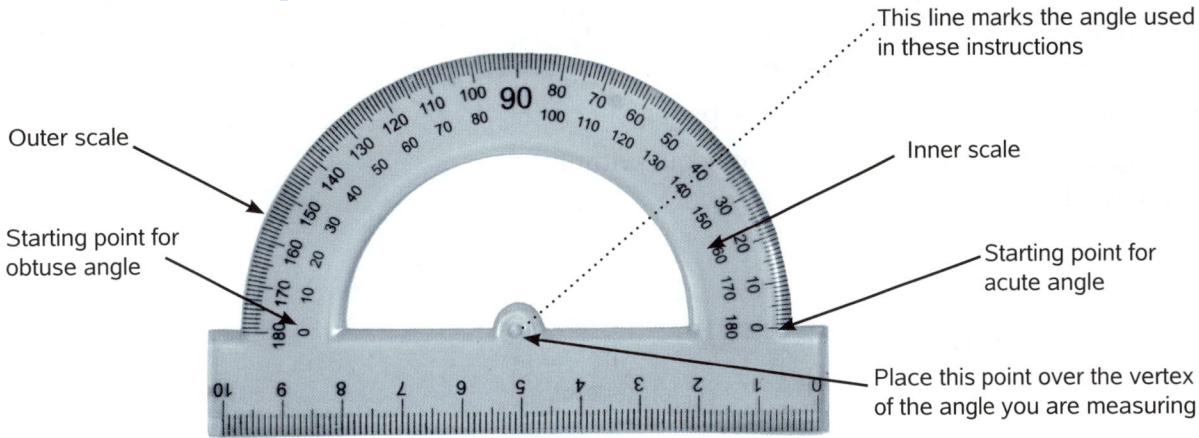

- Outer scale
- Starting point for obtuse angle
- This line marks the angle used in these instructions
- Inner scale
- Starting point for acute angle
- Place this point over the vertex of the angle you are measuring

To measure the smaller (acute) angle on this protractor:
- Look for the zero on the right hand side.
- Imagine the angle opening up, starting at the zero.
- Read the angle on the outer scale. The angle reads 40°.

To measure the larger (obtuse) angle on this protractor:
- Look for the zero on the left hand side.
- Imagine the angle opening up, starting at zero.
- Read the angle on the inner scale. The angle reads 140°.

1.1.2 How to use a drawing compass

Before you use your compass, make sure that:
- The hinge at the top of the compass is tight. A loose hinge will slip.
- The pencil is held in place tightly.
- The point of the pencil is the same length as the point on the compass.

- Hinge
- Point

To use your compass:
- Press down on the point and turn the hinge at the top of the compass to draw a circle.
- Do not hold the compass too tightly.
- Practise until you are comfortable with your compass.

Exercise

2 Are the following definitions true (T) or false (F)?

  a A protractor is used for measuring the length of a line.
  b A pair of compasses is used to draw the arc of a circle.
  c A pen is used to draw graphs.
  d The best diagrams are drawn in pencil.
  e A pencil sharpener makes your pencil blunt.

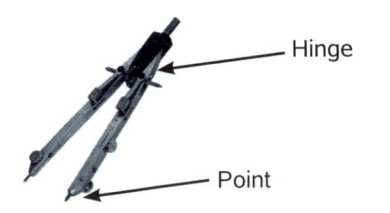

1.2 Types of books and paper used in mathematics

1.2.1 Exercise books

Books have either stapled or spiral binding.

Stapled binding means that you do not lose pages.

Spiral binding means that you can tear pages out without damaging the book.

1.2.2 Types of paper

Type	Sample	Use
5 mm squared paper		Good for general use, to draw diagrams or to write on. Write on alternate lines to make your working clearer.
8 mm lined paper		Good practice for examinations. Most exams are written on this paper.
Graph paper		You can use graph paper to draw clear and accurate graphs, with good axes and scales.
Squared 'French' paper		Good for general use to draw diagrams and write on. Easy to use.

> **KEY WORD**
>
> **Graph paper** squared paper used for drawing graphs

Starting the course ◉ 1

1.2.3 Folders and dividers

You should use a folder to:

- Keep your notes in order.
- Store extra practice materials.
- Keep your work, after your teacher has marked it.

Keeping your work organised will help you when it is time to revise.

1.3 Choosing a calculator

Ask your teacher to give you advice about the type of calculator you need.
Here are some common types of calculators used in everyday life and at school:

Type of calculator		But...
Mobile (cell) **phone** *Battery powered*		Simple sums only. No BIDMAS.
Simple calculator *Battery or solar powered*		Simple sums only. No BIDMAS. Only four operations; +, −, × and ÷. No square root key, trigonometry keys, or statistics etc.
Scientific calculator Correct order of operations, BIDMAS. Includes square root key, trigonometric operations, etc. Has a memory. *Battery or solar powered*		You will need to learn to use it efficiently. Make sure you know the most useful keys and when to use them. Choose one that shows you the complete sum that you are doing, not just the answer.
Graphical calculator Correct order of operations, BIDMAS. Draws graphs. Solves quadratic and simultaneous equations. Includes trigonometric operations, statistical tests and simple spreadsheets.		You will need to learn to use it efficiently. Make sure you know the most useful keys and when to use them. Make sure that you understand the menus and how they work.

Exercise 3 Match the beginning of each sentence with the correct ending.

1 When you draw a graph you can use either…
2 When I am shopping I can use…
3 When Jaime was six he enjoyed using…
4 A scientific calculator is useful when you…
5 Neither a cell phone nor a simple calculator…
6 When you are doing statistical problems…

a …it is useful to have either a scientific calculator or a graphical one.
b …a simple calculator to learn his sums.
c …uses the BIDMAS rules.
d …graph paper or a graphical calculator.
e …need to find the square root of a number.
f …my cell phone to add things up.

Exercise 4 Find the words listed below in the grid.

calculator	compasses	straight	edge	eraser
folder	highlighter	hinge	instrument	pen
pencil	protractor	ruler	set square	sharpener

H	C	M	U	S	E	T	M	C	C	P	R	E	X	F
O	I	T	S	R	Q	J	Z	A	B	R	E	G	I	O
S	X	G	A	E	Q	U	L	U	A	O	N	D	I	L
J	V	S	H	O	S	C	A	Y	J	T	E	E	U	D
B	E	P	W	L	U	S	W	R	J	R	P	I	C	E
R	C	Y	X	L	I	R	A	U	E	A	R	H	Z	R
C	N	I	A	D	V	G	E	P	N	C	A	X	G	A
Q	N	T	E	G	N	I	H	L	M	T	H	O	S	T
U	O	P	E	N	C	I	L	T	U	O	S	I	H	H
R	S	E	T	O	C	G	S	V	E	R	C	G	U	C
T	G	H	R	D	J	L	V	E	Z	R	I	N	Z	R
T	N	E	M	U	R	T	S	N	I	A	O	N	T	U
Z	X	B	U	F	M	Y	X	Z	R	H	E	R	N	B
R	V	G	P	A	X	V	M	T	R	P	J	I	R	I
T	I	J	M	F	U	T	S	C	C	W	O	X	C	Y

Think about the questions from the start of this chapter.
Can you answer them now?
◎ What do you use to measure an angle accurately?
◎ What do you use a drawing compass (pair of compasses) for?
◎ What do you use a scientific calculator for?
◎ Should you draw a graph with a pen or a pencil?

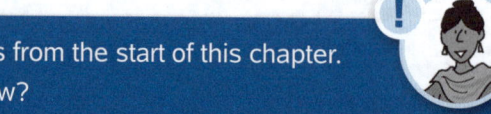

2 Studying mathematics

In this chapter you will answer...
- Have you finished the exercise?
- Did you understand the example?
- Have you brought your algebra book?
- Where is your assignment? Is it ready?

2.1 The basics of studying mathematics

Before you start your mathematics classes here are some important things to remember:

When you learn mathematics you must start at the beginning. Each new idea depends on the one before. You need to understand the basic ideas before you can learn the more difficult ones. Imagine a wall – it will collapse if a brick at the bottom is missing! You need to make sure you really understand each topic that you learn. If you need help, don't be afraid to ask your teacher questions.

It is said that 'mathematics is a universal language' and you may feel that it will be easier to understand in English than other subjects. This can be true for some parts, but you need to be aware of differences in the way some words are used. Some notation may be different too.

Language

In an English lesson, if you say "You and your brother are very similar", *similar* means that you and your brother are very alike, but not identical.

However, in a maths lesson if you say "These two triangles are similar", *similar* means that the two triangles are exactly the same shape. All the angles are the same, but the triangles are different sizes.

Decimals may be written as 52.13 or 52,13 or 52'13 or 52•13.

Intervals may be written as $3 < x < 5$ or [3,5] or]3, 5[.

You will find other examples of differences in language, depending on where you have studied before. Ask your teacher for help if you are confused.

See Chapter 5.

2.2 Studying mathematics in class

Here are some important ideas that will make it easier.

In the lesson:

- Sit next to a friend who you work well with.
- Use a mathematical dictionary.
- Write down any words you do not understand in a notebook.
- Check the Glossary at the back of this book. Translate the words into your first language.
- Copy the examples so that you can study them later.
- Remember that you may have been taught a different method in your previous school.
- Raise your hand and ask questions if you do not understand.
- Don't be scared of being wrong. Learn from your mistakes!
- Make sure that you show all the working in your answers. This helps your teacher to understand how you are thinking and give you more help when you make a mistake.

At the end of the lesson:

- Ask about any words that you didn't understand.
- Prepare for your next lesson. Ask your teacher what you will be studying. Look at your textbook and check any words that you do not know.

KEY WORD

Study learn

KEY WORD

Preparation work done before a lesson

Exercise

1 Draw a line through the odd one out in each list.
   The first one has been done for you.

   a start   begin   commence   ~~finish~~
   b completed   begun   finished   reached the end
   c test   task   homework   preparation
   d assignment   examination   project   coursework
   e correct   wrong   right   true
   f inaccurate   exact   particular   precise
   g teacher   student   pupil   learner
   h understand   comprehend   know   misunderstand
   i centre   middle   central point end
   j the same as   equals   identical   different

The odd one out means the one that is different.

Your teacher may use the word 'work' in different ways.

	It means….
Work out…	Find out by calculation.
Work on…	Give this topic extra study or attention.
Work through…	Follow a logical series of steps to solve a problem.
Working (out)	The steps you use to solve a problem.

KEY WORDS

Exercise a set of practice questions

Assignment a piece of work for you to do on your own

Homework work done after a lesson, usually corrected by your teacher

Working written calculations and equations to show how you have solved a problem

Studying mathematics 2

Exercise 2 Complete the sentences using the words listed:

| work out | work through | work on | working |

a What is $5\frac{1}{3} \div \frac{4}{15}$? Can you _____ the answer?
b In today's lesson, we are going to _____ statistics.
c In mental arithmetic, you _____ the answer in your head.
d When you do an algebra problem, you should show all your _____.

Practise saying these sentences to a friend. Can you think of some more examples?

2.3 Studying mathematics on your own

Mathematics is a skill as well as a school subject.

When you are learning a language or a musical instrument, practice is important. It is just as important when you are learning and understanding mathematics.

Find some time each day to practise and work through examples.

After your class:

◎ Look at the examples you were given in class, and make sure that you understand them.
◎ Work with a friend or a group of friends. Explaining an idea to someone else helps you understand it more clearly.
◎ Read your notebook and look in a dictionary to find the words that you did not understand.
◎ Complete your assignments as soon as possible. You will remember your teacher's explanations better.
◎ If you do not understand, ask your teacher for help.

KEY WORD

Example a problem that has been worked out for you

You cannot learn mathematics just by reading it – you have to do it yourself!

Exercise 3 Match each question to the correct answer.

1 When is the best time to look at the work you completed in class?
2 What should you do if you miss a class?
3 What should you do if you cannot understand the work that you have been given?
4 If you need extra explanations or diagrams where can you look?
5 If there are some words that you do not understand, what can you do?
6 Why should you always write down all the calculations that you have done?
7 Why is it a good idea to work with a friend?

a Ask for help.
b On the internet.
c As soon as you can.
d Look in a mathematical dictionary.
e Your teacher needs to be able to read all your work so s/he can help you.
f Explaining a new idea to someone else helps you to understand it better.
g Copy the work that you have missed.

13

2.4 Using a mathematics textbook

When you read most schoolbooks you can read them quite quickly, and you can sometimes understand new words by their position in the sentence. New ideas are explained in words and pictures.

You need to read a mathematics book in a different way because it explains ideas using numbers or diagrams, and examples as well as words.

You will understand better if you:

- Read slowly.
- Read each section several times.
- Use a notebook and write down any questions that you want to ask your teacher.
- Use a mathematics dictionary to check new words.
- If you need more help, find another book with more examples or an Internet site that explains the subject more clearly.
- Work through the examples as well as reading them. A good way to learn is to:
  - Read the problem.
  - Cover up the solution in the book.
  - Work out the answer by yourself.
  - Check your solution by looking in the book.

Exercise

4 Decode this message.

This is a reminder of the best way to study maths on your own:

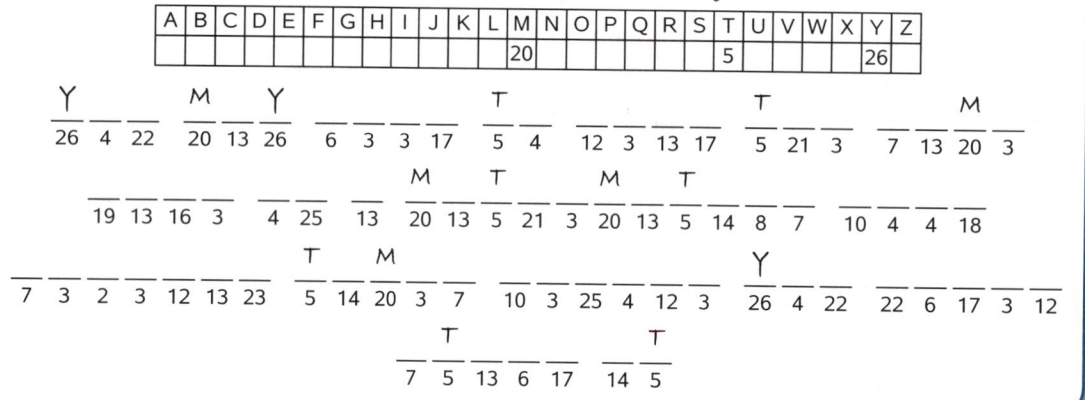

A	B	C	D	E	F	G	H	I	J	K	L	M	N	O	P	Q	R	S	T	U	V	W	X	Y	Z
												20						5						26	

Decoded message: **YOU MAY NEED TO READ THE SAME PAGE OF A MATHEMATICS BOOK SEVERAL TIMES BEFORE YOU UNDERSTAND IT**

2.5 How to keep organised

Keeping organised can make it easier to learn.

Here are some ideas of how to keep organised:

- Draw a plan for your timetable and put it on the wall where you can see it easily.
- Keep a diary, personal organiser or planner. Write down:
  - **When** you are given work or assignments.
  - **When** you need to return the assignment to your teacher.
- Keep your work for each subject organised in folders. Use dividers to separate the work into sections. This way you can separate your notes, your completed work, and work that has been marked and returned to you.
- If you use exercise books, keep the completed ones. Write the topics on the outside and you will be able to review your work when you prepare for a test or examination.
- **Keep everything tidy!**

Studying mathematics 2

Exercise

5 Look carefully at this timetable and answer the following questions:

	Lesson 1	Lesson 2	Lesson 3	Lesson 4	Lesson 5
Monday October 14th	Maths Hand in work from Wed, Oct 9th	Geography	History Essay on Genghis Khan for Thursday	Spanish	Science Read chapter 6 by Friday
Tuesday October 15th	Science	ICT	English Hand in essay on Jane Austen	Maths Exercise 5, page 36 set for Thursday	Spanish Learn new words from page 125

a When was the Maths homework set?
b Who is the subject of the English essay?
c Which page has the new Spanish words for you to learn?
d What is the third lesson on Monday?
e Why must you print off your spreadsheet on Monday?

> Some schools give each pupil a planner to help them organise their work.

Talking points

Draw your own timetable for your week.
Practise asking your classmate questions about their timetable.

2.6 Notation

Lines	A dotted line	....
	A dashed or broken line	– – – – – – –
	A solid line	───────
Brackets	Square brackets	[ ]
	Curly brackets	{ }
Equality/inequality signs	Less than	<
	Greater than	>
	Less than or equals	≤
	Greater than or equals to	≥
	Not equal to	≠
	Approximately equal to	≈

15

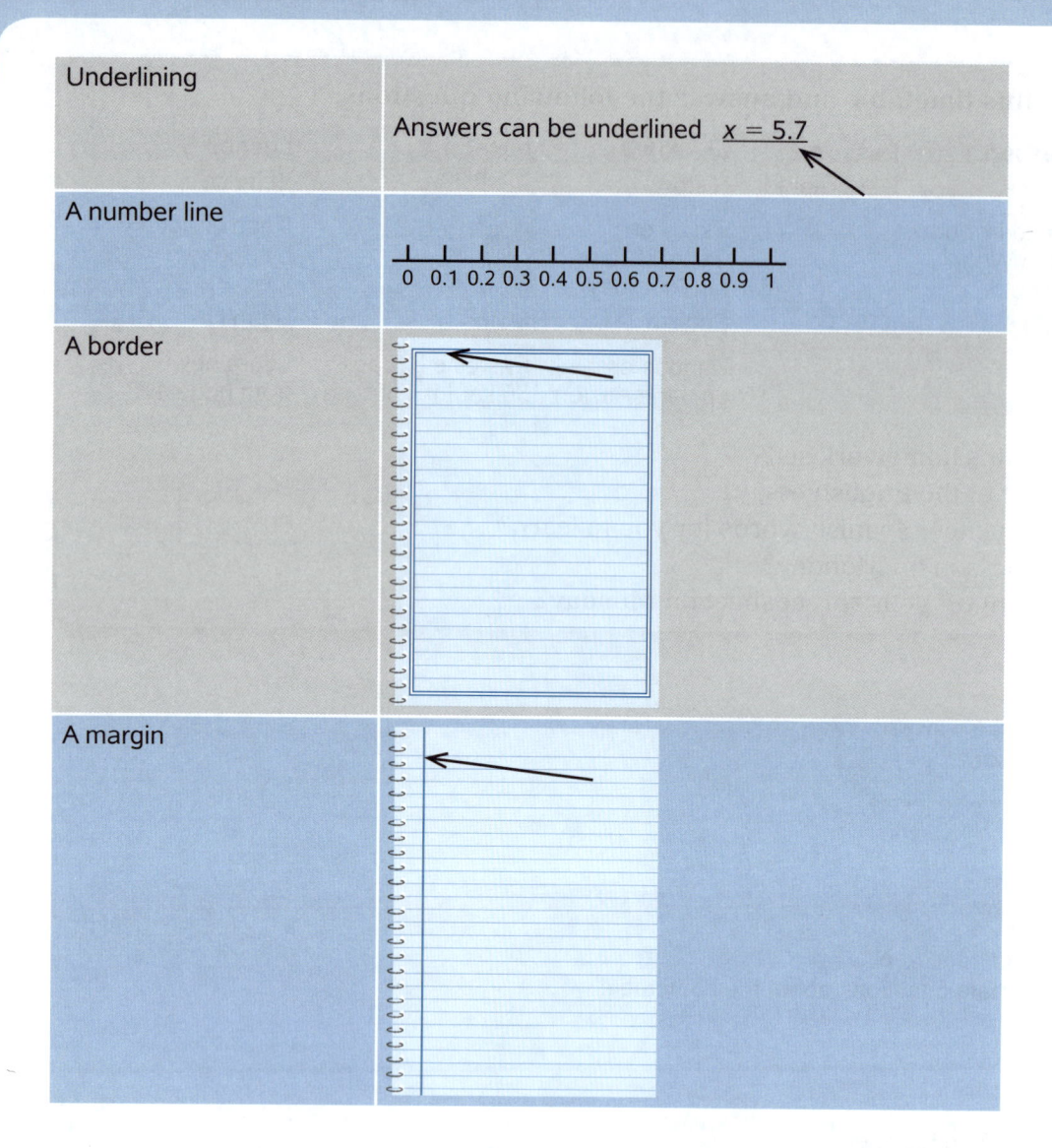

Underlining	Answers can be underlined x = 5.7
A number line	0 0.1 0.2 0.3 0.4 0.5 0.6 0.7 0.8 0.9 1
A border	
A margin	

Think about the questions from the start of this chapter.
Do you understand them now?
- Have you finished the exercise?
- Did you understand the example?.
- Have you brought your algebra book?
- Where is your assignment? Is it ready?

3 Number

In this chapter you will answer...
- Three children share two pizzas. What fraction does each child eat?
- Is −3 an integer?
- What is 10% of $59.00?
- Can you give me a multiple of 7?

3.1 Number sets

-10 -9 -8 -7 -6 -5 -4 -3 -2 -1 0 1 2 3 4 5 6 7 8 9 10

The first numbers that people used were the **counting numbers**: 0, 1, 2, 3, 4, 5, 6, …
Zero has a very special place among these numbers, as it behaves differently.
Some people do not put zero in the counting numbers.

As people used numbers more, **integers** came into use. Integers are whole numbers and include negative numbers for debts, temperature and many other ideas:
… −4, −3, −2, −1, 0, 1, 2, 3, 4, 5 …

Then people started to share, and not all the sums worked out exactly, so **rational numbers** were used. These are also called fractions.

Example

$\frac{1}{2}, \frac{5}{8}, \frac{599}{600}, \ldots$

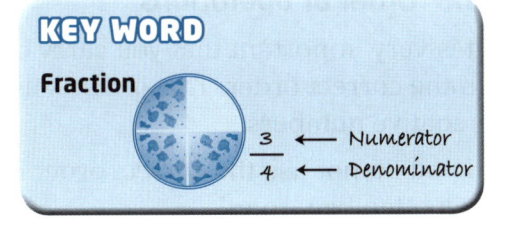

KEY WORD

Fraction

$\frac{3}{4}$ ← Numerator
← Denominator

Talking points

Work with a friend and discuss which type of number you would use:

a to work out your share of something
b when you are working with a calculator
c to add up the number of sweets you have left
d to measure temperature.

3.2 Operations

The four most basic operations in mathematics are:

1 **Add (+)** Other words used are plus, total, the sum of, adding, …

2 **Subtract (−)** Other words used are minus, subtract, take away, difference, deduct, lose, …

3 **Multiply (×)** Other words used are times, product, double, …

4 **Divide (÷)** Other words used are share, halve, equal shares, …

17

Exercise 1 Match each written question to the arithmetic.

Arithmetic	Question
1 $5 + 12 = 17$	a If you share twelve small pizzas between five people, how much pizza does each person get?
2 $12 \div 5 = 2.4$	b If you have twelve Euros and you lose five, how much money do you have left?
3 $5 \times 12 = 60$	c Ali is five years old and Simon is twelve years old. What is the sum of their ages?
4 $12 - 5 = 7$	d In a class of twelve, each person has five pencils. How many pencils are there in total?

Exercise 2 Are the answers to these questions true (T) or false (F)?

Question
a Sam is asked to add twelve and seventeen and then double the answer. She says the answer is fifty-six.
b The product of 12×8 is 96
c I think of a number, add six, halve the total, and get the answer twelve. The number I thought of was twenty.
d The difference between twice eight and three times five is one.

3.3 Order of operations

It is very important that you carry out numerical operations in the correct order. This order is used for both positive and negative numbers.

If you do not use the correct order of operations, the answer will often be wrong!

It helps to remember **B I D M A S**:

Brackets are worked out first
Indices are next
Division
Multiplication
Addition
Subtraction

Be careful:
Simple calculators may not follow BIDMAS, but scientific and graphical calculators are programmed to follow it.

Examples:
1 $3 \times 4 + 5 \times 6 = 12 + 30 = 42$
   Not $3 \times 4 + 5 \times 6 = 12 + 5 \times 6 = 17 \times 6 = 102$
2 $(5 - 12) \times (4 + 1) = -7 \times 5 = -35$
3 $(3^2 - 6)^3 = (9 - 6)^3 = 3^3 = 27$

Exercise 3 Try these without a calculator:

1 $5 \times 6 - 3 \times 4 =$
   a 60   b 108   c 18   d 360

2 $(16 + 9) \div 5 + 3 =$
   a $3\frac{1}{8}$ b 8   c 20.8   d $5\frac{3}{5}$

3 $-2 \times 12 \div 3 \times 4 =$
   a -32 b -2 c -16 d -23

4 $(3 + 3 \times 5)^3 =$
   a 54   b 27000   c 5832   d 3375

3.4 Prime numbers, factors, and multiples

If a whole number divides exactly into another, it is a **factor** of that number.

$12 = 1 \times 12$
$12 = 2 \times 6$
$12 = 3 \times 4$

Example

1, 2, 3, 4, 6, and 12 are all **factors** of 12.

If a number can divide exactly into a second number, the second number is called a **multiple**.

The multiples of 3 are 3, 6, 9, 12, 15, … these are all the numbers in the three times table.

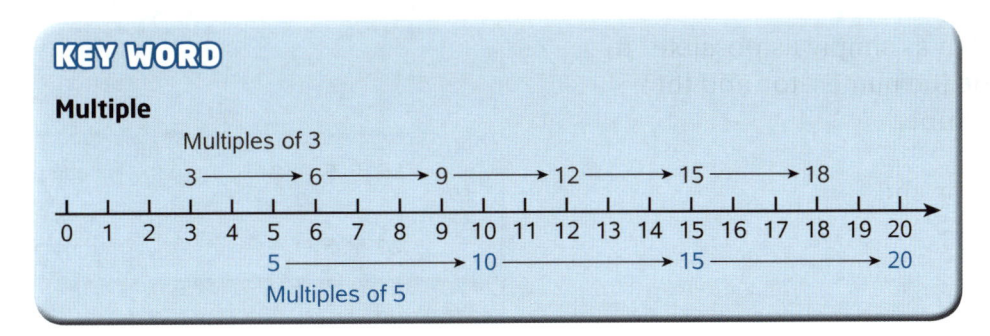

KEY WORD
Multiple

Multiples of 3: 3 → 6 → 9 → 12 → 15 → 18

Multiples of 5: 5 → 10 → 15 → 20

A **prime number** is a number whose only factors are 1 and itself.

Examples

$13 = 13 \times 1$ only   so 13 is a prime number
$12 = 3 \times 4$ or 6×2 or 12×1 so 12 is not a prime number

1 is not a prime number. It is the building block of other numbers and has only one factor – itself.

The first prime numbers are 2, 3, 5, 7, 11, 13, 17, 19, 23, 29, 31, …

Prime factors are the factors of a larger number that are also prime numbers.

Example

You can write 48 as the product of prime factors:

$48 = 2 \times 24$
$ = 2 \times 2 \times 12$
$ = 2 \times 2 \times 2 \times 6$
$ = 2 \times 2 \times 2 \times 2 \times 3$

So, $48 = 2 \times 2 \times 2 \times 2 \times 3$

2	48
2	24
2	12
2	6
3	3
	1

Exercise

4 Work out the following calculations:

1 Which number has the prime factors 2, 3 and 5?
  a 120   b 90   c 160   d 270

2 Look at the following list of numbers:
  1, 2, 5, 9, 18, 31, 49, 120
  a Which of these numbers are prime?
  b Which of these numbers are multiples of three?
  c Which of these numbers are factors of 120?

3 Which number is not a prime factor of 2310?
  a 2   b 5   c 13   d 10

4 Choose one of the following names to complete each of these sentences:

prime number	multiple	factor
square	prime factor	

a The answer to 35 ÷ 7 is a ……………….. .
b 121 is a ……………………………….. .
c 45 is a …………………………… of 9.
d 11 is one of the …………….…… s of 132.
e The ……………….s of 28 are 1, 2, 4, 7, 14, and 28.

3.5 Fractions

A fraction is part of a whole, usually written in two parts. The top part is called the **numerator**, and the bottom part is called the **denominator**.

Example

In the fraction $\frac{3}{5}$ 3 is the numerator
5 is the denominator.

$\frac{3}{5}$ means the same as "three divided by five" or 3 ÷ 5.

Fractions are normally written as simply as possible. To simplify a fraction you divide the numerator and the denominator by the same number.

$\frac{\overset{3}{\cancel{15}}}{\underset{4}{\cancel{20}}} = \frac{3}{4}$ Divide numerator and denominator by 5

$\frac{15}{20} \overset{15 \div 5 = 3}{\underset{20 \div 5 = 4}{=}} \frac{3}{4}$

$\frac{\overset{17}{\cancel{102}}}{\underset{20}{\cancel{120}}} = \frac{17}{20}$ Divide numerator and denominator by 6

$\frac{102}{120} \overset{102 \div 6 = 17}{\underset{120 \div 6 = 20}{=}} \frac{17}{20}$

$\frac{15}{20} = \frac{3}{4}$ and $\frac{102}{120} = \frac{17}{20}$

Mixed numbers have two parts, a whole number and a fraction.

$3\frac{3}{4}$ or $11\frac{2}{5}$

In **improper fractions**, the numerator is larger than the denominator. You can write an improper fraction as a mixed number.

$\frac{15}{2} = 7\frac{1}{2}$ and $\frac{27}{4} = 6\frac{3}{4}$

Fractions can be written as decimals. To change a fraction to a decimal you divide the numerator by the denominator.

$\frac{3}{5} = 3 \div 5 = 0.6$

Exercise

5 Answer these questions.

1 Look at these numbers:
$\frac{15}{30}, \frac{13}{52}, \frac{13}{4}, 2\frac{7}{8}, \frac{98}{99}, 4\frac{5}{7}, \frac{580}{579}$

  a Which of these numbers are mixed numbers?
  b Which of these numbers are improper fractions?
  c Which of these numbers can be simplified?

2 60 ÷ 90 =
  a $\frac{2}{3}$ **b** $\frac{5}{6}$ **c** $\frac{120}{180}$

3 $1\frac{7}{8}$ can also be written as
  a $\frac{15}{8}$ **b** 2.125   **c** 1.875

3.6 Percentages

Percentages are fractions with a denominator of 100.

Example

65% can also be written as $\frac{65}{100}$.

$50\% = \frac{50}{100}$ "/" means divide or divided by

$= 50/100 = 50\%$

Percentages are used to simplify and compare quantities.

Is a mark of 32/40 for History better than a mark of 63/75 for Physics?

$\frac{32}{40} = \frac{80}{100} = 80\%$ and $\frac{63}{75} = \frac{84}{100} = 84\%$

So the Physics mark is better.

Another way of working this out is to multiply the fraction by 100:

$\frac{32}{40} \times 100 = 80\%$ and $\frac{63}{75} \times 100 = 84\%$

> Remember that **per** means **divide** and **cent** means **one hundred**.

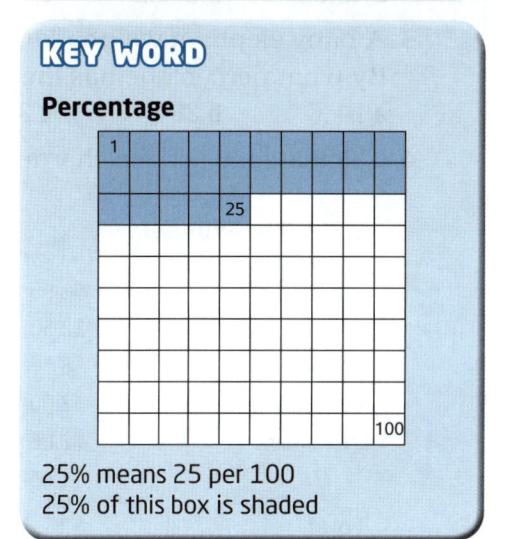

KEY WORD

Percentage

25% means 25 per 100
25% of this box is shaded

Example

◎ To **increase** an amount by a percentage, there are two methods.

You can increase a price of 140€ by 5% as shown.

Add 5% of 140€ to 140€:

5% of 140€ = $\frac{5}{100} \times 140 = 7$€,

140€ + 7€ = 147€

or

Calculate 105% of 140€

(since 100% + 5% = 105%):

105% of 140€ = $\frac{105}{100} \times 140 = 147$€

◎ You can **decrease** an amount by a percentage using similar methods.

You can decrease a weight of 85 kg by 12% as shown.

12% of 85 kg = $\frac{12}{100} \times 85 = 10.2$ kg,

85 − 10.2 = 74.8 kg

or

Calculate 88% of 85 kg

(since 100% − 12% = 88%):

88% of 85 kg = $\frac{88}{100} \times 85 = 74.8$ kg

◎ You can calculate the percentage decrease or increase, if you are given two values.

Eva buys a motorcycle for $600 and sells it for $480. What is her percentage loss?

$600 − $480 = $120

Percentage decrease is $\frac{120}{600} \times 100 = 20\%$ decrease

> Remember:
> $\frac{\text{difference in quantities}}{\text{original quantity}} \times 100$

6 Use percentages to answer these questions.

1 30 km is increased by 6%. What is the result?
  a 500 km   b 31.8 km   c 28.2 km   d 180 km

2 The cost of a shirt is 54 AUD. The cost is reduced by 8%. What is the new cost?
  a 49.68   b 58.32   c 43.2   d 675

3 A baby elephant weighs 110 kg when it is born. Two months later it weighs 136.4 kg. By what percentage has the weight increased?
  a 24%   b 28%   c 36.4%   d 26.4%

4 Calculate the service charge on this restaurant bill:

```
         The White Horse
=====================================
 1 pizza               $6.95
 1 green salad         $2.50
 Casserole of lamb     $8.50
 Vegetables            $2.00
 2 desserts            $2.85
                       $2.85
 -----------           ---------
 Total                 $25.65
=====================================
 15% service charge
```

  a $3.85   b $17.10   c $3.84   d $2.57

Talking points

Try to find three examples of percentages in your local newspaper. Work out three mathematics questions to ask about each of these examples. Then give the examples to your friend and practise asking them the questions.

7 All life on earth needs water, but water is not unlimited. Complete each of these sentences with the correct number. Choose the numbers from the box.

a Water covers about ……. of the Earth's surface, but most of it is too salty to use.

b Of what is left, about …… is in remote areas, and much of that arrives at the wrong time and in the wrong place, as monsoons and floods.

c Humans can use less than ……. of all the Earth's water.

d We use about ……. of the water we have in farming.

e The World Water Council believes that by 2020 we shall need ……. more water than is available if we are to feed the world.

f Only …….. of the world's water is not salty, and two-thirds of that is frozen.

| 0.08% | 66% | 70% | 2.5% | 17% | 20% |

22

3.7 Ratio and proportion

A **ratio** compares quantities using simple numbers.

Example

If concrete is made from water and cement in the ratio 1:4, then the weight of cement is four times greater than the weight of water.

Concrete	Water	Cement
Ratio	1	4
Proportions	1 kg	4 kg

KEY WORD

Ratio

The ratio of girls to boys is 3:1

a To calculate the weight of water for 20 kg of cement,
   $20 \times \frac{1}{4}$ = 5 kg of water

b To make 100 kg of concrete, how much cement will you need?

   1 + 4 = 5 parts in total   *Add the two parts of the ratio.*

   100 ÷ 5 = 20 kg   *Each part weighs 20 kg.*

   4 × 20 = 80 kg cement   *4 parts of cement are needed.*

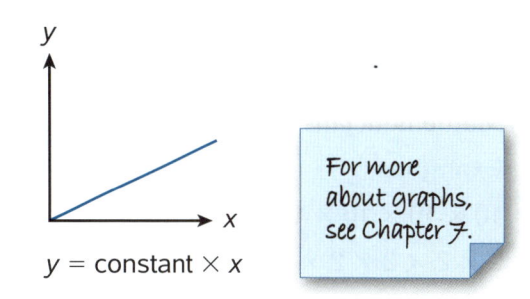

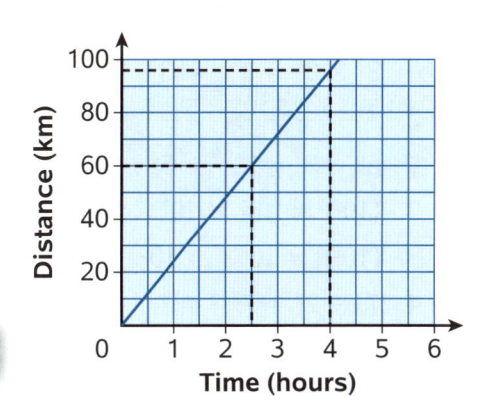

Two quantities are in **proportion** – or proportional – if they change in such a way that one of the quantities is a constant multiple of the other.

Example

The faster I walk, the further I go.
The more petrol I buy, the more it costs.

Direct proportion, also called **direct variation** or **varying directly**, follows the rule that $y = $ constant value $\times x$.

The graph will be a straight line, starting at (0, 0).

$y = $ constant $\times x$

For more about graphs, see Chapter 7.

Example

A journey of 60 km takes $2\frac{1}{2}$ hours. At the same speed, how far could you go in 4 hours?

$2\frac{1}{2}$ hours for 60 km
1 hour for   60 ÷ 2.5 = 24 km
     4 hours: 4 × 24 = 96 km

or

Distance = constant × hours
    60 = c × $2\frac{1}{2}$ *Divide 60 by 2.5*
    24 = c
    D = 24 × 4 = 96 km

8 Answer these proportion questions:

1. For pink paint, mix red paint and white paint in the ratio 1:4. How many cans of red paint do you need to mix with three cans of white paint?
   a $\frac{3}{4}$ can   **b** $\frac{4}{3}$ can   **c** 12 cans   **d** 5 cans

2. For orange paint, mix yellow and red paint in the ratio 2:3. How many litres of red paint will you need for a total 15 litres of orange paint?
   a 5 litres   **b** 9 litres   **c** 6 litres   **d** 8 litres

3. In a storm, 56 cm of water fell in eight hours. How much rain fell in two and a half hours?
   a 20 cm   **b** 14 cm   **c** 18 cm   **d** 17.5 cm

4. A bus uses 35 litres of fuel to travel 126 km. How much fuel will it need to travel 450 km?
   a 125 litres   **b** 1620 litres   **c** 324 litres   **d** 75 litres

3.8 Powers and indices

The words index, power and exponent have exact mathematical meanings that are not the same as their meanings in everyday life.

- An **index** is the superscript number in $3^2 = 3 \times 3 = 9$.
- **Indices** is the plural of index.
- **Power** is also used. For example, "3 raised to the power of 2" is the same as 3^2.
- **Exponent** may also be used instead of the words index or power.

Mathematicians like to write big numbers as simply as possible.

Examples

$10 \times 10 \times 10 \times 10 \times 10 \times 10 = 10^6 = 1\,000\,000 = 1$ million

$2 \times 2 \times 2 \times 2 \times 2 = 2^5 = 32$

The **rules of indices** are the mathematical rules of using numbers with powers or exponents.

Rule 1 $(3 \times 3 \times 3) \times (3 \times 3 \times 3 \times 3) = 3^7$
or $3^3 \times 3^4 = 3^{3+4} = 3^7$

Rule 2 $\frac{5 \times 5 \times 5 \times 5 \times 5 \times 5}{5 \times 5} = 5^4$
or $5^6 \div 5^2 = 5^{6-2} = 5^4$

Rule 3 $(10^2)^3 = 10^2 \times 10^2 \times 10^2 = 10^6$
or $(10^2)^3 = 10^{2 \times 3} = 10^6$

Rule 4 $7^2 \div 7^2 = 7^{2-2} = 7^0$
but $7^2 \div 7^2 = 1$

So, any number to the power zero is equal to one.

Example

$10^0 = 1, 5^0 = 1, 123^0 = 1, -8^0 = 1$

You can carry out index, or power, calculations on a calculator. The key will be marked y^x or x^y or $\wedge$

$\sqrt{49} = 7$
$7^2 = 49$

3 is called the base, 2 is the index

A **square number** is a number with index 2.
$1^2 = 1, 2^2 = 4, 3^2 = 9, ...$

A **cubic number** is a number with index 3.
$1^3 = 1, 2^3 = 8, 3^3 = 27, ...$

When two numbers with the **same** base are **multiplied** together, you **add** the indices.

When two numbers with the **same** base are **divided**, you **subtract** the indices.

When a number with an index is raised to another index, you **multiply** the indices.

A number divided by itself equals 1.

Number ● 3

Exercise

9 Calculate:

1. $5^3 \div 5^6 =$
   - **a** 5^3
   - **b** $5^{\frac{1}{2}}$
   - **c** 5^2
   - **d** 5^{-3}

2. $10^2 \times 10^8 =$
   - **a** 10^{10}
   - **b** 10^{-6}
   - **c** 10^{18}

3. $(7^2)^4 =$
   - **a** 49^2
   - **b** 7^6
   - **c** 7^2
   - **d** 7^8

4. $(13^0)^8 =$
   - **a** 1
   - **b** 13^8
   - **c** 8
   - **d** 13

3.9 Accuracy

You often need to simplify numbers, especially after using a calculator. You can do this by **rounding** to a given number of **decimal places** or to a given number of **significant figures**.

Decimal places

When you round to a given number of decimal places, you use the decimal point as reference.

Examples

a Write 54.687 correct to one decimal place.

54.687 → 54.7 (1 d.p.)	54.6∣87 → 54.7	6 → 7 because 8 > 5

b Write 3.14159 correct to two decimal places.

3.14159 → 3.14 (2 d.p.)	3.14∣159 → 3.14	4 is not changed, because 1 < 5

Significant figures

When you are rounding to a given number of significant figures, it is important not to change the size of the number.
i.e. Millions must remain millions, tenths must stay as tenths, etc.

Examples

a Write 65 432 correct to three significant figures (3 s.f.).

65 432 → 65 400	65 432 → 65 400	3 < 5, and 65 400 is closer to 65 432 than 65 500

b Write 0.00007658 correct to two significant figures (2 s.f.).

0.00007658 → 0.000077	0.00007658 → 0.000077	5 follows 6, and changes that number only

25

Standard form

Very large numbers, or very small ones, can be easier to understand when written in standard form. It is also easier to compare numbers if you write them in standard form.

Examples

a Write 782 000 in standard form.

| 782 000 = 7.82 × 100 000
= 7.82 × 10^5 | 782 000. = 7.82 × 100 000
= 7.82 × 10^5 | $6.321 × 10^5$ is entered as 6.321 EXP 5 or 6.321 EE 5
or
$6.321 × 10^5$ is entered as
6.321 EXP 5
or 6.321 EE 5

The key sequence depends on the type of calculator |

b Write 0.000521 in standard form.

| 0.000521 = 5.21 ÷ 10 000
= 5.21 × 10^{-4} | 0.000 521. = 5.21 ÷ 10000
= 5.21 × 10^{-4} | $4.98 × 10^{-3}$ is entered as 4.98 EXP−3 or 4.98 EE −3
or
$4.98 × 10^{-3}$ is entered as
4.98 EXP − 3
or 4.98 EE − 3 |

Exercise

10 Calculate:

1 54.6874 to 2 decimal places is
   a 54.79   b 54.69   c 54.68   d 54.70

2 0.042189 to 4 decimal places is
   a 0.04219   b 0.0422   c 0.00432   d 0.042

3 1 258 300 to 3 significant figures is
   a 126   b 1 250 000 c 300   d 1 260 000

4 0.000029815 to 2 significant figures is
   a 0.000030 b 0.00   c 0.00003   d 0.000029

5 $9.83 × 10^4$ as an ordinary number is
   a 9830   b 98300   c 9830000   d 98.3 × 1000

6 In standard form the number 0.00000608 is
   a $6.08 × 10^{-5}$ b $608 × 10^{-8}$ c $6.08 × 10^{-6}$ d $60.8 × 10^{-7}$

Number 3

Comprehension

Facts about planets

The figures are given in standard form to 3 significant figures.

Planet	Distance from the sun	Diameter	Mass
Mercury	5.79×10^7 km	4.88×10^3 km	3.30×10^{23} kg
Venus	1.08×10^8 km	1.21×10^4 km	4.87×10^{24} kg
Earth	1.50×10^8 km	1.28×10^4 km	5.97×10^{24} kg
Mars	2.28×10^8 km	6.79×10^3 km	6.42×10^{23} kg
Jupiter	7.79×10^8 km	1.44×10^5 km	1.90×10^{27} kg
Saturn	1.43×10^9 km	1.20×10^5 km	5.68×10^{26} kg
Uranus	2.87×10^9 km	5.12×10^4 km	8.68×10^{25} kg
Neptune	4.50×10^9 km	4.95×10^4 km	1.02×10^{26} kg
Pluto	5.91×10^9 km	2.27×10^3 km	1.27×10^{22} kg

11 Use the table above to answer these questions. Cross out the wrong word.

  a Mercury is *heavier/lighter* than Mars.
  b *Uranus/Pluto* is the planet furthest away from the sun.
  c The planet with the *largest/smallest* diameter is Jupiter.
  d The planet nearest to the sun is *Venus/Mercury*.
  e The distance between Earth and *Mercury/Jupiter* is 6.29×10^8.
  f The mass of Jupiter is about 300 times greater than that of *Earth/Neptune*.

3.10 Problem solving

Problems may be given in words, and then need to be translated into mathematics before you can answer. They will often use unfamiliar words for simple ideas such as adding or dividing, ratio, or proportion.

To work on word problems:

1 Read the question carefully two or three times.
2 Highlight any words that you do not know.
3 Ask about these words, or look them up.
4 Write the calculation in maths language.
5 Look at the answer – does it make sense?

Examples

a A boy walks 1.5 km to a bus stop. He travels three times as far in the bus as he did on foot. How far does he travel in total?

   "Three times as far" means $3 \times 1.5 = 4.5$

   "Total" means add, $1.5 + 4.5 = 6$ km

b A football team played fifteen matches and won nine of them. How many matches did the team lose?

   $15 - 9 = 6$ matches lost

Exercise

12 Solve these word problems.

  a Three quarters of the hockey team and their friends stay to eat after the match. Seven go home. How many stay?
  b Rita runs a 400 m race in 63 seconds. When she runs again she has decreased her time by 5%. How long does she take now?
  c At the end of one year £100.00 invested at an interest rate of 5% will be worth £105.00. What will it be worth after three years?
  d A recipe for pastry says "three parts of fat are needed for four parts of flour". How much flour is needed for 60 grams of fat?

e A can of drink contains 0.33 litres of lemonade. How many cans can be filled from a container of 240 litres?
  f The body of a barn owl is approximately 35 cm long. Its wingspan is about 87.5 cm. What is the ratio of the wingspan to the body?
  g If the planet Jupiter has a mass of 1900 $\times 10^{24}$ kg, and Mercury has a mass of 0.33 $\times 10^{24}$ kg, what is the difference in their masses? Give your answer in standard form.
  h A human hair has a diameter of 0.002 cm. Scientists have created threads that are 2500 times thinner than a human hair. What is the diameter of each thread? Give your answer in standard form.

1729 – a very special number

In 1919, the English mathematician G. H. Hardy was visiting his friend and colleague Srinivasa Ramanujan in hospital in London. Srinivasa Ramanujan was born in Madras in India but came to Cambridge to work and do more research. Both he and Hardy were fascinated by prime numbers and the random way in which they appear among the counting numbers. The two men worked together to see if they could find a pattern for the order of prime numbers and find a formula that would give larger and larger prime numbers.

Hardy arrived in a taxi, and told Ramanujan that the number of the taxi was 1729, a very uninteresting one. Ramanujan disagreed,

"No, Hardy, it is a very interesting number. It is the smallest number expressible as the sum of two positive cubes in two different ways"

Ramanujan was able to see the patterns in numbers very easily and had understood that

1729 = $12^3 + 1^3$ and 1729 = $10^3 + 7^3$

13 **Cross out the incorrect word in each of these sentences.**

  a A *cubic/square* number is a number that is multiplied by itself three times.
  b A prime number can only be *divided/multiplied* by itself and by one.
  c One *is/is not* a prime number.
  d Prime numbers occur in a *regular/irregular* pattern.
  e The *factors/multiples* of 1729 are 7, 13, and 19.
  f Adding two prime numbers greater than 2 together will always give an *odd/even* number.

Answer these questions.

  g Where was Srinivasa Ramanujan born?
  h Where did he and G.H. Hardy meet?
  i What word did G. H. Hardy use to describe the number of the taxi?
  j What type of numbers interested the two mathematicians so much?

Think about the questions from the start of this chapter.
Can you answer them now?
◉ Three children share two pizzas. What fraction does each child eat?
◉ Is −3 an integer?
◉ What is 10% of $59.00?
◉ Can you give me a multiple of 7?

3 Consolidation: Number

Need more practice? Review and check your understanding here.

Exercise 3.1

The exercise does not need a calculator.

1. Use all the digits 1, 3, 5 and 4 to make:
   a. the largest number possible
   b. the smallest number possible
   c. an even number
   d. a multiple of 5
   e. an odd number less than 3000

   What is the difference between the largest number and the smallest number?

2. Put these numbers in order, starting with the lowest one:
   23, −58, $3\frac{1}{4}$, −3, 0, 8.75, 37

3. a. If the temperature last night was −2 °C, how much has it risen if the temperature is now
      i. 5 °C   ii. 10 °C   iii. −1 °C?
   b. If the temperature at noon was 22 °C, how much has it dropped if it is now
      i. 15 °C   ii. 11 °C   iii. −2 °C?

4. Start with the number 12
   a. Double the number.
   b. Add 6.
   c. Halve your answer to (b).
   d. Subtract 3 from your answer to (c).

   What is your answer now?

   Try starting with a different number – can you explain what is happening?

5. Work these sums out – remember the BIDMAS rules!
   a. $(12 + 6) − 5 =$
   b. $2 + 8 \div 4 =$
   c. $30 \div 5 + 42 \div 6 =$
   d. $(15 + 3) + (7 − 3) =$
   e. $(4 + 5)^2 − 3^3 =$

6. Put brackets in the correct place to make these expressions true.

   Examples

   $4 + 5 + 1 \times 5 = 34$ needs these brackets $4 + (5 + 1) \times 5 = 34$

   a. $8 + 4 \div 2 + 7 = 13$
   b. $8 + 4 \div 2 + 7 = 17$
   c. $8 + 4 \div 2 + 1 = 4$

7. Look at these numbers: 187, 294, 450, 389
   a. Which number is a prime number?
   b. Which number is a multiple of 11?
   c. Which number can be divided by both 6 and 7?
   d. Which number uses only the prime factors 2, 3, and 5?

8 a Is 5 a prime factor of 7000? **c** Is 7 a prime factor of 647?
b Is 11 a prime factor of 528? **d** Is 2 a prime factor of 34?

9 Write each of these numbers as a product of its prime factors.

Example

$48 = 2 \times 2 \times 2 \times 2 \times 3$
$= 2^4 \times 3$

a 64 **b** 315 **c** 210 **d** 1764

10 a Take any three-digit number – don't use zero, and start with all the digits different.
  b Reverse the number.
  c Take the smaller number away from the larger one.
  d Take the answer to (c), reverse it and then add these two numbers together.
  e What is the answer?

Try with different starting numbers – what do you notice?

11 A palindrome is a word or number that reads the same going forwards or backwards.

MUM, DAD, RADAR, KAYAK, 1331, 20902……. are all palindromes.

There are many interesting websites about palindromic numbers.

Use a search engine to find them.

You can convert any number into a palindromic one, though it may take several stages.

1 Take any number.
2 Reverse the digits.
3 Add the numbers from (a) and (b) together.
4 Look at this new number – is it a palindrome? If not, take the answer to (c) and repeat steps (b) to (d).

Example

```
  69        165        726       1353
 +96       +561       +627      +3531
 165       726       1353       4884
```

Exercise 3.2

You will need a calculator for some of the questions. Give your answers to 1 decimal place.

1 Look at this list of fractions: $\frac{3}{4}, 1\frac{7}{8}, \frac{25}{26}, 2\frac{2}{3}, \frac{19}{12}, \frac{9}{8}, 9\frac{1}{8}, \frac{4}{5}$

Put the fractions in the correct column of this table:

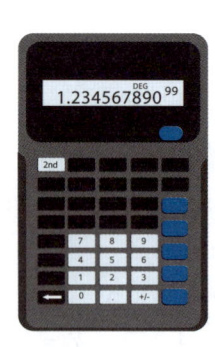

Improper fraction	Mixed number	Fraction less than 1

Consolidation: Number ◎ 3

2 Look at this:

If $\frac{15}{4} = 3\frac{3}{4}$, match each improper fraction with the correct mixed number.

Mixed number	Improper fraction
$5\frac{1}{3}$	
	$\frac{13}{8}$
	$\frac{100}{7}$
$2\frac{3}{5}$	
$8\frac{4}{7}$	
	$\frac{21}{4}$

Choose one of these numbers to fill in the blank spaces:
$14\frac{2}{7}$, $\frac{16}{3}$, $\frac{13}{5}$, $5\frac{1}{4}$, $1\frac{5}{8}$, $\frac{60}{7}$

3 What are the missing numbers (marked ?) for these equivalent fractions?

a $\frac{3}{5} = \frac{?}{15} = \frac{?}{100}$

b $\frac{?}{4} = \frac{30}{8} = \frac{90}{?}$

c $\frac{?}{7} = \frac{10}{?} = \frac{25}{35}$

d $\frac{3}{?} = \frac{?}{16} = \frac{75}{100}$

$\frac{3}{5} = \frac{6}{10} = \frac{9}{15}$ are equivalent fractions.

4 Calculate the following:

a $\frac{3}{5}$ of 210€

b $\frac{5}{8}$ of 128 kg

c $\frac{5}{9}$ of 360°

d $\frac{3}{7}$ of 84 km

e $\frac{4}{11}$ of 165 tonnes

5 Look at these pairs of fractions and put the correct symbol (<, > or =) between them.

Example

$1\frac{1}{4} < 1\frac{1}{3}$

a $\frac{15}{14}$ ...... $\frac{14}{15}$

b $3\frac{3}{8}$ ...... $\frac{27}{8}$

c $\frac{1}{81}$ ...... $\frac{1}{80}$

d $\frac{3}{7}$ ...... $\frac{5}{8}$

e $\frac{4}{7}$ ...... $\frac{32}{56}$

f $\frac{2}{3}$ ...... $\frac{66}{100}$

6 Complete this table. The first row has been done for you.

	Fraction	Decimal fraction	Percentage
a	$\frac{3}{8}$	0.375	37.5%
b	$\frac{14}{25}$		
c			33%
d		0.45	
e	$\frac{11}{20}$		
f		1.6	

$\frac{3}{8} \times 100 = \frac{300}{8} = 37.5\%$

And $3 \div 8 = 0.375$

31

7 a Henry gains a mark of 25 out of 40 for his Spanish spelling test, and a mark of 38 out of 50 for his maths test. Which result is better? Why?

b Jo's class has 14 boys and 16 girls.

  i What percentage of the class are boys?

  ii Four girls leave the class. What percentage of the class are girls now?

c 60% of a basket of apples are green, the rest are red. If there are 15 green apples, how many apples are there altogether?

8 Keri estimates that there are approximately 15 000 people watching a hockey match. She estimates that 3 900 are children, and 6 600 are men. The rest of the crowd are women.

a What percentage of the crowd are children?

b What fraction of the crowd are men?

c How many women does Keri think are at the match?

9 Write each of these ratios in its simplest form.

Example

12:18 = 2:3

a 13:52
b 30:90
c 27:63
d 12 km:45 km
e 45 mins:3 hours

10 a The ratio of butter to flour in a cake is 1:3. If you use 210 grams of flour, how much butter do you need?

b The ratio of boys to girls in a class is 3:4. There are twelve boys. How many girls are there?

c When Jim makes jam he uses 4 kg of sugar for each 5 kg of fruit. If he has 8 kg of cherries, how much sugar will he need?

11 Hana is 15 years old and her brother Hue is 9.

a What is the ratio of their ages?

Their grandfather gives them 1200 HKD and divides the sum in the ratio of their ages.

b How much does he give Hue? How much does Hana receive?

c What will the ratio of their ages be six years from now?

d How much does their grandfather give each grandchild in six years time?

12 A toy shop buys toys for €16 each, and puts them on sale at a price of €20 each.

a What percentage profit does the shop expect to make?

Not all the toys are sold, so the shop tries to sell the remaining toys for €18 each.

b What is the percentage decrease from the first price to the second?

c What is the percentage profit that the shop makes on the lower price?

13 In 2009 the BBC World Service reported that the price of 1 tonne of rice had risen from $370 to $1 000.

After the rice harvest the price fell to $608.

  a What was the percentage rise in the price of rice before the harvest?

  b What was the percentage drop after the harvest?

    The price was expected to rise again by 3%

  c What would the new price be?

14 A4 paper is 297 mm long and 210 mm wide.
A5 paper is 210 mm long and 148 mm wide.

  a What is the ratio of the lengths of A4 and A5 paper? Give your answer to 2 decimal places.

  b What is the ratio of the widths of A4 and A5 paper? Give your answer to 2 decimal places.

  c What do you notice?

  d Find the area of each size of paper, then divide the larger area by the smaller one.

  e Write down the answer to 3 significant figures.

  f There is a link between your answers to (a), (b), and (c). Can you find it?

Exercise 3.3

You will need a scientific calculator for this exercise.

1 Use your calculator to find the answers to these questions.

For each one, give your answer to:

  i the nearest whole number

  ii one decimal place

  iii 4 significant figures

Example

$\sqrt{5} + \sqrt{7} = 4.8818193$

  i 5 to the nearest whole number

  ii 4.9 to one decimal place

  iii 4.882 to four significant figures

  a $15 \div 7$

  b $\sqrt{(4 + 13)} - 1$

  c $2\pi + \sqrt{5}$

  d $(\sqrt{5} + \sqrt{7})^2$

  e $\frac{1 + \sqrt{5}}{2}$

  f 7π

2 Which of these numbers are not written in standard form?

  a 6.0×10^5

  b 38.2×10^{-4}

  c 0.618×10^3

  d 5.601×10^6

  e 3.98×10^0

3 Write these numbers in order, starting with the smallest.

5.7×10^6, 3.2×10^2, 4.5×10^{-6}, 3.8×10^{-2}, 5×10^0, 5.75×10^5

Extension

The Golden Ratio has fascinated mathematicians, artists and architects as well as musicians and philosophers for centuries.

Some scholars think that it was used to calculate the proportions of the Parthenon in Athens. It was certainly studied by Plato and Pythagoras, and was an inspiration to artists such as Leonardo da Vinci.

The Golden Ratio is the solution to the equation $x^2 - x - 1 = 0$ and is given as

$\varphi = 1.61603\ldots$ or $\varphi = \frac{1 + \sqrt{5}}{2}$

Any rectangle using the ratio for its length and width has a very pleasing shape, so it is used widely for things like credit cards, stamps, picture frames or window frames.

Many books have been written about the golden ratio, and it is a good subject for a mathematics project.

However, be careful if you look it up on the internet – there are more than thirty seven million eight hundred thousand results!!

4 Use the Standard Form key on your calculator to answer these questions. It is marked EE or EXP.

Give your answer in Standard Form.

a $(4.2 \times 10^3) \times (5.5 \times 10^5) =$

b $(5.5 \times 10^5) \div (4.0 \times 10^6) =$

c $(6.82 \times 10^{-2}) + (3.91 \times 10^{-3}) =$

d $(9.43 \times 10^3) - (9.08 \times 10^2) =$

e $(1.47 \times 10^{10}) \times (5.2 \times 10^6) =$

5 The speed of light is 3×10^5 km/sec. Calculate how long it takes for light to travel from the Sun to:

a Mercury, which is 5.79×10^7 km from the Sun.

b Pluto, which is 5.91×10^9 km from the Sun.

c What is the difference between the two times?

6 a What is the value of:

i $5^2 \times 4^2$

ii $5^2 - 4^2$

iii $2^4 \times 2^2$

iv $2^4 + 2^2$

v 10^5

vi $8^2 \div 2^6$

b Which is larger, 3^2 or 2^3?

c Which is smaller $(5^3 \div 5^4)$ or $(5^4 \div 5^3)$?

d Which of these numbers is equal to one?

$7^2 \div 2^7$, $6^3 \div 6^3$, $5^2 \times 4^0$, $2^5 \times 0$, $8^5 \times 1$, $(7^3)^0$

7 A drop of water has a volume of 5×10^{-2} cm³. A litre is 1000 cm³.

a If a bucket has a volume of 15 litres, how many drops does it hold?

b If a shower uses 70 litres of water, how many drops does it use?

c If a bath has a volume of 220 litres, how many drops does it hold?

d If a tap is losing a drop of water every second, how many drops does it lose in one hour?

e What volume of water does it lose in one hour?

Extension

8 A nanometre (nm) is 1 billion times smaller than a metre, so 1 nanometre = 1×10^{-9} metres.

It is the measurement used when scientists are measuring the length of atoms and molecules, things that are too small to see unless you are using a special atomic force microscope.

According to Albert Einstein, one sucrose molecule is approximately 1 nm long.

a If a sugar cube is 1 cm long, calculate how many molecules of sucrose there are along one side of the cube.

b How many molecules are there in one whole cube?

4 Algebra

In this chapter you will answer...

- If $a = 2$ and $b = -3$, what is a added to b?
- You think of a number, double it and add three. The answer is seven. What is the number that you thought of?
- The formula for the area of a circle is pi(π) multiplied by the radius squared. What is the value of π?
- 96, 48, 24,... What is the next number in the sequence?

4.1 Why do we use algebra?

Here are some ideas that your teacher may give you for learning algebra. Do you agree?

1. Algebra is fun – you can use it to solve puzzles.
2. Writing in letters is quicker than writing in words.
3. It is logical. You learn rules which always work.
4. It is efficient. It says many things very quickly.
5. It makes ideas easier to remember.
6. It is used to programme a computer.
7. It will be useful in the future. Doctors, engineers, nurses, business people, etc all use formulae.

KEY WORDS

Formula a rule given in a short form by numbers and letters
E.g.
The area of a circle = $\pi \times r^2$

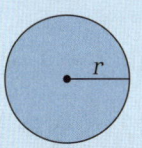

Formulae is the plural of formula

Exercise

1. Here are some examples that show how letters can be shorter than words. Match the phrases with the letters that can be used in their place.

   You can use x, y, n, or any other letter.

1	A number plus two	a	$n - 7$
2	Three times a number	b	$\frac{n}{3}$
3	Seven subtracted from a number	c	$n + 2$
4	A number divided by three	d	$x + y$
5	A number taken away from seven	e	a^2
6	Two different numbers added together	f	$3n$
7	A number multiplied by itself	g	$7 - n$

KEY WORDS

Term each part of a line of algebra.
E.g.
In $3x - 5 = 7$, $3x$, -5, and 7 are all terms
Like terms terms which involve the same letter or symbol (and the same index)
E.g.
$3y$, $5y$, $-2y$ are all (a)like.
$3x$, 5, $-8x^2$ are not like terms.
Expressions are algebraic rules that do not have an equals sign in them
E.g. $2x + y$

Talking points

Think of seven more examples in words. Read out your examples and try to get your friend to write them as algebra. Be careful - it's not easy!

35

4.2 Simplifying algebraic expressions

You can add **like terms**, terms that have the same letters, but different numbers.

Remember: the + or − sign belongs to the letter <u>after</u> the sign.

Examples

Adding and subtracting

1. $5a + 3a + a = 9a$ $(5 + 3 + 1 = 9)$
2. $5a − 3a + a = 3a$ $(5 − 3 + 1 = 3)$
3. $3pq + 2pq − 6p = 5pq − 6p$ 'pq' terms are different from 'p' terms.
4. $2x^2 − x + 1 = 2x^2 − x + 1$ no change because each term is different, x^2 and x are not like terms.

Multiplying

1. $3x \times 6x = 3 \times 6 \times x \times x = 18x^2$ You can leave out the $\times$ sign.
2. $3m \times 5n = 3 \times 5 \times m \times n = 15mn$ Write letters in alphabetical order (m before n)
3. $7 \times 7y^2 = 49y^2$

Dividing

Since $\frac{y}{y} = 1$ and $\frac{x^2}{x^2} = 1$ or $\frac{\text{one symbol}}{\text{the same symbol}} = 1$

Then $\frac{15x^2y^3z}{3xyz} = \frac{15}{3} \times \frac{x^2}{x} \times \frac{y^3}{y} \times \frac{z}{z} = 5 \times x \times y^2 = 5xy^2$

> **KEY WORD**
> **Brackets** these tell you which part of the sum to do first. There are different types of brackets.

Brackets

When there is a single bracket, you multiply each term inside the bracket by the term outside.

(inside)   ( ) outside

1. $3(x − 2y) = 3 \times x − 3 \times 2y = 3x − 6y$
2. $3a(a + b) = 3a \times a + 3a \times b = 3a^2 + 3ab$
3. $7(2a + b) − 3(a − b) = 7 \times 2a + 7 \times b − 3 \times a − 3 \times (−b)$
   $= 14a + 7b − 3a + 3b$
   $= 11a + 10b$

> Be careful $(−3 \times −b) = +3b$

Exercise

2 Evaluate:

1. $12a − 2b + a − b =$
      a $10ab$ **b** $13a − 3b$ **c** $13a − b$

2. $5x^2 + 2xy − y^2 =$
      a $5x^2 + 2xy − y^2$ **b** $6x^2y^2$ **c** $4x^2 + 2xy$

3. $6x \times x \times 2y =$
      a $12xy$ **b** $8xy^2$ **c** $12x^2y$

4. $\frac{24m^2n^3}{3m^3n} =$
      a $6mn$ **b** $\frac{8n^2}{m}$ **c** $8mn$

5. $4(3x − 2y) =$
      a $12y − 3x$ **b** $12x − 8y$ **c** $4xy$

6. $5(f + 2g) − 3(3f − 2g) =$
      a $−4f + 4g$ **b** $14f + 4g$ **c** $−4f + 16g$

4.3 Substitution

You can put numbers in the place of the letters in an expression, so that the algebra becomes a sum. This is called substitution.

KEY WORD

Substitution putting a number in the place of a letter

Examples

1 If $x = 5$, then $4x = 4 \times 5 = 20$
   And $4x^2 = 4 \times 5^2 = 4 \times 5 \times 5 = 4 \times 25 = 100$

2 If $a = 3$ and $b = 7$,
   $a + b = 3 + 7 = 10$
   $a - b = 3 - 7 = -4$

Consecutive numbers follow in order.

Examples

8, 9, 10, 11, ... or 23, 24, 25, 26, ... are consecutive numbers.

In algebra, if the first number in a list of consecutive numbers is x, then the next is $x + 1$, then $x + 2$, etc.

Talking points

Discuss with a friend. Consider the following:

- $x, x + 2, x + 4, x + 6$.......could be consecutive odd numbers, or consecutive even numbers.
- How can you use algebra to write a number that is always even?

Odd numbers are 1, 3, 5, 7, ...
Even numbers are 2, 4, 6, 8, ...

4.4 Using formulae

For more about geometry see Chapter 5.

A formula is a short and simple way to explain and remember a complicated idea.

- You can say "to find the circumference of a circle you must double (×2) the length of the radius, then multiply by pi (π)".

  C is the Circumference, r is the radius and π is pi.

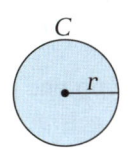

  You can also write this as a formula: $C = 2\pi r$

  ### Example

  If the radius of a circle is 7 cm, then the circumference is given by

  $C = 2 \times 7 \times \pi = 14\pi = 44$ cm

  If you remember the formula, you remember how to do the sum.

- You can say "to find the volume of a cube, you multiply the length of the sides together three times"

  You can also write this as:

  Volume = s^3 where s = length of each side

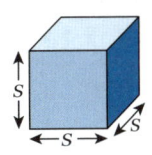

  ### Example

  If $s = 10$ cm, $V = 10 \times 10 \times 10 = 1000$ cm³
  If $s = 1.5$ m, $V = 1.5 \times 1.5 \times 1.5 = 3.375$ m³

◉ To use a formula, you replace each letter with the matching value.

Example

The area of a triangle is $A = \frac{1}{2}bh$,

where **b** is the length of the base, and **h** is the height of the triangle.

If $b = 8\,cm$ and $h = 5\,cm$, $A = \frac{1}{2} \times 8 \times 5 = 20\,cm^2$.

3 Which formula would you use to work out each of the following examples?

a $V = \pi r^2 h$, **b** $a^2 + b^2 = c^2$, **c** $A = \pi r^2$, **d** $s = \frac{d}{t}$, **e** $C = 2\pi r$, **f** $A = \frac{(a+b)}{2}h$

Problem	
1 The area of a trapezium	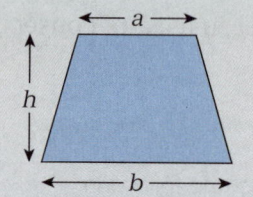
2 The area of a circle	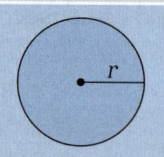
3 The speed of a car	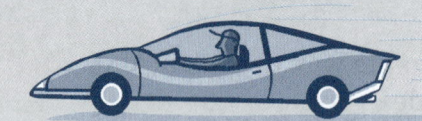
4 The circumference of a circle	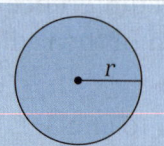
5 The length of the the hypotenuse, c	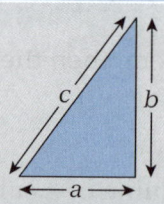
6 The volume of a cylinder	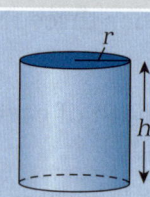

4.5 Finding a formula

Sometimes you need to find out a formula for yourself before you can use it to solve a problem.

If you are asked to find your own formula:

- Read the question carefully.
- Check any difficult words.
- It may help to draw a picture if you can.
- Substitute letters and numbers for words.

> **KEY WORD**
>
> **Solve** find the answer to a problem in numbers

> **KEY WORD**
>
> **Perimeter** the length around the whole outline of a shape

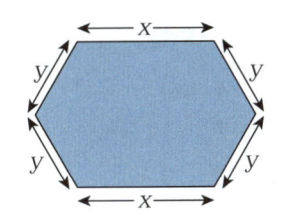

Example

A shape with six sides (a hexagon) has two sides that are x cm long and four sides that are y cm long. Find a formula for the perimeter of the shape.

Let P be the perimeter of the hexagon.

$P = x + y + y + x + y + y$

$\quad = 2x + 4y$

What is the perimeter of the hexagon if $x = 7$ cm and $y = 11$ cm?

$P = 2 \times 7 + 4 \times 11 = 14 + 44 = 58$ cm

You can also work backwards to find the lengths of the sides when you know the perimeter.

If the perimeter of the shape is 42 cm, and the shorter sides are 6 cm, what is the length of the longer sides?

$42 = 2x + 4 \times 6$

$42 = 2x + 24$

$18 = 2x$

$9 = x$

> Replace P with 42 and x with 6.

So, the longer sides are 9 cm.

Exercise

4 Decide for each word problem if the given formula is true (T) or false (F).

a The area of a rectangle with length $(x - 4)$ cm and width x cm	$A = x^2 - 4x$
b The perimeter of a rectangle, with length $(x - 4)$ cm and width x cm	$P = 2(x - 4) + x$
c The area of a triangle with a base of y cm and height of $(y - 2)$ cm	$A = y(y - 2)$
d The third angle of a triangle with two angles of $f°$	Angle $= 180° - 2f$
e The volume of a box that is z cm wide, $(z - 2)$ cm high and $(z + 5)$ cm long	$V = z(z + 5)(z - 2)$
f The area of the base of a box that is z cm wide, $(z - 2)$ cm high and $(z + 5)$ cm long	$A = (z - 2)(z + 5)$

4.6 Linear equations

In a linear equation:
- There is one equation and one answer.
- There is an equals (=) sign.
- The quantities on one side balance the quantities on the other.

To solve equations, you need to do the same thing to both sides.
Keep each operation on a new line and show your working. Always check your answers.

Examples

1. $x + 7 = 12$
    $x + 7 - 7 = 12 - 7$
    $\underline{x = 5}$
    Check: $5 + 7 = 12$ ✓

2. $x - 3 = 9$
    $x - 3 + 3 = 9 + 3$
    $\underline{x = 12}$
    Check: $12 - 3 = 9$ ✓

3. $4x = 20$
    $\frac{4x}{4} = \frac{20}{4}$
    $\underline{x = 5}$
    Check: $4 \times 5 = 20$ ✓

4. $\frac{x}{7} = 5$
    $\frac{x}{7} \times 7 = 5 \times 7$
    $\underline{x = 35}$
    Check: $35 \div 7 = 5$ ✓

KEY WORDS

Equation An equation tells you that the terms on each side of the equals sign (=) are the same.
E.g. $3x - 5 = 7$ is an equation. It is only true if $x = 4$

Take 7 away from each side of the equation.

Substitute $x = 5$ in the original equation to check your answer.

Add 3 to both sides.

Divide both sides of the equation by 4.

Multiply both sides of the equation by 7.

Remember:
- $+$ and $-$ are "inverse" operations: adding and subtracting are opposites, and one 'undoes' the other.
- $\times$ and $\div$ are "inverse" operations: multiplying and dividing are opposites, and one 'undoes' the other.
- Work through equations with a new step on every row.
- Underline the answer to make your work clear.
- You can check if your answer is correct by working backwards.

Opposites are a very important idea in mathematics
E.g.

correct/ incorrect	multiply/ divide	equal/ unequal
square/ square root	add/ subtract	do/undo

Example

$2x + 1 = 15$
$2x = 14$
$\underline{x = 7}$

Check: $2 \times 7 + 1 = 15$

Algebra 4

Exercise 5 Solve these equations:

1. $3x - 2 = 19$
   - a $x = 8$
   - b $x = \frac{17}{3}$
   - c $x = 7$

2. $5(x + 1) = 35$
   - a $x = 6$
   - b $x = 7$
   - c $x = 8$

3. $2x + 1 = x + 11$
   - a $x = 4$
   - b $x = 10$
   - c $x = 6$

4. $25 - 3x = 22$
   - a $x = 9$
   - b $x = 1$
   - c $x = 3$

4.7 Equations and word problems

Exercise 6 Here are some more word problems to practise.
Match each problem to the equation and then match the equation to the answer.

Problem	Equation	Answer
a Think of a number, add two, double that answer and then subtract six. The answer is forty two.	$2(n + 3) + 2n = 42$	$n = 12$
b A rectangle has a perimeter of forty-two centimetres. The rectangle is three centimetres longer than it is wide. How wide is it?	$2(n + 2) - 6 = 42$	$n = 9$
c A triangle has one angle of forty-two degrees. The other two angles are the same size. How big are they?	$3n + 6 = 42$	$n = 69$
d Three consecutive even numbers add up to forty-two. What is the first number?	$2n + 42 = 180$	$n = 22$

4.8 Simultaneous equations

Simultaneous equations have two equations with two unknown values.

There are only two values that are true for both equations.

To find the solution, you work with both equations at the same time, which is why they are called "simultaneous".

If $a + b = 10$ and $a - b = 2$,

the only values that are true for both equations are $a = 6$ and $b = 4$.

To work with two equations at the same time, there are two common methods you can use:

- elimination
- substitution

Elimination method.

$$a + b = 10 \quad (1)$$
$$a - b = 2 \quad (2)$$

Add equations (1) and (2):

$$a + b + a - b = 10 + 2$$
$$2a = 12$$
$$\underline{a = 6} \text{ and } \underline{b = 4} \text{ from equation (1)}$$

> By adding equation (1) and equation (2) you eliminate b.

Substitution method.

$$a + b = 10 \quad (1)$$
$$a - b = 2 \quad (2)$$

Rearrange equation (2) to find an expression for a:

$$a = 2 + b \quad (3)$$

Substitute this value for a into equation (1):

$$(2 + b) + b = 10$$
$$2 + 2b = 10$$
$$2b = 8$$
$$\underline{b = 4} \text{ and } \underline{a = 6} \text{ from equation (3)}$$

> You substitute $(2 + b)$ for a.

Check:

Substitute $a = 6$ and $b = 4$ into (1): $4 + 6 = 10$ ✓
Substitute $a = 6$ and $b = 4$ into (2): $6 - 4 = 2$ ✓

so the answers are right.

Simultaneous equation problems can be given in algebra or in words.

In algebra:

$$2x + y = 11 \quad (1)$$
$$x - 3y = 9 \quad (2)$$

If you add or subtract these equations you will still have x's and y's.

You need to work an extra step.

Equation (1) × 3: $6x + 3y = 33 \quad (3)$

Add equations (2) and (3):

$$x - 3y = 9 \quad (2)$$
$$6x + 3y = 33 \quad (3)$$
$$7x = 42$$

$$x = 6 \text{ and } y = 11 - 2 \times 6 = -1 \text{ (from equation 1)}$$

> Equations (2) and (3) both include '3y' so you can now use the elimination method.

Check: $2 \times 6 + (-1) = 11$ and $6 - 3(-1) = 9$, so the answers are right. ✓

In words:

Two oranges and three apples cost twenty-two cents. If an orange costs one cent more than an apple, how much does each cost?

"Translate" into algebra:

$$2f + 3g = 22 \quad (1)$$
$$f - g = 1, \text{ or } f = g + 1 \quad (2)$$

> f represents an orange and g represents an apple.

Use the substitution method:

then $2(g + 1) + 3g = 22$
$$5g + 2 = 22$$
$$5g = 20$$
$$g = 4 \text{ and } f = 4 + 1, f = 5$$

Check: $2 \times 5 + 3 \times 4 = 10 + 12 = 22$, and $5 - 4 = 1$, so the answers are right ✓

Algebra 4

Exercise 7 Put these sentences in the correct order to show the steps for solving simultaneous equations.
- Eliminate by adding or subtracting the equations.
- Multiply one or both equations by the correct number so that the numbers in front of the terms to be eliminated are the same.
- Label the equations (1) and (2).
- Check your answers using the equations that you started with.
- Substitute your first answer in equation (1) or (2) to find the second answer.

Exercise 8 Match the right equations to each problem:

1 Three times a number is added to four times another number to give 40. The sum of the two numbers is 13. Find the numbers.	a $4x + 3y = 45$
	b $x + y = 13$
2 Four mangoes and three bananas cost 45 cents. One mango and two bananas cost 20 cents. How much does each fruit cost?	c $x + y = 13$
	d $x + 2y = 20$
3 One large sack of corn and one small sack of corn cost 13 dollars. The difference in price between the cost of three large sacks and four small sacks is 11 dollars. How much does each sack cost?	e $3x - 4y = 11$
	f $3x + 4y = 40$

4.9 Inequalities

Not all equations have equal signs. In some equations the value of one side is less than the value of the other.

These are called **inequalities**.

There are four inequality symbols to learn:

<	Less than	$x < 3$	
>	More than	$x > 4$	
≤	Less than or equal to	$x \leq 5$	
≥	More than or equal to	$x \geq -2$	

On a number line, an open circle is used for **less than** and **more than** symbols: (○).

A solid circle is used for **greater than or equal** and **less than or equal** symbols: (●).

You solve inequalities in the same way as linear equations.
You can draw the answer on a number line.

Examples

$$3x + 4 \geq 13$$
$$3x \geq 9$$
$$x \geq 3$$

Subtract 4 from both sides.

Divide both sides by 3.

Be very careful with the negative letters!

$$5 - x < 7$$
$$5 - x + x < 7 + x$$
$$5 < 7 + x$$
$$-2 < x$$
$$x > -2$$

Add x to both sides.

Take 7 from both sides.

Now read the inequality backwards!

x can also take integer values, so $x = -1, 0, 1, 2, 3, ...$
Why is x not equal to -2?

Exercise

9 Read these sentences and cross out the wrong word(s) in each one.

  a Five is *greater/less* than zero.
  b Twenty is *greater/less* than two.
  c If $2x + 3 \geq 15$ then x is *greater than/less than* or equal to six.
  d If $5 - 3x \leq 2$ then x is *greater than/less than* or equal to one.

Exercise

10 For each number line shown below, write out the answer in words and list some integer values. The first has been done for you.

		x is less than 5	....0, 1, 2, 3, 4
a			
b			
c			
d			

4.11 Sequences

A set of numbers that follows a pattern is called a sequence.

1	2	3	4	5	6	7	8	9	10	11	12	13	14
1	3	5	7	9	11	13	15	17	19	21	23	25	27
2	3	5	7	11	13	17	19	23	29	31	37	41	43
1	1	2	3	5	8	13	21	34	55	89	144	233	377
1	3	6	10	15	21	28	36	45	55	66	78	91	105
2	4	8	16	32	64	128	256	512	1024	2048	4096	8192	

Algebra 4

◎ Some sequences have special names.

Example

Natural numbers	1, 2, 3, 4, 5, …
Even numbers	2, 4, 6, 8, 10, …
Odd numbers	1, 3, 5, 7, 9, 11, …
Prime numbers	2, 3, 5, 7, 11, 13, …
Fibonacci numbers	1, 1, 2, 3, 5, …

> Fibonacci was an Italian mathematician who lived around 1200 CE.
>
> In the Fibonacci sequence, each number is the sum of the two numbers before.
>
> $1 + 1 = 2, 1 + 2 = 3, 2 + 3 = 5, …$

◎ Some sequences have a special name based on their shape:

Example

Triangle numbers: 1, 3, 6, 10, …

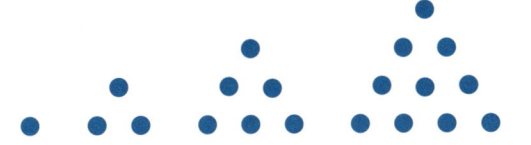

Square numbers: 1, 4, 9, 16, …

> Remember: $1 \times 1 = 1^2 = 1$, $2 \times 2 = 2^2 = 4$, $3 \times 3 = 3^2 = 9$, …

You can describe sequences in different ways.

◎ Some sequences have a rule that helps you work out the next number:

Example

5, 9, 13, 17, 21, ……	Add on four each time
99, 94, 89, 84, 79, …..	Subtract five each time
3, 6, 12, 24, 48, …….	Multiply by two each time

◎ Some sequences have a formula:

Example

If the nth term is $4n - 3$,

The <u>first</u> term is $\quad 4 \times \underline{1} - 3 = 1$

The <u>second</u> term is $\; 4 \times \underline{2} - 3 = 5$

The <u>third</u> term is $\quad 4 \times \underline{3} - 3 = 9$

So the sequence is 1, 5, 9, 13, 17, …

◎ Some sequences have pictures :

+3   +3

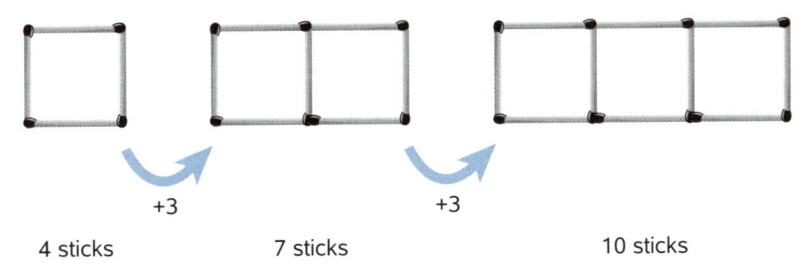

4 sticks   7 sticks   10 sticks

The formula is $3n + 1$, so the <u>fourth</u> shape will be $3 \times 4 + 1 = 13$

Or you can think of it like this:

n	1	2	3	4
$3n$	3	6	9	12
$3n + 1$	4	7	10	13

> For each new pattern you add on 3; this gives $3n$.
>
> $3n + 1 = 4$, the first pattern.

Exercise

11 Look at the table at the beginning of this section, then answer these questions.

1. Can you name the sequences in the table?
   Can you find a rule for each one?

2. One of the sequences is different – it is "the odd one out" and has no rule.
   Which one is different?

3. The sequence below is called the "Lucas number sequence", after the mathematician François Lucas who studied it:
   2, 1, 3, 4, 7, 11, 18, 29, 47, 76, 123, 199, 322, 521, …
   a. How did Lucas build this sequence?
   b. What is the sixth number of the sequence?
   c. There is one number that is even and prime – what is it?
   d. 123 is a multiple of two prime numbers. What are they?
   e. Which number is one less than two hundred?
   f. There is a link between the Fibonacci numbers and the Lucas numbers. Can you find out about it?

4. Here is another sequence that does not follow any of the rules in this section:
   13, 1113, 3113, 132113, …
   Try speaking the numbers. What do you notice?

Comprehension

Diophantus

Diophantus was a Greek mathematician who worked at the Library of Alexandria in Egypt in the third century CE. He is often called "the father of algebra" and wrote thirteen books called "The Arithmetica". Most of the books were lost but six survived and were studied by other mathematicians through the ages.

This study of his work has been very important in history. Much of the mathematics studied in the world today is based on it. Copies of "The Arithmetica" were used in Europe from the 1500s after they had been translated into Latin from Arabic.

Diophantus was also studied by Arab mathematicians such as al-Khwārizmī, who is also given the name "the father of algebra" by some scholars, because he used the ideas and improved them. Al-Khwārizmī lived about five hundred years after Diophantus and worked in Baghdad.

Before Diophantus everyone wrote out equations completely in words. He had the idea of using short forms of words and symbols for operations that he used many times, though his methods would still look very difficult and different from the ones used in schools today.

In modern times, Diophantine equations are special ones that have solutions only in whole numbers.

The following puzzle is said to have been engraved on his tombstone. This is a translation of the puzzle:

'Here lies Diophantus,' the wonder behold.

Through art algebraic, the stone tells how old:

God gave him his boyhood one sixth of his life,

One twelfth more as youth while whiskers grew rife;

And then yet one-seventh ere marriage begun;

In five years there came a bouncing new son.

Alas, the dear child of master and sage

After attaining half the measure of his father's life chill fate took him.

After consoling his fate by the science of numbers for four years, he ended his life.'

12
a Where did Diophantus work?
b Who is also called "the father of algebra"?
c How many books did Diophantus write?
d Why are Diophantine equations special?
e Which mathematician worked on the ideas of algebra first?
f What do the words 'youth', 'sage' and 'fate' mean in the puzzle?
g How long was he married before his son was born?
h Which fraction is larger, $\frac{1}{6}$ or $\frac{1}{12}$?
i How else can you write 'a half'?
j Can you work out how old Diophantus was when he died?

Think about the questions from the start of this chapter.
Can you answer them now?

◎ If $a = 2$ and $b = -3$, what is a added to b?
◎ You think of a number, double it and add three. The answer is seven. What is the number that you thought of?
◎ The formula for the area of a circle is pi(π) multiplied by the radius squared. What is the value of π?
◎ 96, 48, 24,... What is the next number in the sequence?

4 Consolidation: Algebra

Need more practice?
Review and check your understanding here

Exercise 4.1

You will need a scientific calculator for questions 7 to 12.

1. Rewrite (a) to (f) in algebra symbols.

   Example

   "A third of a number added to five" becomes $\frac{n}{3} + 5$

   a Half a number subtracted from seven.
   b A number which is doubled, then added to three.
   c The square root of a number.
   d A number which is added to three before the result is then doubled.
   e A number which is added to seven, and then the result is squared.
   f A number which is multiplied by three and then added to seven. The result is halved.

2. Simplify the following expressions by collecting like terms together.

   a $5x - 3x + 2y - y$
   b $5m + 2n + 7n - 3m$
   c $5ab + 4ab + 2a - 3b$
   d $8x^2 - 2y^2 + y^2 - 3x^2$
   e $7x^2 + 3xy - 4x^2 + y^2$
   f $12m^2 - 6m + m + m^2$
   g $11a^2 - 9ab - 5b^2$

   xy and 2xy are like terms
   x^2 and 2x are not like terms

3. Simplify the following expressions.

   a $5x \times 3x$
   b $8m \times 3n \times 2n$
   c $12xy \times 3x^2y$
   d $(7x^2)^2$
   e $(3ab)^3$
   f $\frac{11x^2y^3}{2xy}$
   g $15m^3n^2 \div 3m$

4. Expand the brackets.

   a $4(x + 3)$
   b $3x(x - 1)$
   c $7(y^2 - 2y)$
   d $5(3a + 4)$

5. Expand the brackets, then simplify by collecting like terms:

   a $7(x - 2) + 3(x + 2)$
   b $5(y + 4) - 2(y + 1)$
   c $3(a + 5) - 2(a - 1)$
   d $6(b - 2) - 3(b - 4)$

   Expand means multiply out. Remember to multiply each term outside the brackets by each term inside the brackets.

Consolidation: Algebra 4

6 If $a = 2$, $b = 3$, $c = 5$ and $d = 0$, calculate the value of

a $a + b$

b $a + b - c$

c $a^2 + b^2$

d $d(a + c)$

e $b + c - d$

f $(a \times b) + (b \times c)$

g $b^2 + d^2$

h $\frac{(a + b)}{c}$

Remember the order of operations BIDMAS.

7 The formula for the circumference of a circle is $C = 2\pi r$.

a If $r = 12$ m, calculate C, and give your answer to 1 decimal place.

b If $C = 28$ cm, calculate r, and give your answer to 3 significant figures.

8 The formula for speed is $speed = \frac{distance}{time}$.

a If you travel 18 km in 3 hours, calculate your speed.

b If you travel for 8 hours at 35 kph, calculate your distance.

c If a giant tortoise walked 4.5 m at a speed of 10 cm per second, how long did he take?

9 The formula for the volume of a cylinder is $V = \pi r^2 h$.

(Give your answers to 3 significant figures.)

Be careful — look at the units!

a If $r = 8$ cm and $h = 12$ cm, calculate V.

b If both the radius and the height are 7.5 cm, calculate V.

c If the height is 11 cm and the radius is half this value, calculate V.

10

(rectangle with width $(w + 4)$ cm and height w cm)

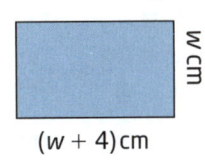

a Find a formula for the perimeter of the rectangle ($P = $).

b If $w = 8$ cm, calculate P.

c Find a formula for the area of the rectangle ($A = $).

d If $w = 9$ cms, what is the area?

11

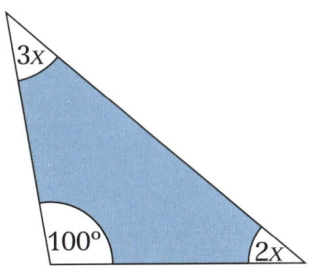

(triangle with angles $3x$, $100°$, $2x$)

a Write a formula for x

b What is the value of x?

12 A box is x cm wide, $(x + 5)$ cm long and $(x - 2)$ cm high.

a Write a formula for the volume of the box ($V = $)

b If $x = 7$ cm, calculate V.

Exercise 4.2

The exercise does not need a calculator.

1 Solve these equations. All the answers are integers.
- **a** $3x + 1 = 10$
- **b** $4y - 5 = 11$
- **c** $5a + 7 = 2$
- **d** $3(x - 7) = 15$
- **e** $4(a + 8) = 16$
- **f** $\frac{x-7}{2} = 8$
- **g** $\frac{2b + 5}{3} = 7$

2 Solve these equations. The answers may be integers or fractions.
- **a** $3y - 8 = 2$
- **b** $5b + 2 = 6$
- **c** $3(m - 1) = 27$
- **d** $\frac{4x + 5}{2} = 12$

3 Solve these equations.
- **a** $7x + 4 = x + 28$
- **b** $8m - 3 = 4m + 5$
- **c** $6z - 6 = 2z - 1$
- **d** $5c + 19 = 2c - 2$

Example: $5x + 3 = 2x - 2$
$5x - 2x = -2 - 3$
$3x = -5$
$x = -\frac{5}{3} = -1\frac{2}{3}$

4 Solve these equations.
Be careful about the negative (−) signs!
- **a** $5 - 2x = 4$
- **b** $8 = 4 - y$
- **c** $12 - 3x = 4$
- **d** $10 + 3z = 24 - 4z$

Example: $8 - 2g = 7$
$8 - 7 = 2g$
$1 = 2g$
$g = \frac{1}{2}$

5 The perimeter of a rectangle is 48 cm.
The width is x cm, and the length is 6 cm longer.
- **a** Write an equation for x.
- **b** Solve your equation to find the value of x.

6 The angles of a triangle are θ, $(\theta - 30)$, and $(\theta + 45)$ degrees.
- **a** Write an equation for θ.
- **b** Solve your equation to find the value of θ.

7 Zak multiplies a number by seven and then adds five to the result. His total is nineteen.
- **a** Write an equation, using N for Zak's number.
- **b** Solve his equation to find the value of N.

8 Solve these simultaneous equations:

a $a - b = 8$ $a + b = 18$	**b** $m + 3n = 10$ $-2m + n = 1$
c $2x - y = 7$ $x + y = 2$	**d** $4f - 2g = 2$ $f + g = 5$

9 Read each question carefully and use the information to make two equations. Solve these equations to find both variables.

  a The sum of two numbers is thirteen. Four times the first number added to twice the second number is thirty-eight. What are the numbers?

  b The difference between two numbers is six, and twice their sum is thirty-two. What are the numbers?

  c Two cans of cola and one pizza cost $5. Two pizzas and three cans of cola cost $9.25. What is the cost of a can of cola, and what is the cost of a pizza?

10 Rewrite these statements using the correct symbol: $<, >, \leq, \geq, \neq$

  a x is less than or equal to 3
  b y is greater than -2
  c π is not equal to 3
  d z is greater than or equal to zero
  e g is less than 17

11 Rewrite these algebra statements in words:

  a $x < 10$
  b $\frac{1}{3} \neq 0.33$
  c $y \geq 3$
  d $k > -5$
  e $d \leq 0$

12 Solve these inequalities. Illustrate your answer with a number line.

  a $x + 2 > 3$
  b $3 + 2x \leq 7$
  c $2(x + 2) \geq x + 6$
  d $4x + 2 > x + 10$
  e $2 < 4 - x$

> Example: $2x + 5 < 15$
> $2x < 10$
> $x < 5$
>
> $-2\ -1\ \ 0\ \ 1\ \ 2\ \ 3\ \ 4\ \ 5\ \ 6\ \ 7$

13 Read the instructions, then write the first five terms of the following sequences:

  a Start with three and add two each time.
  b Start with forty-nine and subtract five each time.
  c Start with two, and multiply by four each time.
  d Start with seven hundred and twenty-nine, and divide by three each time.
  e Start with two, and square the number each time.

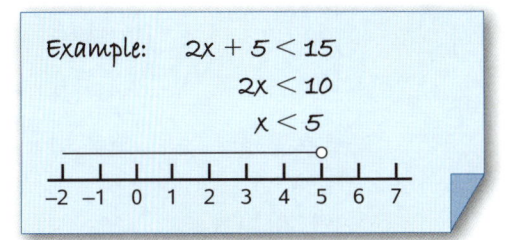

> Example: "Start with twenty-four and divide by two each time", becomes 24, 12, 6, 3, 1.5, ...

14 Write the rule for each of these sequences:

  a 12, 7, 2, -3, ...
  b 1.5, 3, 6, 12, ...
  c 64, 32, 16, 8, ...
  d 7, 10, 13, 16, ...
  e 14, 13.5, 13, 12.5 ...

15 You are given the formula for the *n*th term of a sequence. Write down the first five terms.

Example: If the nth term is 3n + 2, the sequence is 5, 8, 11, 14, 17...

  a The *n*th term is $6n - 3$.

  b The *n*th term is $n^2 + 1$.

  c The *n*th term is $50 - 4n$.

  d The *n*th term is $\frac{1}{n}$.

Extension

Pascal's Triangle is named after the French mathematician Blaise Pascal (1623 − 1662 CE) although it was known and used much earlier than that.

  a Can you find out how it works?

  b Can you complete some extra rows?

  c Can you find any sequences in the triangle?

  d Can you find any other pictures of Pascal's triangle?

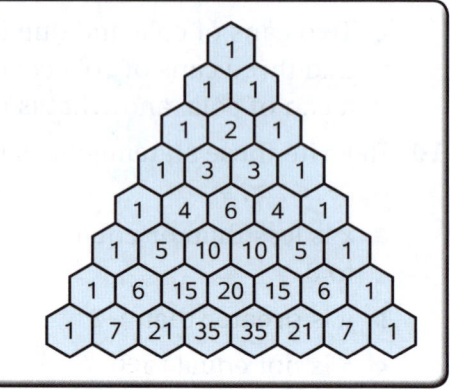

5 Geometry

In this chapter you will answer...

- What is the sum of the angles in a triangle?
- How many sides are there in a regular heptagon?
- What is the name of the line from the centre of a circle to the edge?
- How many millimetres are there in a metre?
- What is the formula for the volume of a cone?
- How many lines of symmetry are there in a square?

5.1 Angles

Angles are used to measure turning and rotation.

Angles are measured in **degrees**. The symbol for a degree is a small circle to the right of the number.

Example

You write fifty degrees as 50°.

- An **acute** angle is less than 90°.
- A **right** angle is exactly 90°.
- An **obtuse** angle is less than 180° but more than 90°.
- A **straight** angle is exactly 180°.
- A **reflex** angle is less than 360° but more than 180°.
- A **full rotation** is 360°.

acute   right   obtuse

straight   reflex   full rotation

Geometry can be useful!

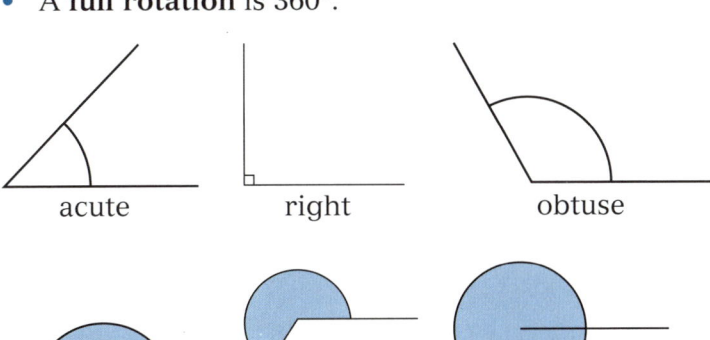

Be careful! When teachers talk about geometry they use many words that may be familiar, or seem easy to find in a dictionary. But these words have exact mathematical meanings and you need to make sure that you understand the 'maths word', not just the English word.

Talking points

Research and discuss with the class why 360° is used for a full circle.

53

1 Use the diagrams to complete this table.

Clock face	Name of angle	Size of angle
Example	Right angle	90° 270°
a		240°
b		

Clock face	Name of angle	Size of angle
c		225°
d		
e		

5.2 Angles between straight lines

When two straight lines cross, angles are made that have special names and connections.

Vertically opposite angles are equal, so $a° = b°$

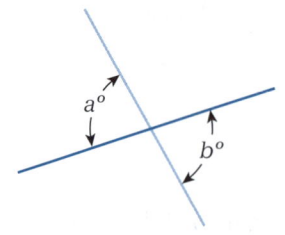

5.3 Angles in parallel lines

When a straight line crosses parallel lines, the angles also have special properties.

1 Alternate angles are equal, so $f° = g°$

Alternate angles make a **Z** shape

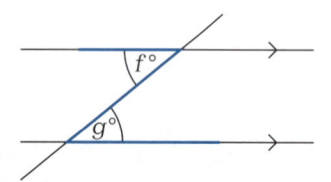

2 Corresponding angles are equal, so $m° = n°$

Corresponding angles make an **F** shape

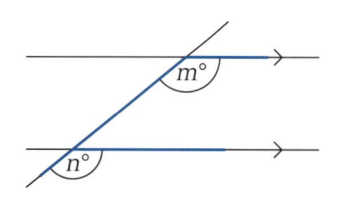

KEY WORD

Parallel Lines are parallel if they are always the same distance apart and will never meet.
E.g. Railway lines are parallel.

Geometry 5

2 Look at these letters carefully.
Then choose a word(s) from the box to complete each sentence.

| acute | obtuse | right-angles | parallel |
| 360° | reflex | full-turn | 180° |

The first one has been done for you.

I LOVE MATHS

a **M** has three <u>acute</u> angles.
b **T** has two .... angles.
c **M**, **H** and **E** have .... lines.
d **A** has two .... angles.
e The .... angles in **E** add up to .... degrees.
f **I** is a straight line with an angle of .... degrees.
g **V** has one .... angle and one .... angle.
h **O** contains a .... with an angle of ....

5.4 Triangles

A triangle is the simplest type of polygon. It has three straight sides and three angles.

The angles in a triangle add up to 180°.

There are different names for particular triangles:

- In a **scalene** triangle, all the angles are different sizes and all the sides are different lengths.

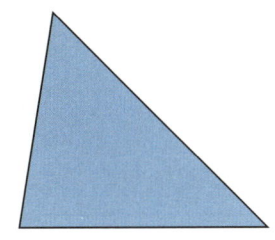

- In an **equilateral** triangle, all the sides are the same length and all the angles are the same size.

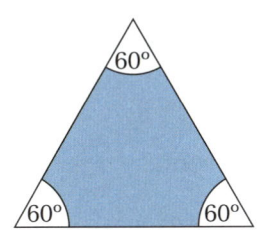

KEY WORD

Polygon a shape with three or more straight sides

Why does a polygon have to have at least three sides? Can you draw a polygon with two straight sides?

55

- In an **isosceles** triangle, two angles are the same size and two sides are the same length.

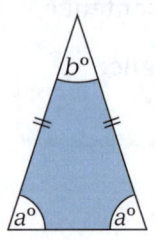

- In a **right-angled** triangle, there is one angle of 90°.

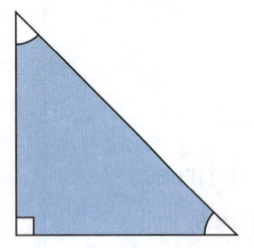

The Greeks and Romans thought that Geometry was the most important science.

The Greek and Roman languages have given the different angles and triangles their special names.

- An **acute** angle is sharp and the Latin adjective for 'sharp' is 'acutus'.

- A **reflex** angle bends backwards and the Latin verb for 'bend' is 'flectere'.

- A **scalene** triangle is not regular and the Greek adjective for 'uneven' is 'scalenos'.

- An **isosceles** triangle has two sides that are the same length, and the Greek words for 'equal' and 'legs' are 'iso' and 'sceli'.

Exercise

3 Find the name of each triangle.
   a "I am the most elegant triangle, as two of my sides are always the same."
   I am a/an .... triangle.
   b "I am the most reliable triangle, as I am always the same shape, even when I am a different size."
   I am a/an .... triangle.
   c "I am the most interesting triangle as I am always different."
   I am a/an .... triangle.
   d "I am the most upright triangle, as I always stand straight".
   I am a/an .... triangle.
   e "I am very special, as I am both upright and elegant."
   I am a/an .... triangle.

5.5 Quadrilaterals

A quadrilateral is a polygon with four straight sides and four angles.

The angles of a quadrilateral add up to 360°.

There are eight different types of quadrilateral and each one has its own name and properties:

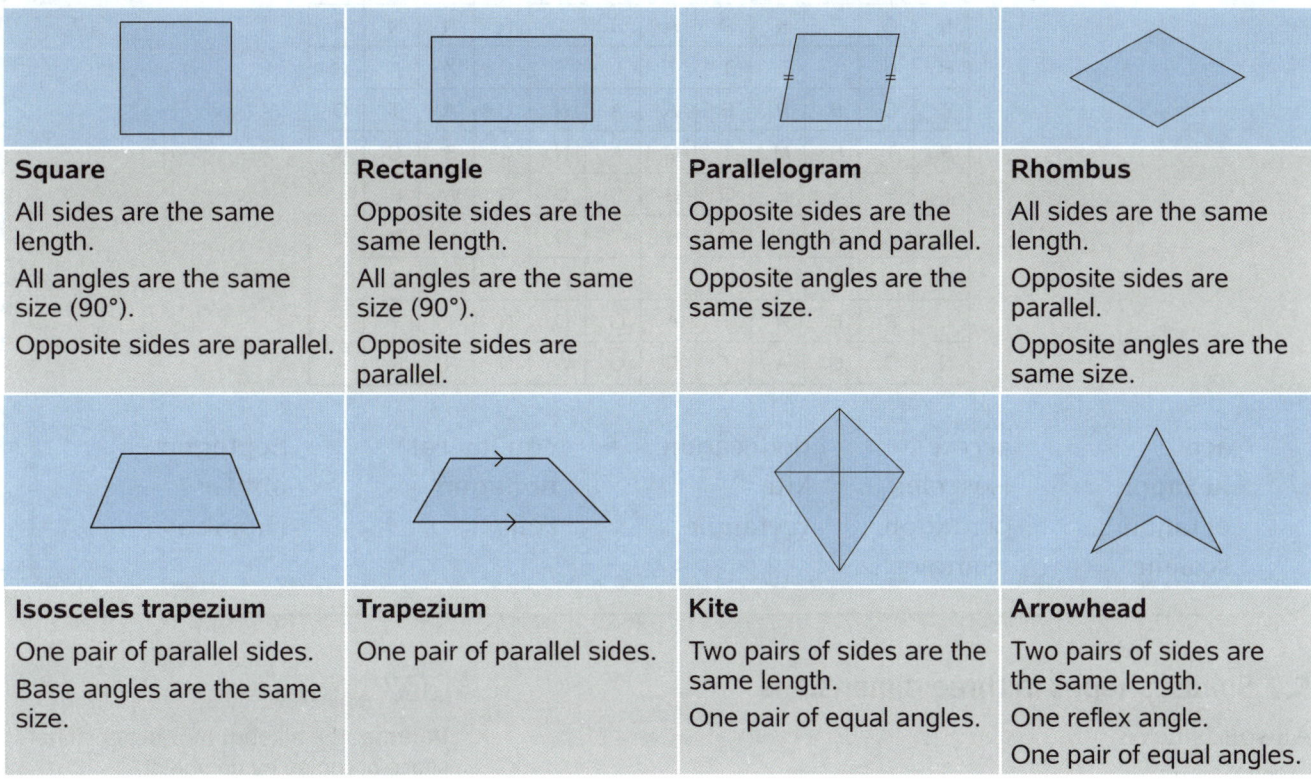

Square	Rectangle	Parallelogram	Rhombus
All sides are the same length. All angles are the same size (90°). Opposite sides are parallel.	Opposite sides are the same length. All angles are the same size (90°). Opposite sides are parallel.	Opposite sides are the same length and parallel. Opposite angles are the same size.	All sides are the same length. Opposite sides are parallel. Opposite angles are the same size.

Isosceles trapezium	Trapezium	Kite	Arrowhead
One pair of parallel sides. Base angles are the same size.	One pair of parallel sides.	Two pairs of sides are the same length. One pair of equal angles.	Two pairs of sides are the same length. One reflex angle. One pair of equal angles.

Arrowheads are special as they are **concave**.
All the other quadrilaterals are **convex**.

5.6 Polygons with more than four sides

'Polygon' is the name for any shape that is drawn with straight sides.

A **regular** polygon has equal sides and equal angles.

In Geometry 'equal' means the same size or the same length. The names of the polygons come from Greek or Latin words:

> **KEY WORD**
>
> **Regular** a polygon is regular if all its angles are the same size and all its sides are the same length

Number of sides of the polygon	Number	Latin name of the number	Greek name of the number	Name of Polygon
3	3	Tres	Tria	Triangle
4	4	Quattuor		Quadrilateral
5	5		Pente	Pentagon
6	6		Hexi	Hexagon
7	7		Hepta	Heptagon
8	8	Octo	Octo	Octagon
9	9	Novem		Nonagon
10	10	Decem	Deca	Decagon
12	12	Duodecem	Dodeca	Dodecagon
20	20		Ikosi	Icosahedron

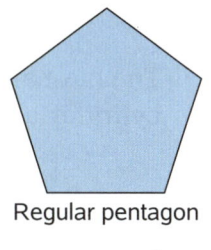

Regular pentagon

Irregular pentagon

Exercise

4 Wordsearch. Find the names of the angles and polygons.

S	C	A	L	E	N	E	T	N	Y	E	H
N	O	G	A	C	E	D	O	D	Q	L	E
X	S	V	T	J	O	G	W	U	F	G	X
S	C	E	K	R	A	B	I	N	N	N	A
R	U	I	L	T	I	L	T	O	X	A	G
E	Q	B	P	E	A	A	N	U	A	T	O
F	T	E	M	T	C	A	N	C	S	C	N
L	H	I	E	O	G	S	U	G	W	E	I
E	X	R	K	O	H	T	O	X	L	R	S
X	A	Z	N	Q	E	R	W	S	N	E	Y
L	P	E	N	T	A	G	O	N	I	Y	U
N	O	G	A	T	C	O	W	O	R	R	A

acute	arrow	dodecagon	equilateral	heptagon
hexagon	isosceles	kite	nonagon	obtuse
octagon	pentagon	rectangle	reflex	rhombus
scalene	triangle			

5.7 Solids: shapes in three dimensions

All solids have:

◎ **faces**, the flat surfaces
◎ **edges**, where the faces meet
◎ **vertices (plural of vertex)**, the points where the edges meet.

A solid is a shape formed in three dimensions.

1 A solid with six square faces is called a **cube**.

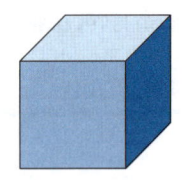

2 A **cuboid** has six faces which are rectangles or squares.

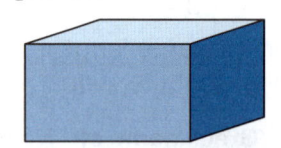

3 The base and top of a **cylinder** are circles.

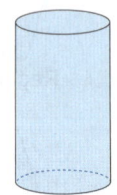

4 The base of a **pyramid** may be a square, or a rectangle.

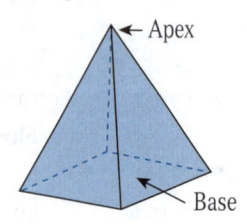

← Apex
← Base

KEY WORDS

Volume the amount of 3-dimensional space occupied by an object

Capacity the amount of space that something contains

Be careful! A shape has volume (the amount of space that it takes up) and capacity, which is the amount that it contains.

5 A pyramid with a triangular base is called a tetrahedron.

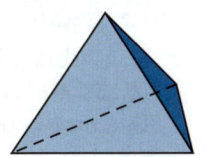

6 A triangular prism has a triangle as its cross section. The cross section is the same for the whole length.

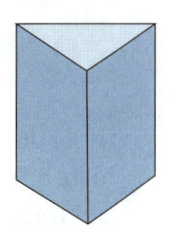

> A polyhedron is a solid with flat sides. A cylinder is not a polyhedron.

Exercise

5 Complete this table, and work out the number in the last column for each shape.

	Shape of faces	Number of faces (F)	Number of edges (E)	Number of vertices (V)	F + V − E
a Cube	Square				
b Cuboid			12		
c Square-based pyramid	One square Four triangles				
d Triangular prism		5			
e Tetrahedron				4	

Euler's Formula

The value of F + V − E for any straight-sided solid is called 'Euler's formula'.

In Exercise 5, did you get the same value each time?

> Leonhard Euler, (1707–83) was a Swiss mathematician who made a lasting contribution to the development of mathematics.

5.8 Circles

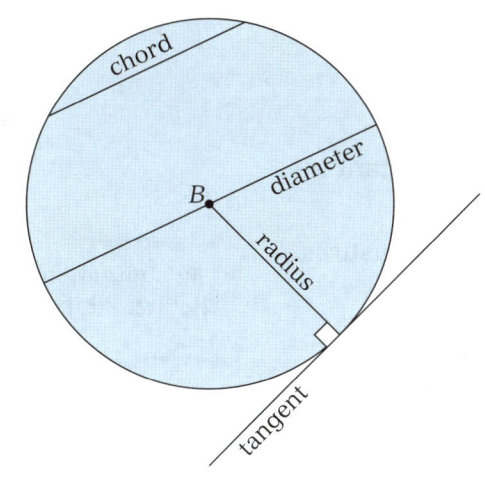

The **radius** of a circle is the distance from the centre of the circle to the **circumference**.

The **circumference** of a circle is the perimeter, or outside edge.

The **diameter** of a circle is a straight line through the centre from one edge to the opposite edge.

A **chord** is a straight line joining two points on the **circumference**.

A **tangent** touches the **circumference** and makes a **right angle** with the **radius** at the point of contact.

Important formulae:

Circumference = π × diameter   or   Circumference = 2 × π × radius

$C = \pi d$ or $C = 2\pi r$

π is a special number.

> Remember:
> In algebra, when letters are joined up this means multiply.

Facts about π (pi)

- π is the number found when the circumference of a circle is divided by the length of its diameter.
- A circle with a diameter of one metre will have a circumference of 3.14 (3 d.p.) metres.
- This idea has been used for at least 4,000 years.
- It has been known from early times that the value of π was a little bit more than 3.
- The first person to use the symbol π was William Jones in 1706. He used the Greek letter for P to represent perimeter.
- π-day is celebrated each year on March 14th.
- Using a computer π has been calculated to 51 billion places.
- π is an irrational number. It cannot be written as a fraction and no pattern has been found for the order of the numbers. The first 10 figures for π are 3.141592654…

> Why March 14th?

Talking points

Knowledge of geometry helps architects to design attractive buildings.

Work with a partner and find five examples of famous buildings that you both like. Try to identify as many of the shapes and angles as you can.

5.9 Metric measures

People measure things every day. It is also an important idea in mathematics.

Metric measures are the standard international measures for length, mass and volume.

These are the names of the standard units:

Length		Mass		Volume	
Millimetre	(mm)	Milligram	(mg)	Millilitre	(ml)
Centimetre	(cm)			Centilitre	(cl)
Metre	(m)	Gram	(g)		
Kilometre	(km)	Kilogram	(kg)	Litre	(l)
		Tonne	(t)		

> The standard units measure mass, not weight. Do you know why?

Milli- and kilo-

Many units of measurement begin with milli- or kilo-.

'**Mille**' means one thousand in Latin   A **milli**metre is $\frac{1}{1000}$ of a metre

'**Khilloi**' means one thousand in Greek   A **kilo**gram is 1000 grams,
a **kilo**metre is 1000 metres

'**Centum**' means one hundred in Latin   A **centi**metre is $\frac{1}{100}$ of a metre

Exercise

6 Which unit would you use to measure these? Choose from the list of units in the box.

kilometres   grams   litres   centimetres   millilitres   millimetres   kilograms

		Unit
a	The distance between Athens and Rome	
b	The volume of liquid in a can of cola	
c	The mass of a shark	
d	The length of a fishing rod	
e	The mass of a shoe	grams
f	The volume of water in a pond	
g	The width of a leaf	

Exercise

7 Complete these sentences with the correct units.

a The distance to the bus stop is 700 ....

b The mass of a newborn baby is 3.2 ....

c The length of a pencil is 13 ....

d To cook rice measure 800.......... of water for 250 .... of rice.

e The mini-bus needs 45 .... of diesel.

5.10 Mensuration

Mensuration is the mathematical system of rules for finding areas and volumes.

You can use formulae to calculate area and volume.

If you choose the correct formula, you will get the correct answer!

- Length:
  - use: mm, cm, m, km
  - There is only one length measurement

- Area:
  - use: mm², cm², m², km²
  - Area formulae need **2** length measurements multiplied together

- Volume:
  - use mm³, cm³, m³, km³.
  - Volume formulae need **3** length measurements multiplied together
  - Volumes are also measured in millilitres and litres.   1 ml ≡ 1 cm³

  1 litre ≡ 1000 cm³

Area is 2-dimensional.
Volume is 3-dimensional.

Area Formulae

Look at the diagrams – you will see **two** lengths marked on each one.

In polygons the two measurements are always at 90°. Circles are different.

	Formula	Diagram
The area of a rectangle	$A = bh$	
The area of a triangle	$A = \frac{1}{2}bh$	
The area of a circle The radius is multiplied by itself	$A = \pi r^2$	
The area of a parallelogram	$A = bh$	
The area of a trapezium	$A = \frac{(a+b)}{2}h$	

Remember:
$r^2 = r \times r$

Volume Formulae

Look at the diagrams. You will see **three** lengths marked on each solid, unless there is a circular base.

	Formula	Diagram
The volume of a cube	$V = s^3$	
The volume of a cuboid	$V = lbh$ because volume = length × breadth × height	
The volume of a prism	$V = $ Area of cross-section × length	
The volume of a cylinder A cylinder is also a prism	$V = \pi r^2 h$	

Geometry 5

	Formula	Diagram
The volume of a cone	$V = \frac{1}{3}\pi r^2 h$	
The volume of a pyramid The formula is like the one for the cone	$V = \frac{1}{3} \times$ area of base $\times h$	

To calculate areas and volumes:

1 Look at the shape, or read the question carefully.
2 Do you need to find an area or a volume?
3 Find the formula for the shape you are using.
Copy the formula.
4 Put the numbers from the diagram or question into the formula.
5 Calculate the value.
6 Check the units.

Example

The base has a radius of 10 cm, the height is 12 cm.
Find the volume.

1 What do you need to find?   You need to find the volume.
2 What shape is it?   This shape is a cone.
3 What is the formula?   The formula is $V = \frac{1}{3}\pi r^2 h$
4 $V = \frac{1}{3} \times \pi \times 10 \times 10 \times 12$
5 $V = 400\pi$
6 $V = 1257 \text{ cm}^3$

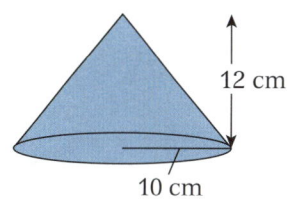

Exercise

8 Complete the table.

The formulae, the answers and the units are given in this box:

The formulae are:	$A = s^2$, $A = \dfrac{(a+b)}{2} h$, $V = \pi r^2 h$, $A = bh$, $C = 2\pi r$, $V = \text{base area} \times \text{height}$
The answers are:	49, 4.5, 503, 195, 405, 39
The units are:	cm², m³, mm², m³, cm, cm²

Description	Formula	Answer	Units
a A bicycle wheel has a diameter of 62 cm. How far does it travel in one turn?			
b The parallel sides of a trapezium are 5 cm and 8 cm. The distance between the parallel sides is 6 cm. What is the area of the trapezium?			
c A triangular prism has a length of 3 m. The base of the triangle measures 2 m and the height is 1.5 m. What is the volume?			
d Each square on a chessboard measures 7 cm. What is the area of each square?			
e A cylindrical storage tank has a height of 10 m. The radius of the base is 4 m. Find the volume.			
f If the base of a parallelogram measures 27 mm and the height is 15 mm, what is its area?			

5.11 Symmetry

Line Symmetry

A shape with line symmetry can be folded in half so that the two halves match exactly.

The line of symmetry is like a mirror that reflects one side to match the other.

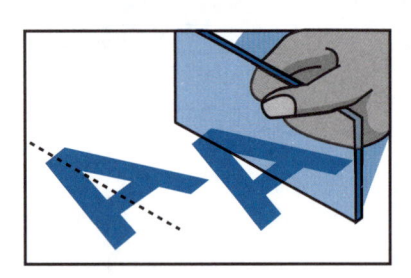

KEY WORDS

Mirror image an image which is like a reflection in a mirror. Everything is the same, except reversed.

Mirror line a line dividing a diagram or picture exactly in half

Shapes may have more than one line of symmetry.

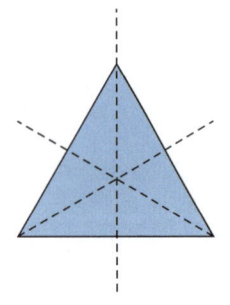

Rotational symmetry

A shape has rotational symmetry if it repeats itself more than once in every full turn (360°).

This shape has a rotational symmetry of order 4. If you turn it, it will look exactly the same every 90°.

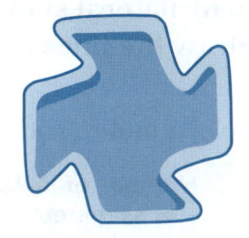

*It is possible to have line symmetry **and** rotational symmetry.*

Exercise

9 Complete this table by listing the letters of the alphabet that match the description of symmetry.

a One line of symmetry	A, T, … ?
b Two lines of symmetry	H, … ?
c Rotational symmetry of order 2	N ? ? ?
d Rotational symmetry of order 4	H, … ?
e More than 4 lines of symmetry	… ?
f No lines of symmetry, no rotational symmetry	F, G, … ?
g Two lines of symmetry, rotational symmetry of order 2	… ?

Talking points

Work with a partner.

a Take a piece of paper and fold it in half.

Draw a shape on the folded paper, starting and finishing at the fold line.

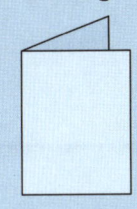

Cut out your shape and open it out.

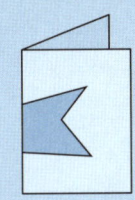

Your shape has one line of symmetry.

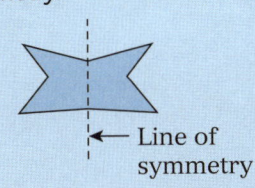

← Line of symmetry

b Make other shapes with one line of symmetry.

c By folding your paper twice, make shapes with two lines of symmetry.

d How can you make shapes with four lines of symmetry?

10 Write the name of each quadrilateral shown in this table.
On a copy of the shapes, draw the lines of symmetry and write the order of rotational symmetry.

Quadrilaterals may have line symmetry, rotational symmetry or both.

		Name	Number of lines of symmetry	Order of rotational symmetry
a			2	2
b				
c				
d				
e				
f		Arrowhead		

Think about the questions from the start of this chapter.
Can you answer them now?
◎ What is the sum of the angles in a triangle?
◎ How many sides are there in a regular heptagon?
◎ What is the name of the line from the centre of a circle to the edge?
◎ How many millimetres are there in a metre?
◎ What is the formula for the volume of a cone?
◎ How many lines of symmetry are there in a square?

5 Consolidation: Geometry

Need more practice?
Review and check your understanding here

Exercise 5.1

1 Look at the diagrams below to remind you that:
  ◎ The angles on a straight line add up to 180°
  ◎ The angles round a point add up to 360°

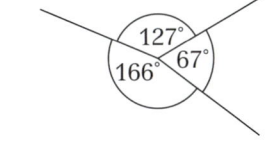

158° + 22° = 180°   127° + 67° + 166° = 360°

Use the value of the given angles to calculate the size of every other angle.

a   37°

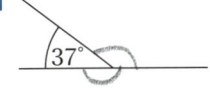

b   105°, 127°

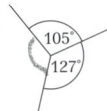

c   112°, 112°

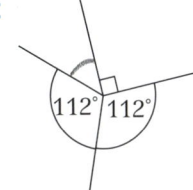

d   132°

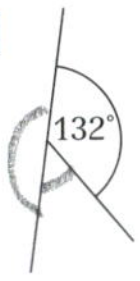

2 Use the value of the given angles to calculate the size of every other angle.

a   64°

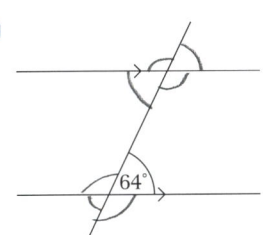

b   141°

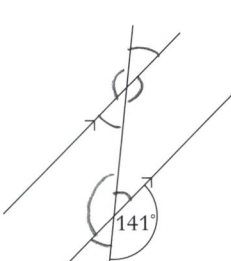

c   67°

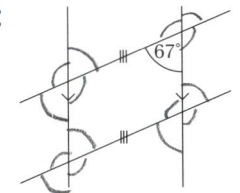

d   61°, 66°

67

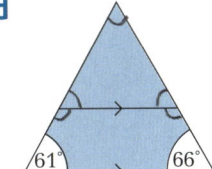

3 These diagrams show the four different types of triangle.

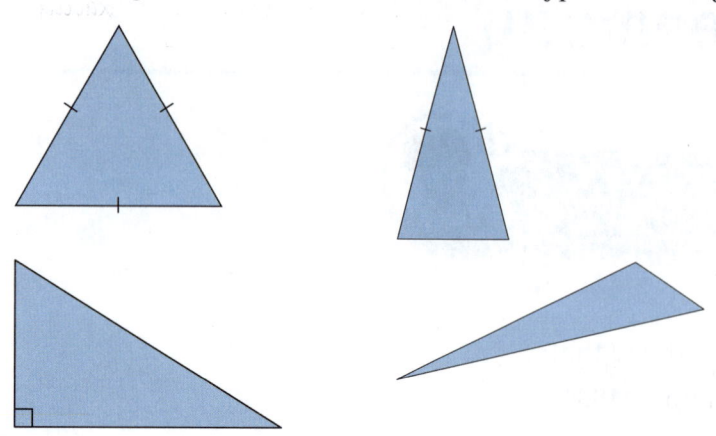

Look at the diagrams and then choose the correct word to complete the following sentences.

| scalene | length | isosceles | right-angled | three |
| two | equilateral | different | angles | |

You may need to use a word more than once.

a A/n ……………………triangle has …………… angles of 60°. The sides of the triangle are all the same………………

b A/n …………………… triangle has two sides that are the same……………and …………angles that are the same size.

c A triangle with an angle of 90° is called a/n ……………………… triangle.

d In a/an ………………… triangle all the sides are …………… lengths and none of the …………… are the same.

e The angles of a triangle add up to ……………

4 Use the information from question 3 to find the size of each unmarked angle in these diagrams.

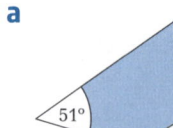

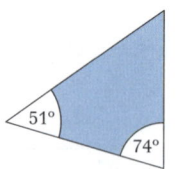

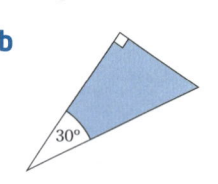

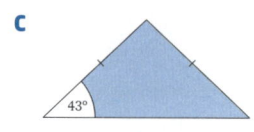

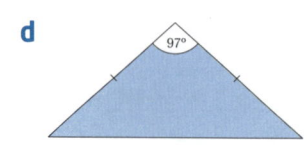

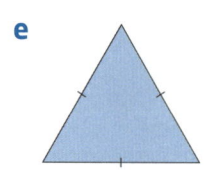

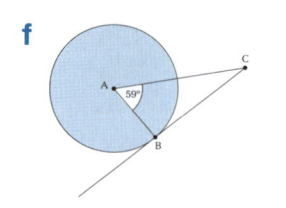

a 51°, 74°

b 30°

c 43°

d 97°

e

f 59°

5 Five lines are drawn between the vertices of a regular pentagon and its centre. The pentagon is divided into five congruent triangles.

> Congruent triangles are exactly the same shape and size.

If the length of the line HI is the same as the length of the line GI:

a What other lines are the same length?

b What type of triangle is drawn?

c What is the size of the angles at the centre of the pentagon?

Example

The angles DIE, EIF, …

d What is the size of each internal angle?

Example

The angles DEF, EFG, …?

The lines DE and EF are extended to give external angles.

e What is the size of each external angle?

Example

MEF, LFG……

f What do the external angles add up to?

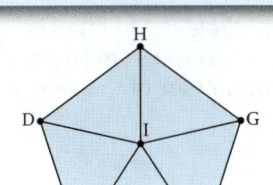

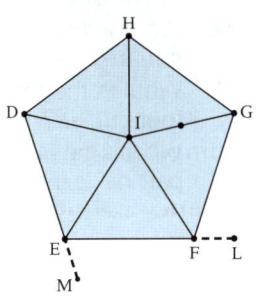

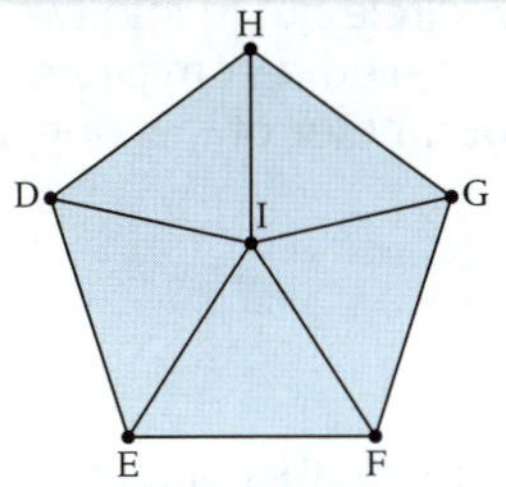

6 Look at the diagram of a regular hexagon.

a Can you give the name of the triangle AGF?

b What do you notice about the length of the sides of the triangle CGD?

c Can you calculate all the angles of triangle AGF?

d What are the external angles of the hexagon?

e What do the external angles add up to?

f Is this true for all regular polygons?

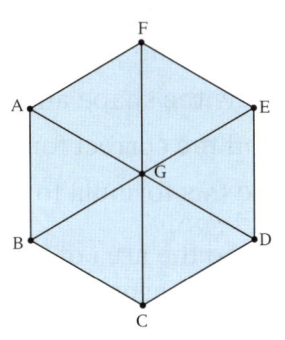

Extension

7

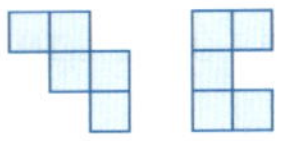

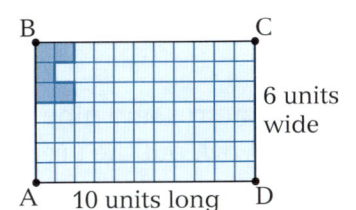

These are pentominos, shapes created by linking five squares together using the edges of the squares.

There are twelve different shapes altogether. Can you find them? Be careful about rotations or reflections.

When you have found all twelve shapes, you can fit all the pentominos into a rectangle, 10 units long and × 6 units wide. It is easier to do this if you cut them out, rather than draw them!

Exercise 5.2

You will need a calculator for this exercise.
Give your answers to 3 significant figures.

1 The radius of a circle is 12 cm. Find its circumference and its area.

2 The diameter of a circle is 8m. Find its circumference and its area.

3 A circle has a circumference of 44 cm.

a What is the radius of the circle?

b What is the diameter of the circle?

4 The distance from the centre of a circle to its circumference is 2.5 m. Calculate the area of the circle.

5 A circle cut in into two equal pieces is called a semicircle. What is the perimeter of this semicircle?

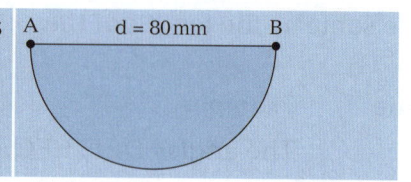

A   d = 80 mm   B

6 Look at this diagram.
  a What is the area of the square?
  b What is the total area of the four circles?
  c What is the area of the shaded part inside the square?

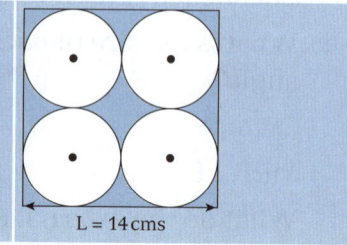

L = 14 cms

Reading Practice!
Read these questions carefully, then:
- Identify the shape
- Draw the shape and mark the measurements
- Find the correct formula
- Use this formula to calculate the area or volume.

7 Find the area of a parallelogram with a base that measures twelve centimetres and a height that measures seven centimetres.

8 A right-angled triangle has a base measuring two and a half metres, and a height of one and a half metres. Calculate the area.

9 Calculate the volume of a cylinder. The height of the cylinder is twelve millimetres and the radius of the base is five millimetres.

10 A trapezium has parallel sides that measure seven centimetres and nine centimetres. The distance between the parallel sides is five centimetres. Work out the area of the trapezium.

11 A box has a length of fourteen centimetres, a width of ten centimetres, and a height of eight centimetres. What is the volume of the box?

12 What is the volume of a pyramid with a square base of eight centimetres and a height of five and a half centimetres?

13 Find the area of a carpet that is three and a quarter metres long, and two and one third metres wide.

Similar shapes
14 a Calculate the area of a square with sides of 3 cm.
  b Calculate the area of a square with sides that are 9 cm long.
  c Write the ratio of their areas in its simplest form.

15 a Calculate the volume of a cube with sides of 4 cm.
  b Calculate the volume of a cube with sides of 8 cm.
  c Write the ratio of the volumes in its simplest form.

70

16 Fill in this table. Some of the entries have been made for you.

Ratio of length	Ratio of area	Ratio of volume
1 : 2	1 : 4	
1 : 3		1 : 27
1 : 5		
1 : a	1 : a^2	

Practical mensuration

17 Matt is building a rocket. The rocket is made from a cone and a cylinder.

The radius of the cone and cylinder is 3.5 cm.

The height of the cylinder is 30 cm.

The length of the rocket is 40 cm.

Find the volume of the rocket.

18 Jasmina is making a kite. She uses two sticks and some thick paper.

One stick is 30 cm long and the other is 50 cm long.

Label this diagram with the lengths. AB is 14 cm.

What is the area of the paper used in the kite?

> **Extension**
>
> The Platonic solids are the five solid shapes that were studied by the mathematicians in Greece, more than two thousand years ago.
>
> The flat 2-D (two dimensional) diagrams are called 'nets' and if you copy them onto thick paper and then fold them, you can make the solid shapes.
>
> Can you find out the name of each solid?

Name of solid	3-D image	Net

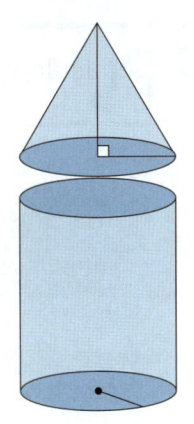

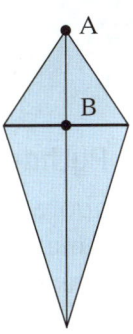

6 Pythagoras' theorem and trigonometry

> **In this chapter you will answer...**
> - Can you use Pythagoras' theorem without a right-angled triangle?
> - If a triangle has sides of 7 cm, 5 cm and 10 cm, does it contain a right angle?
> - What is the value of sin 30°?
> - If you are given the opposite and adjacent sides of a triangle, which trigonometry ratio do you use?
> - How do you find $\theta°$ if you know the value of $\cos \theta$?

6.1 Pythagoras' theorem

Pythagoras' theorem may be the oldest practical mathematical idea in the world. It has been used for at least 4,000 years.

The Egyptians used it to build the pyramids and to plan their fields after the floods each year.

The Babylonians used it to build their cities and gardens.

The Chinese called it the '*kou ku*' theorem about 3,000 years ago.

It was used in India more than 2,000 years ago to build altars and temples.

You can find evidence that Pythagoras' theorem is true for all right-angled triangles in many books. There are many different proofs, some use algebra or diagrams; others are more practical.

Look on the Internet for a film of Dr Jacob Bronowski - he shows the theorem using tiles.

Here is one proof:
The diagram on the right has a square, KLMN, drawn inside a larger square, GHIJ.

The length GK = a and the length KH = b, so GH = $a + b$

The area of the large square, GHIJ: $(a + b)^2 = a^2 + 2ab + b^2$
The area of the centre square and four triangles:

$$c^2 + 4 \times \tfrac{1}{2} ab = c^2 + 2ab$$

These areas are the same:

$$c^2 + 2ab = a^2 + 2ab + b^2$$

therefore $\quad \underline{c^2 = a^2 + b^2}$

Subtract 2ab from both

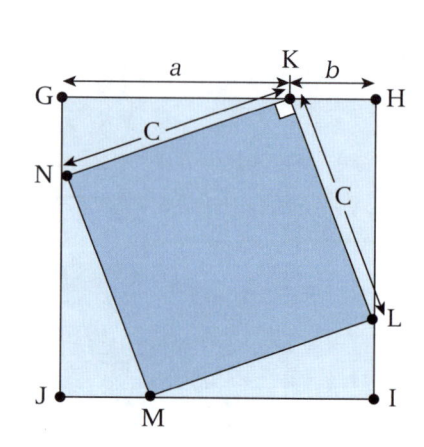

6.1.1 Pythgoras' triples

Archaeologists have found clay tablets from Babylon listing groups of numbers that fitted the rule

$$c^2 = a^2 + b^2$$

These were used by architects and engineers.
Here are some examples of Pythagoras' triples:

   3, 4, 5
   5, 12, 13
   8, 15, 17
   7, 24, 25

$3^2 + 4^2 = 25 = 5^2$

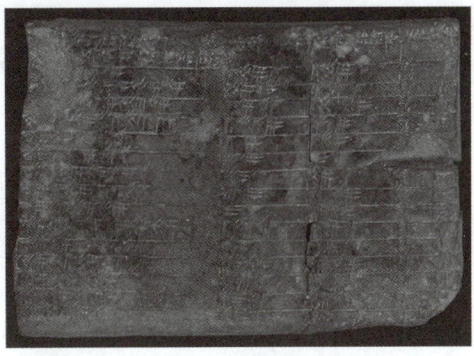

Plimpton tablet 322. These may be lists of Pythagoras' triples for use in Babylon.

In Egypt, a rope with 13 evenly spaced knots was extended and the corners pinned with sticks. If the sticks were placed so that the sides were three units, four units and five units long, then one of the vertices was a right angle. This was an easy and accurate way for builders to measure a right angle.

Example

$3^2 + 4^2 = 9 + 16$
$ = 25$
$ = 5^2$

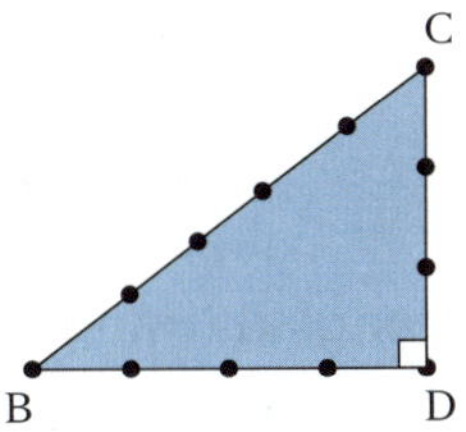

6.1.2 To use Pythagoras' theorem

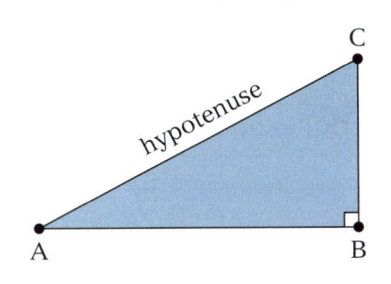

In every right-angled triangle:

The **longest** side is opposite the right angle (90°).

The longest side is called the **hypotenuse**.

The shortest side is opposite the smallest angle.

KEY WORD

Hypotenuse the side opposite the right angle in a right-angled triangle

This means that we can use the written rule:

"In any right-angled triangle, the area of the square on the hypotenuse is equal to the sum of the squares on the other two sides"

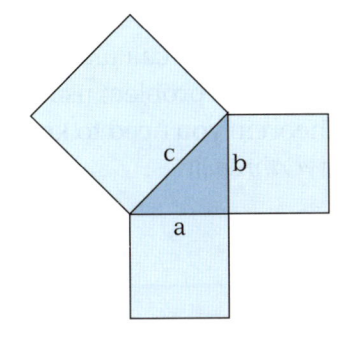

$a^2 + b^2 = c^2$

Examples

1 Calculate the length of the hypotenuse in a triangle with sides of 5 cm and 12 cm.

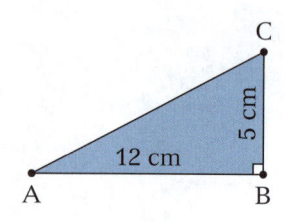

$a^2 + b^2 = c^2$
$5^2 + 12^2 = 25 + 144$
$ = 169$
$ = 13^2$

The length of the hypotenuse is 13 cm.

To find the hypoteneuse you need to find c.
$c^2 = 169 = 13^2$

2 A right-angled triangle has a hypotenuse of 12 m. The height of the triangle is 5 m. How long is the base?

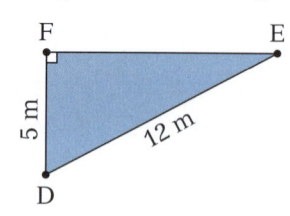

$a^2 + b^2 = c^2$
$5^2 + b^2 = 12^2$
$b^2 = 12^2 - 5^2$
$b^2 = 144 - 25$
$b^2 = 119$
$b = \sqrt{119}$
$b = 10.9\,m$

Subtract the shorter side.

Always look at your answer to check that it makes sense. Is the hypotenuse the longest length?

3 A triangle has sides of 1.5 m, 2 m and 2.5 m. Is it a right-angled triangle?

2.5 m is the longest side, so if the triangle is right-angled, then this must be the hypotenuse.

If the triangle has an angle of 90°, $1.5^2 + 2^2$ will be the same as 2.5^2

$1.5^2 + 2^2 = 2.25 + 4 = 6.25$

$2.5^2 = 6.25$ so $1.5^2 + 2^2 = 2.5^2$ and the triangle contains a right angle.

Exercise

1 Here are some sentences about Pythagoras' theorem. Choose the right word(s) or number for each sentence.

a The hypotenuse is the *longest/shortest* side of a right-angled triangle.
b A right angle is an angle of *180°/90°*.
c You *do/ do not* need to know the size of an angle in the triangle to use Pythagoras' theorem.
d To use Pythagoras' rule, a triangle *must / must not* contain a right angle.
e In the Pythagoras triple (7, 24, 25) twenty-five is the *largest/smallest* number.
f The proof of Pythagoras' theorem is true for *all/some* right-angled triangles.
g At least 4,000 years means that the rule has been used for *less than/more than* 4,000 years.
h Pythagoras was from *Greece/ India*.
i A triangle with sides of 3 m, 4 m and 6 m *will/will not* contain a right angle.
j In a triangle with sides of 8 cm, 15 cm, and 17 cm, the hypotenuse is *15/17* cm long.
k For the final answer in a problem using Pythagoras' theorem, you must remember to use the *square/square root* key on your calculator.
l To solve a problem using Pythagoras' theorem you need to know the lengths of *two/three* lines.

6.2 Trigonometry

- Trigonometry, like Pythagoras' theorem, is a very old system. It grew from different mathematical traditions, in particular those of Egypt, Mesopotamia and India.
- Pythagoras' theorem uses only the sides of a right-angled triangle; trigonometry uses both the sides and the angles.
- The earliest document that uses trigonometry may be the Ahmed Papyrus which dates from 1,650 BCE.
- From ancient times, similar triangles have been used to solve practical problems in geometry, building, astronomy and navigation.
- The mathematician Thales used the lengths of shadows to calculate the heights of the pyramids in Egypt. It was also important to be able to calculate the length of shadows when constructing a sundial.

"Trigonometry is not the work of any one person or nation. Its history spans thousands of years and has touched every major civilization."

Exercise

2 Try this practical activity with a friend. Copy this triangle two or three times. You can make it as large as you like, but don't make it too small!
Angle CAB is 35°, angle ACB is a right angle.

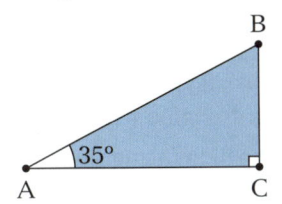

Measure the lengths of AB, BC and AC as accurately as you can.

Calculate the values of $\frac{CB}{AB}$, $\frac{CB}{AC}$ and $\frac{AC}{AB}$ to two decimal places for each triangle.

Compare your results with those of your friend. What do you notice?

You should discover that $\frac{CB}{AB}$ is approximately 0.57, $\frac{CB}{AC} \approx 0.70$ and $\frac{AC}{AB} \approx 0.82$

Is this a surprise? The triangles are all similar, so the ratio of their sides stays the same, however large, or small, they are.

This result is the basis of the trigonometry you will study in class.

The ratios you have found are called **sine**, **cosine** and **tangent**.

They are written as 'tan', 'sin', and 'cos' on your calculator keys.

tan sin cos

$\approx$ is the sign for approximately

For trigonometry problems, the right-angled triangle is always marked as shown in this triangle:

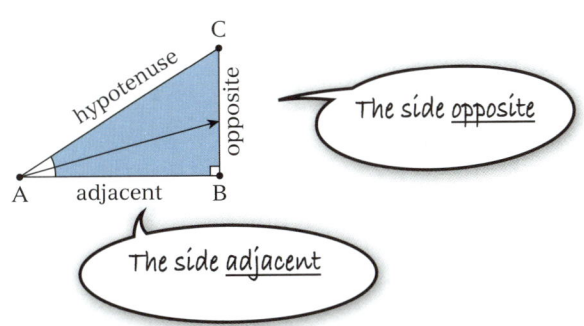

The side *opposite*

The side *adjacent*

And the ratios are defined as:

$$\text{sine} = \frac{\text{opposite side}}{\text{hypotenuse}}$$

$$\text{cosine} = \frac{\text{adjacent side}}{\text{hypotenuse}}$$

$$\text{tangent} = \frac{\text{opposite side}}{\text{adjacent side}}$$

6.2.3 How do you remember the formulae?

- Some people remember the letters **SOH CAH TOA**.
- Some people use a mnemonic, a special phrase like "**S**illy **O**ld **H**arry, **C**aught **A** **H**erring, **T**ripped **O**ver **A**unty".
- Some people remember the shape.

		Which Ratio?
	The hypotenuse is not marked or used.	Use the tangent
	The line opposite the given angle is used with the hypotenuse.	Use the sine
	The angle between the hypotenuse and the adjacent line is used.	Use the cosine

SOH $\sin = \dfrac{opp}{hyp}$

CAH $\cos = \dfrac{adj}{hyp}$

TOA $\tan = \dfrac{opp}{adj}$

KEY WORDS

Adjacent the side next to the given angle in a right-angled triangle

Opposite the side facing the given angle in a right-angled triangle

Exercise

3

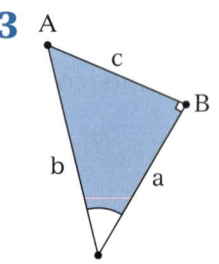

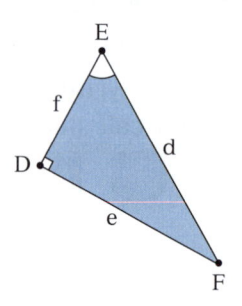

Look at the triangles above and use them to complete the following sentences.

The first sentence has been completed for you.

a In triangle ABC, side **b** is the *hypotenuse*.

b In triangle DEF, side **e** is the .... side

c In triangle ABC, side **a** is the .... side

d In triangle ABC, the ratio $\dfrac{a}{b}$ is called the ....

e In triangle ABC, the ratio $\dfrac{c}{b}$ is called the ....

f In triangle DEF, the ratio $\dfrac{e}{f}$ is called the ....

g In triangle DEF, the sine ratio is given by $\dfrac{?}{d}$

h In triangle DEF, the cosine ratio is given by $\dfrac{?}{?}$

Remember: **SOH CAH TOA**

6.2.4. Using your calculator

You will need a scientific or graphical calculator with keys marked **sin**, **tan** and **cos**.

You will also need a key marked **2nd function**, **inverse**, or **shift**.

Make sure that your screen is showing DEG for degrees. This is very important if you have to reset your calculator.

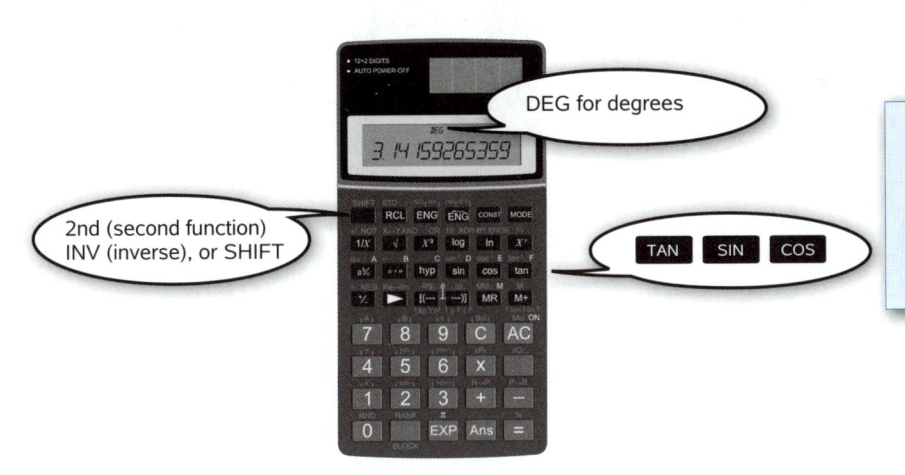

- DEG for degrees
- 2nd (second function) INV (inverse), or SHIFT
- To find the angle you must use the inverse.
- $\cos^{-1}$ is the inverse of cos, and is printed above the cos key on your calculator.

Examples

1

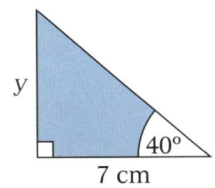

$$\tan = \frac{\text{opposite}}{\text{adjacent}}$$

$$\tan 40° = \frac{y}{7}$$

$$7 \times \tan 40° = y$$

$$y = 5.87 \text{ cm} \quad (3 \text{ s.f})$$

Look at the diagram.
Choose the correct formula.
Write down the formula and fill it in.

2

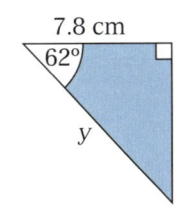

$$\cos = \frac{\text{adjacent}}{\text{hypotenuse}}$$

$$\cos 62° = \frac{7.8}{y}$$

$$y = \frac{7.8}{\cos 62°}$$

$$\underline{y = 16.6 \text{ cm}}$$

Take care!!

Check your key sequence:

[7] [.] [8] [÷] [cos] [6] [2]

3 If you know the length of two lines in a triangle, you can find the angles.

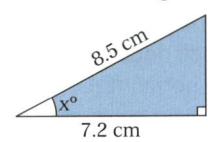

$$\cos x = \frac{\text{adjacent}}{\text{hypotenuse}}$$

$$\cos x = \frac{7.2}{8.5} = 0.84705$$

$$\underline{x = 32.1°}$$

This is the angle whose cosine is 0.84705.

There are two key sequences you can use:

Either: [7] [.] [2] [÷] [8] [.] [5]

followed by [2nd] [cos] [0] [.] [8] [4] [7] [0] [5]

Or: [2nd] [cos] [(] [7] [.] [2] [÷] [8] [.] [5] [)]

Exercise 4

1. tan 89° is
   - a 1.686
   - b 5.729
   - c 57.29

2. sin 90° is
   - a 0.894
   - b 1
   - c 0.156

3. If sin 30° = $\frac{1}{2}$, cos 60° is
   - a 0.8660
   - b 1.732
   - c $\frac{1}{2}$

4. If tan θ = 0.6758, θ is
   - a 34.1°
   - b 1.5943
   - c 0.5943

5. To find the length of BC in this triangle, use:
   - a sin
   - b cos
   - c tan

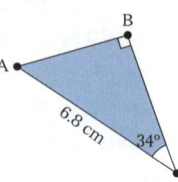

6. To find the size of angle B in this triangle, use:
   - a sin
   - b cos
   - c tan

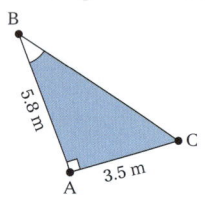

6.2.5 Problems in Words

Your teacher will give you problems that are written in words.

Trigonometry problems are most interesting when they are practical.

To answer them correctly:
- Read the problem
- Sketch a diagram – mark all the information
- Choose your formula
- Complete the calculation.

Example

The Petronas Towers in Kuala Lumpur are 450 m high. If Meena stands 1500 m away from them, what is the angle of elevation when she looks at the top of one of the towers?

$$\tan e = \frac{\text{opposite}}{\text{adjacent}}$$
$$\tan e = \frac{450}{1500}$$
$$e = 0.3$$
$$\underline{e = 16.7°}$$

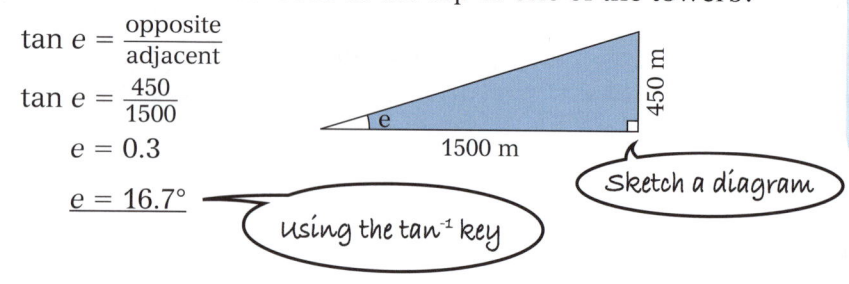

using the tan⁻¹ key

Sketch a diagram

KEY WORDS

Angle of elevation the angle formed when you look up at something from the horizontal

Angle of depression the angle formed when you look down at something from the horizontal

Exercise

5 Read each problem, and then match the problem to the correct diagram and the correct answer.

Problem	Diagram	Answer
A ladder rests against a wall, making an angle of 70° with the ground. If the ladder is six metres long, how far up the wall does it reach?	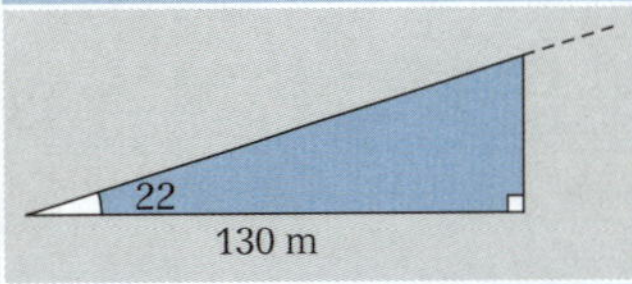 (triangle with 22°, 130 m)	52.5 m
Miki is lying on top of a cliff, looking down at a boat. The cliff is 65 m high and Miki's angle of depression is 22°. How far away is the boat?	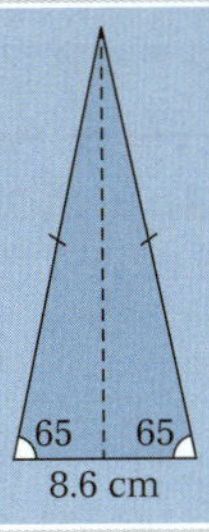 (isosceles triangle with 65°, 65°, base 8.6 cm)	5.64 m
A rectangular field is 210 m long and 130 m wide. What angle does the diagonal make with the longer side?	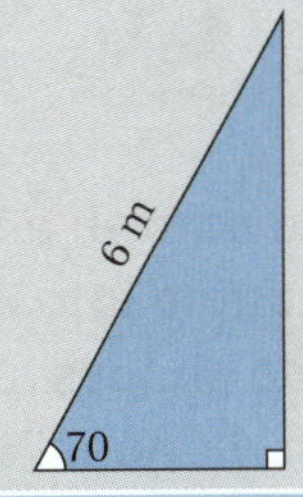 (triangle with 6 m, 70°)	161 m
The base angles of an isosceles triangle are 65°. The base measures 8.6 cm. How long are the equal sides?	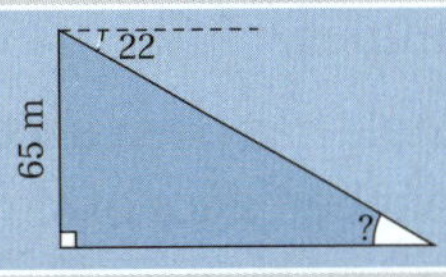 (triangle with 65 m, 22°, ?)	31.8°
The shadow of a tree is 130 m long. The sun is shining at an angle of 22°. How tall is the tree?	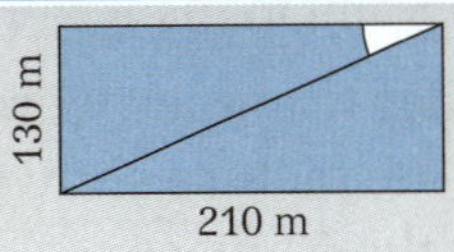 (rectangle 130 m × 210 m with diagonal)	10.2 cm

6.2.6 Exact Values in Trigonometry

You can use the properties of two particular triangles to find exact values for some angles.

1. Take a right-angled isosceles triangle with sides of one unit.
   This gives you a triangle with two 45° angles.

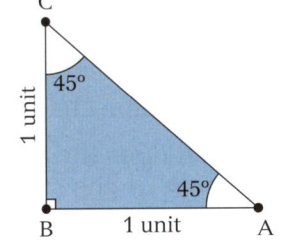

   Using Pythagoras' theorem,
   $$AC^2 = 1^2 + 1^2 = 2$$
   $$AC = \sqrt{2}$$
   So, $\sin 45° = \cos 45° = \dfrac{1}{\sqrt{2}}$

2. Take an equilateral triangle with sides of two units.
   Cut the triangle in half.
   This gives you two right-angled triangles with one angle of 60°, and one angle of 30°.

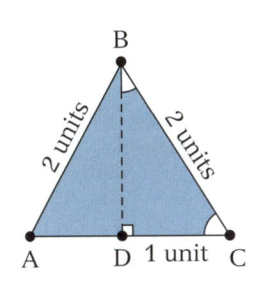

   Using Pythagoras' theorem,
   $$BD^2 = 2^2 - 1^2 = 3$$
   $$BD = \sqrt{3}$$
   So, $\tan 60 = \dfrac{\sqrt{3}}{1} = \sqrt{3}$

Exercise

6 Look at the diagrams on the previous page and use them to complete this table.

Angle	sin	cos	tan
a 30°			
b 60°			$\sqrt{3}$
c 45°		$\frac{1}{\sqrt{2}}$	

Comprehension

Triangulation – ancient and modern

The triangle is the strongest geometric shape, and the most stable. Its shape can only be changed if one of the sides or vertices is broken.

Think how easily you can squash a square into a rhombus or a rectangle into a parallelogram. Four-sided shapes are only strong if they are given a diagonal and changed into two triangles.

The strength of the triangle has been used since ancient times, and the mathematics of similar triangles has been important in many areas.

In **ancient** times similar triangles were used to calculate heights. The picture shows a method explained by the Chinese mathematician Liu Hui in the third century CE. You can see how the method was used to find the height of a cliff which was too difficult to climb.

Triangles were used by the Dutch mapmaker, Gemma Frisius in 1533 CE. to make accurate maps of the area where he lived. Two hundred years later, triangulation was being used all over the world to make maps of countries and continents.

In **modern** times, triangulation is the basis of GPS systems and cell phone networks.

If the emergency services need to find someone who is lost or injured, they can use two or three base stations to find the exact position of a cell phone. The diagram shows the position of a cell phone from three base stations at A and B and C.

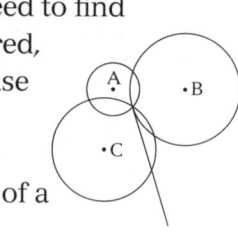

Position of cellphone

7
a Which shape is stronger, a quadrilateral or a triangle?

b Are similar triangles the same size or the same shape?

c Are congruent triangles the same size or the same shape?

d When does the third century begin? In 200 CE or 300 CE?

e Was Liu Hui using right-angled triangles in his calculations?

f Does the triangle used to find the position of a cell phone have to contain a right angle?

g How many base stations do you need to find the position of a cell phone?

Think about the questions from the start of this chapter.
Can you answer them now?
- Can you use Pythagoras' theorem without a right-angled triangle?
- If a triangle has sides of 7cm, 5 cm and 10 cm, does it contain a right angle?
- What is the value of sin 30°?
- If you are given the opposite and adjacent sides of a triangle, which trigonometry ratio do you use?
- How do you find $\theta°$ if you know the value of $\cos \theta$?

6 Consolidation: Pythagoras' theorem and trigonometry

Need more practice?
Review and check your understanding here

Exercise 6.1

1 Find the length of y in each of these triangles. Give your answer to 3 s.f.

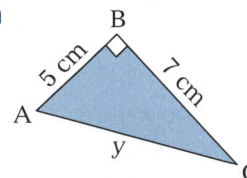

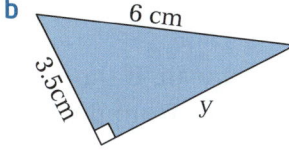

   a Triangle ABC with right angle at B, AB = 5 cm, BC = 7 cm, AC = y

   b Right-angled triangle with one side 3.5 cm, hypotenuse 6 cm, other side y

2 One of these triangles is a right-angled triangle. Which one?

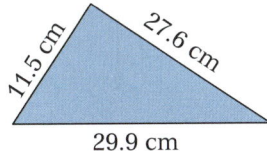

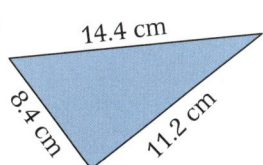

   a Triangle with sides 11.5 cm, 27.6 cm, 29.9 cm

   b Triangle with sides 14.4 cm, 8.4 cm, 11.2 cm

3 Mark the right angles and then use Pythagoras' theorem. Give your answers to 3 s.f.

   a ABCD is a rhombus.
   AC is 12 cm long,
   BD is 8 cm long.
   How long is BC?

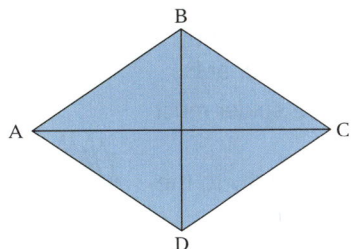

   b ABC is an isosceles triangle.
   AC is 14 cm long,
   BC = AB = 9.4 cm.
   How long is BD?

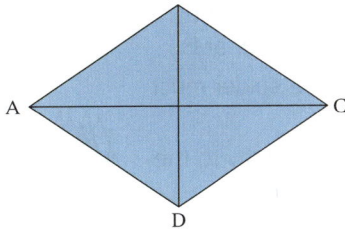

   c FG is the tangent to the circle, centre E.
   The radius of the circle is 5.5 cm.
   If EF is 8.4 cm, find the length of FG.

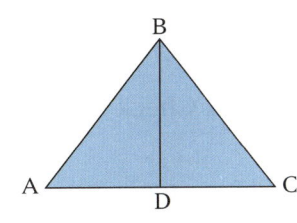

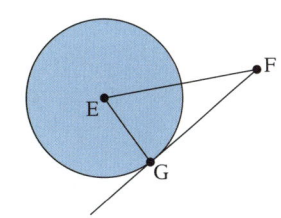

81

Reading Practice

Read these questions carefully, then:

- Draw a diagram. Look for the right angle. Drawing an extra line may help.
- Mark the measurements.
- Use Pythagoras' theorem.

4 A rectangle is seven metres wide and nine metres long. Find the length of the diagonal.

5 A square has diagonals that are seven and a half centimetres long. What is the length of each side?

6 An equilateral triangle has sides that are ninety millimetres long.

   a Find the height of the triangle.

   b Find the area of the triangle.

7 A ladder, seven metres long, rests against a wall. If the base of the ladder is two and a quarter metres from the wall, how high does the ladder reach?

8 a Using this diagram, give the co-ordinates of the points A, B and C.

   b Use Pythagoras' theorem to find the lengths of AB, BC and AC.

   c Is triangle ABC a right-angled triangle?

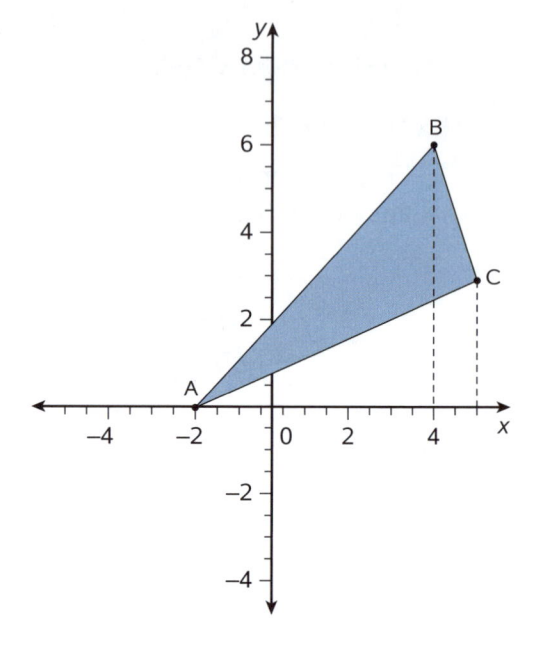

> **Extension**
>
> **This is the first line of a poem by Mary Howitt -**
> "Will you walk into my parlour?" said the spider to the fly.
> The room is 5 m long, 3.5 m wide and 2.8 m high. The spider is at A, a corner at the bottom of the room, and the fly is up in the farthest corner at B.
>
> **a** What is the shortest distance that the spider must walk to catch the fly?
>
> **b** What is the shortest distance from the fly to the spider?

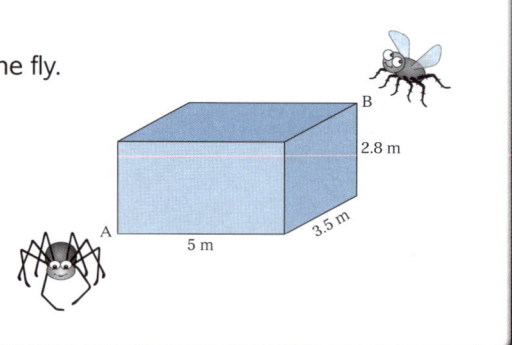

Exercise 6.2

1 Use your calculator to find these values. Check that your calculator is set in degrees first. Give your answers to 4 d.p.

   a tan 55°   **b** cos 15°   **c** tan 85°   **d** sin 20°   **e** cos 90°   **f** sin 62°

2 Use your calculator to find these angles. Greek letters, $\theta, \alpha, \beta, \phi$ etc are symbols that are often used for angles. Give your answers to 1 d.p.

   a If $\tan \theta = 4.00$, $\theta = ?$ **d** If $\cos \theta = 0.337$, $\theta = ?$

   b If $\sin \phi = 0.205$, $\phi = ?$ **e** If $\sin \beta = 1.01$, $\beta = ?$

   c If $\tan \alpha = 0.985$, $\alpha = ?$ **f** If $\cos \beta = 0.8660$, $\beta = ?$

3 Find the length *y* in each triangle. Give your answer to 1 d.p.

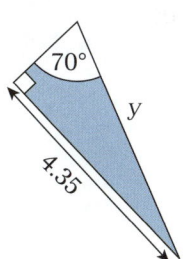

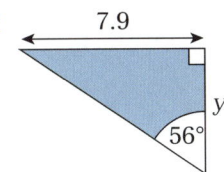

a (right angle at top, 38° at bottom right, base 6.8, y is the vertical side)

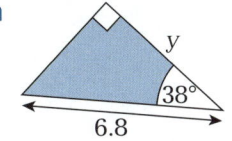

b (70° at top, right angle marked, 4.35 is one side, y is the other)

c (7.9 along the top, right angle, 56° at bottom, y is a side)

d (isoceles triangle, 53° at right, base 9.6, y is the equal side)

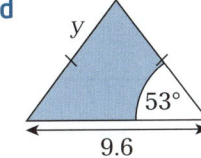

4 Find the size of the marked angle(s) in each triangle.

a (sides 4.8 and 5.9, right angle)

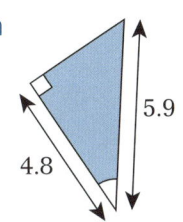

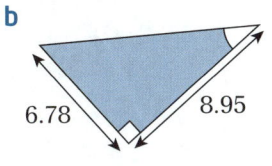

b (sides 6.78 and 8.95, right angle)

c (sides 4.3 and 3.8, right angle)

d (isoceles, 17 cm across top, 12 cm slant sides)

5

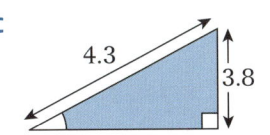

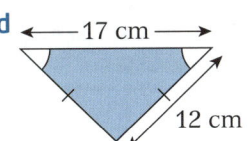

5° 15°

35 m

C   A   B

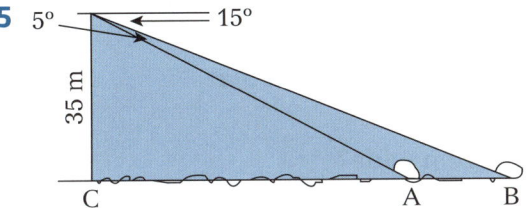

Paula is standing on a cliff looking down at the two rocks at A and at B.

Her angle of depression to the rock at B is 15°, and to the rock at A is 20°.

The cliff is 35 m high.

  a How big are the acute angles at A, B and the angle at C?

  b Calculate the lengths CB and CA.

  c What is the distance between the two rocks?

6 If EG is 15 m,

  a calculate *h*.

  b calculate the area of the triangle EFG.

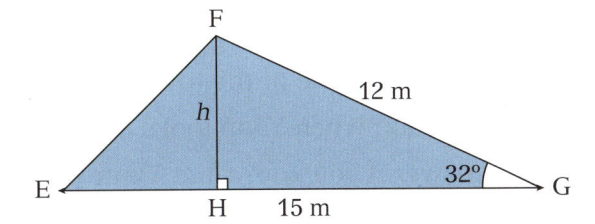

(Triangle EFG with F at top, FG = 12 m, angle at G = 32°, FH = h perpendicular to EG, HG = 15 m, right angle at H)

83

7 Using the exact value of tan 30° that you found in the Pythagoras Chapter, what is the area of this isosceles triangle?

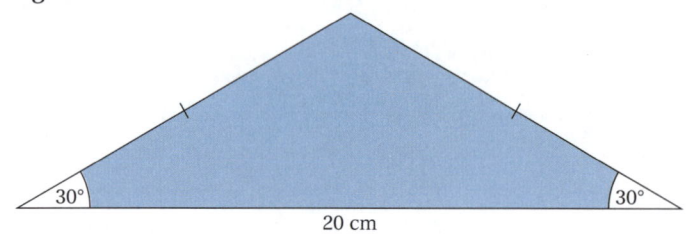

30°   30°
20 cm

> **Extension**
>
> Jo is building a sundial. The central part of the sundial that tells the time is called the 'gnomon' and the flat base is marked out to tell the time.
>
> She decides to make it from paper first, and to test whether she has the shapes and sizes correct.
>
> She knows that, where she lives, the angle of the gnomon has to be 52°, and she wants the base of the gnomon to be 15 cm long.
>
> How high should the gnomon be?
>
> If you look on the Internet, you will find projects and information about how to build different sundials. You will notice that most of them use trigonometry to work out the size and angle of the gnomon.

Exercise 6.3

These problems use either Pythagoras' theorem, or trigonometry, or both.

Look carefully at the diagram or draw your own, and mark on the information that you are given.

1 a How long is the diagonal of a rectangle, 25 cm long and 14 cm wide?

 b What is the size of the angle between the diagonal and the longest side?

2 A ship starts its journey at port A, sails west for 40 km, then sails south for 28 km to port B. It then turns back to port A.

 a What is the distance from port A to port B?

 b What angle does the return journey make with the line marking North?

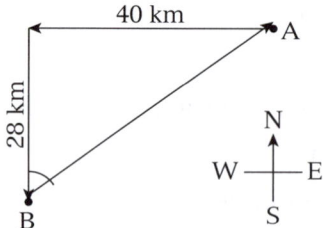

3 The Eiffel tower in Paris is 324 m high.
If Yann is standing 900 m from the base of the tower:

 a Calculate the angle of elevation when Yann looks at the top of the tower.

 b Do you get a different answer if you know that Yann is 2 m tall?

84

4 An obtuse-angled triangle ABC has an angle of 30° at A.
AB measures 11 cm, and AC measures 15 cm.
Mark this information on the diagram.
Calculate:
   a the height of the triangle, the line CD
   b the length AD
   c the length BD
   d the length CB
   e the area of the triangle ABC.

5 Felix is standing on the bank of a river, looking at a tree directly opposite him. The river is 450 m wide. There is another tree 250 m along on the opposite bank.
   a Draw a diagram showing all this information.
   b Calculate the distance from Felix to the second tree.
   c If Felix turns to look at the second tree, what angle does he turn through?

Extension

All these triangles are isosceles triangles.
Calculate the length of the hypotenuse of the smallest triangle.
Use this value to calculate the length of the hypotenuse for the other triangles.
If your answers are correct, you will get a sequence of numbers:
Can you find a rule for the sequence?

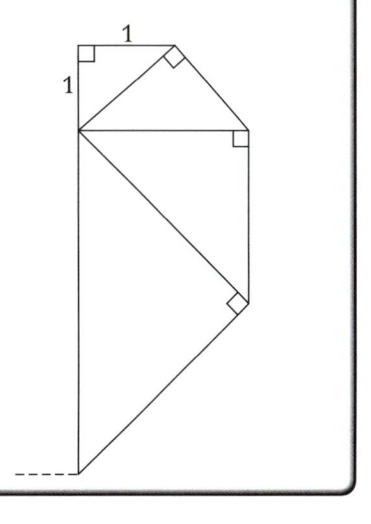

7 Graphs

In this chapter you will answer...

- If a line has the equation $y = 2x - 1$, what is the value of y when $x = 5$?
- When you draw a travel graph, do you plot the time along the x-axis or the y-axis?
- If a graph has the equation $y = x^2 + x - 1$, will the line be straight or curved?
- When you plot the point $(-4, 1)$ is the point in the first or second quadrant?

7.1 Conversion graphs

You can use a straight-line graph to convert (or change) one unit to another.

Example

This graph converts £ sterling to Indian rupees.

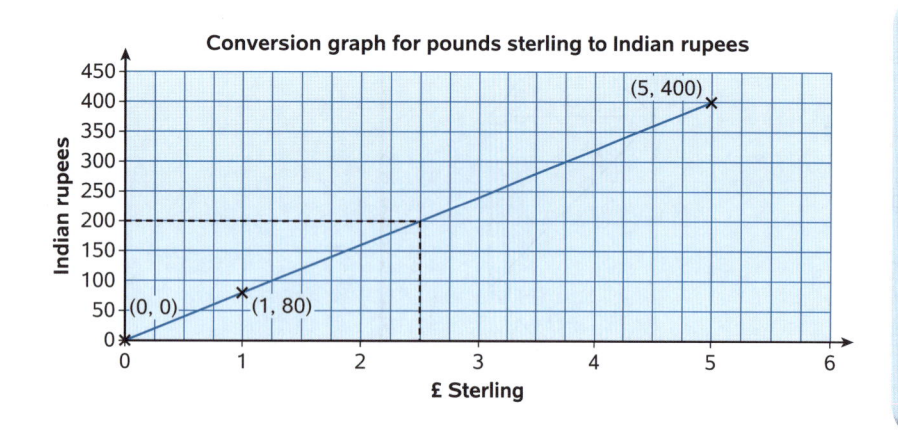

£1 ≡ 80 rupees

Conversion graph for pounds sterling to Indian rupees

KEY WORDS

Axis, axes(pl) the reference line on a graph

Plot draw each exact point on a graph or map

Origin the starting point on a line or graph, on a graph it is the point (0,0)

Horizontal axis the axis going across (often called the x-axis)

Vertical axis the axis going up (often called the y-axis)

Look at the graph and notice:

- £ sterling are plotted on the horizontal axis.
- Indian rupees (INR) are plotted on the vertical axis.
- The graph has a title and the axes are given labels.
- The plotted line starts at the origin (0,0) because £0 = 0 INR. The other points to plot are (1, 80) and (5, 400).

To convert £2.50 to rupees:

1 Draw a dotted line up (↑) from £2.50 on the x-axis to the conversion line.

2 Draw a dotted line along (←) from the conversion line to the vertical axis.

3 Record where this horizontal line meets the y-axis.

This shows that £2.50 ≡ 200 INR

To convert 350 rupees to £s:

1 Draw a dotted line along (→) from 350 rupees on the y-axis to the conversion line.

2 Draw a dotted line down (↓) from the conversion line to the horizontal axis.

3 Record where this vertical line meets the x-axis.

This shows that 350 INR ≡ £4.40

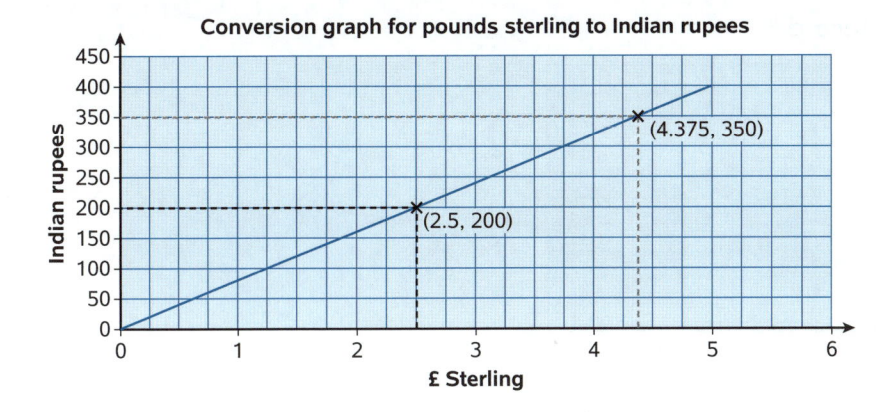

Graphs ● 7

Conversion graph for pounds sterling to Indian rupees

Exercise

1 This graph converts temperatures that have been measured in degrees Celsius (°C) to degrees Fahrenheit (°F).

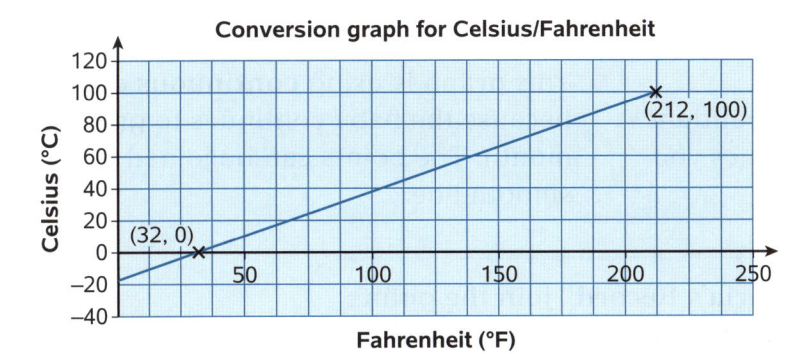

Conversion graph for Celsius/Fahrenheit

0 °C = 32 °F   Freezing point
100 °C = 212 °F   Boiling point

Use the graph to choose the correct word for these sentences.

a 0 °C is the *freezing/boiling* point of water.
b 50 °F is the same temperature as *20/10* °C.
c Fahrenheit is plotted along the *horizontal/vertical* axis.
d The line *is/is not* drawn through the origin.
e 80 °F is *hotter/colder* than 80 °C.
f 0 °F is a *positive/negative* number in degrees Celsius.

7.2 Real life graphs

Real life graphs are graphs that represent a real life situation.

Real life graphs:

- Show information that you have collected.
- Track the development of a situation.

Example

Inez wants to know whether her newborn baby Maria is growing healthily.

A record of Maria's weight on a graph can help her.

This is the record of Maria from her birth until her first birthday:

Age (months)	0	1	2	3	4	5	6	7	8	9	10	11	12
Weight/mass (kg)	2.9	3.2	3.8	4.4	5.0	5.5	6.2	6.6	7.2	7.6	8.3	8.6	8.9

87

Baby Maria's Record

Important facts to remember:

- The **month** is called the **independent** variable because it is the variable that you (or Inez) can choose.
- Plot the **independent** variable on the horizontal axis.
- The weight (or mass) is called the **dependent** variable because it depends on the times you choose.
- Plot the **dependent** variable on the vertical axis.
- Give the graph a title so that the information is easy to understand.
- This graph is using **continuous** data because the baby continues to grow every month. The points can be joined by a smooth line.

Exercise

2 On a copy of the graph 'Baby Maria's Record', join the points with a smooth line. Use your line to estimate answers to the following questions.

a How much did Maria weigh when she was $7\frac{1}{2}$ months old?

b How old was Maria when she weighed 6 kg?

c Can you use this graph to predict Maria's weight when she is
 i 13 months old?
 ii 18 months old?

d If you answered 'no' to c (ii), why not?

e This sentence describes the graph, but the words are jumbled up. Put the words in the correct order.
"A continuous smooth can be baby's as the curve growth is drawn."

7.3 Distance-time graphs

A graph which uses distance and time can tell the story of a journey.

Time is the independent variable.

Distance is the dependent variable.

You can plot two journeys on the same graph.

Graphs 7

3 Roshan leaves his home at 0900. He cycles for two hours to his grandparents' house, which is 30 km away. He spends 30 minutes with his grandmother. He then cycles a further 6 km to see his grandfather, who is fishing. This takes him thirty minutes. Roshan fishes for two hours with his grandfather and then he returns home. This takes him another one and a half hours.

Here is a graph of Roshan's journey:

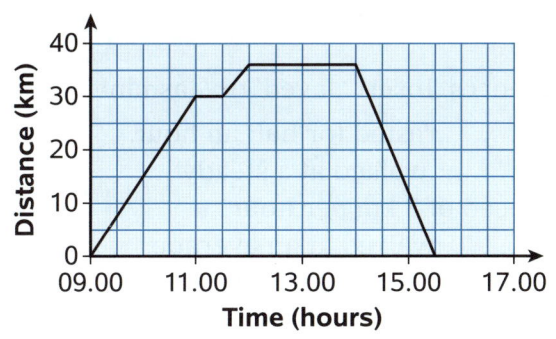

Complete these sentences about Roshan's journey. Choose the correct word or number from the box for each sentence:

a Roshan cycles .... on his way home.
b On his way to visit his grandparents, Roshan is travelling at .... km per hour.
c From 1100 until 1130, the graph is flat because Roshan is............
d Roshan has travelled ....km in one day.
e Roshan's average speed is ....

| 72 | 15 | 18 | faster | resting |

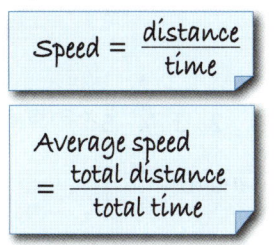

$$Speed = \frac{distance}{time}$$

$$Average\ speed = \frac{total\ distance}{total\ time}$$

Talking points

Ask your classmate questions to work out how they travel to school, and how long it takes. Plot both your journeys on the same graph.

Then work out the answers to the following questions:

1 Whose journey is shorter in distance?
2 Whose journey is shorter in time?

Present your graph to the rest of the class.

4 Javed and Jasmina are walking towards each other.
   This graph shows their journeys:

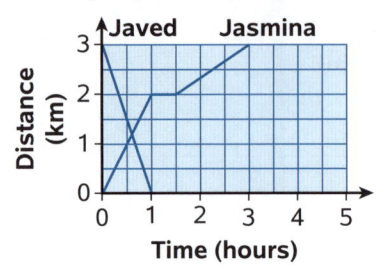

   Use the graph to complete these sentences. Insert 'Javed' or 'Jasmina'.

   a J...... walked steadily for an hour, then rested before continuing.
   b J...... walked steadily for an hour, but did not rest.
   c J...... walked faster than J.............
   d J......... rested for half an hour.
   e J.......... walked at a steady speed of 3 km per hour.
   f J.......... walked at an average speed of 1 km per hour.

   'Walked steadily' means 'Walked at a constant speed'.

7.4 Co-ordinates

Co-ordinates are pairs of numbers that fix a point on a graph.

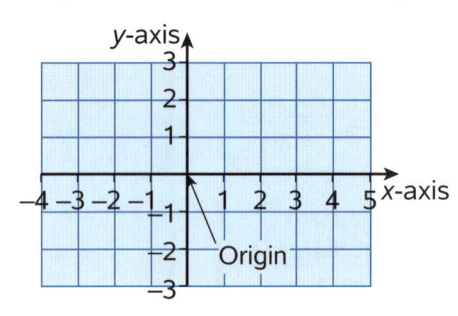

To fix a point you need two directions.

(2, 3) means that you start at (0, 0).

You then move along (→) 2 and up (↑) 3.

(−3, −2) means that you start at the origin.

You then move back (←) 3 and down (↓) 2.

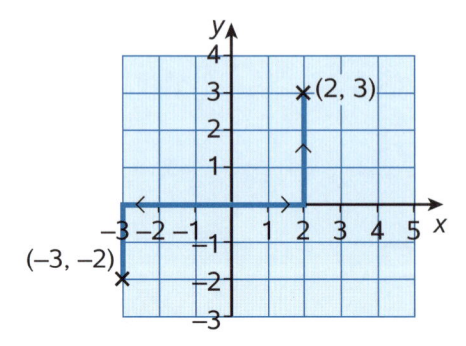

*To remember the right order for co-ordinates say "**Along** the corridor, and **up** the stairs".*

KEY WORD

Quadrant one of the four divisions of a graph:

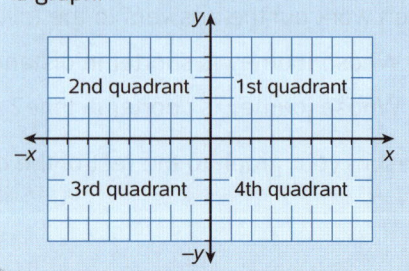

2nd quadrant | 1st quadrant
3rd quadrant | 4th quadrant

Exercise

5 Plot the co-ordinates correctly, then name the shape.

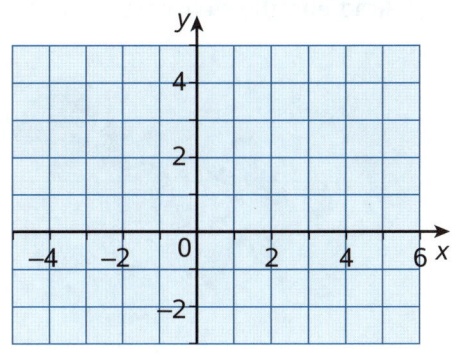

Shape A (0, 0) (6, 2) (0, 3) (3, 4)

Shape B (−1, 0) (−3, 2) (−3, −2) (−5, 0)

Shape A is a ....
Shape B is a ....

7.5 Straight line graphs

A **linear function** written as $y = 3x + 2$ connects the x- and y- co-ordinates and gives you the rule to calculate a sequence of points.

Linear function. Some books call this 'the equation of a straight line'.

The rule is saying "To calculate the y co-ordinate, multiply the x value by 3 and then add 2".

The function is called 'linear' because this sequence of points will plot a straight line.

*Remember:
The x-coordinate comes before the y-coordinate.*

If $x = 1$, $y = 3 \times 1 + 2 = 5$ so the co-ordinates are (1, 5)
If $x = 2$, $y = 3 \times 2 + 2 = 8$ so the co-ordinates are (2, 8)
If $x = -1$, $y = 3 \times (-1) + 2 = -1$ so the co-ordinates are (−1, −1)

You can draw the line by plotting the points (−1, −1), (1, 5), and (2, 8) and then joining them with a straight line:

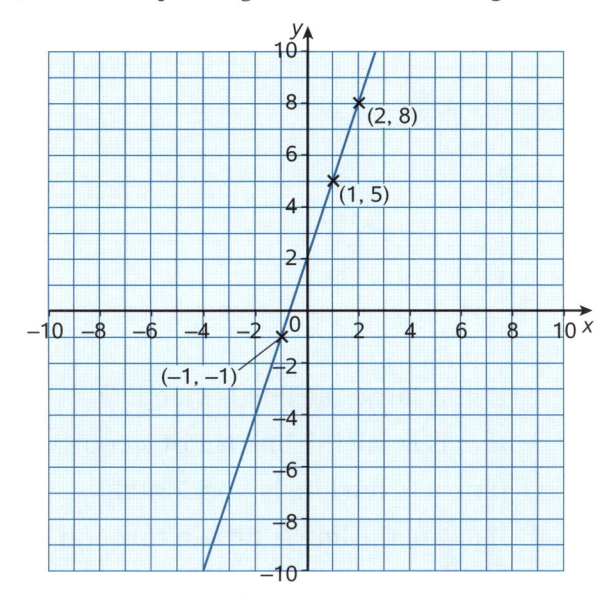

91

The line has a **gradient** of 3.

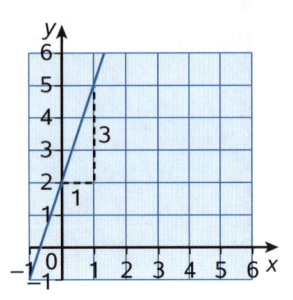

The line has an **intercept** of + 2.

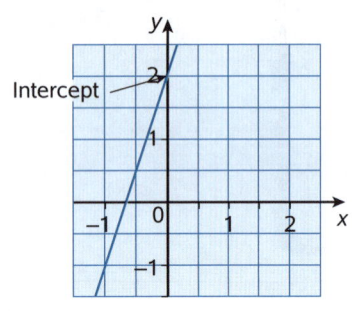

The equation of a line is usually given as $y = mx + c$.

The letter m represents the **gradient**.

The letter c represents the **intercept** on the y-axis.

KEY WORD

Gradient the steepness of a line.

Steep slopes have large gradients.

Gentle slopes have small gradients.

Exercise

6 You are given the function $y = 5 - x$.

Use this grid to calculate some points on the line:

x	y = 5 − x	
x = −1	y = 5 − (−1) = 6	(−1, 6)
x = 1	y = 5 − 1 = ……	…………
x = 2	y = 5 − …… = ……	…………

Plot the graph on a set of axes.
Complete the following sentences.
a The gradient of this graph is …………
b The y-intercept is …………………………

KEY WORD

Intercept the point where a line crosses the horizontal or vertical axis

When you draw a linear graph, it is useful to look at the function you are given and notice that:

◎ If m is negative the line slopes down from left to right.

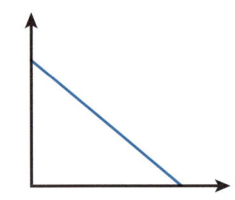

◎ If m is positive the line slopes up from left to right.

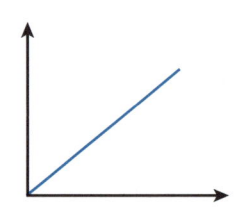

◎ If m is large the line is steep.
◎ If m is small the line is not steep.
◎ If $m = 0$, the line is horizontal.
◎ If $c = 0$, the line is drawn through the origin (0, 0).

Graphs ● 7

> How many points do you think you would need to plot to draw a straight line?
>
> How many points do you think you should plot to make sure that the line you have drawn is correct?

Exercise

7 Without drawing the lines, answer the following questions about these linear functions:

$y = -2x + 3$ $y = 4 - 2x$ $y = x + 11$ $y = 9x$ $y = 6 - x$ $y = \frac{1}{2}x + 5$ $y = 4$

a Which graph(s) slope(s) up from left to right?	
b Which graph is drawn through the origin?	
c Which graph is the steepest?	
d Which graph is the flattest?	
e Which graph(s) slope(s) down from left to right?	
f Which graph is horizontal?	

Exercise

8 Here are some anagrams of words used in this Chapter. Solve the anagrams, then match the words to the correct picture or definition.

> An anagram is when the letters of a word, or words, are put in a different order, e.g. an anagram of 'the eyes' is 'they see'.

NIOIRG		(2, 10) (5, 6)
NEPCTETIR		$17 = 4x - 3$
ENUCSQEE		(graph)
IOARNCTDEOS		(0, 0)
DNIAGTRE		$m = 12$
XEAS		(graph)
AUQONEIT		(1, 1) (2, 2) (3, 3)…..
ALIRNE ONUFINCT	LINEAR FUNCTION	$y = mx + c$
SEPET		(graph)

93

7.6 Curved graphs

Mathematicians and scientists use graphs to connect two different variables.

Example
Distance with time or the temperature outside an aeroplane with its height above sea level.

The connection may (or may not) give a straight line.

When you throw a ball or a stone, it follows a curved path called a **parabola**.

The parabola is also called a **quadratic function**.

It has the general equation $y = ax^2 + bx + c$

$y = x^2$, $y = 2x^2 + x$, and $y = x^2 - 2x + 3$ are all examples of quadratic functions.

To plot the path of a parabola, it useful to make a table.

Example
Plot the graph of $y = x^2 - 2x - 3$ for values of x $-2 \leq x \leq 4$.
Complete the table. Look for patterns and sequences to help you.

x	−2	−1	0	1	2	3	4
x^2	4	1	0	1	4	9	16
−2x	4	2	0	−2	−4	−6	−8
−3	−3	−3	−3	−3	−3	−3	−3
$y = x^2 - 2x + 3$	5	0	−3	−4	−3	0	5

$-2 \times -2 = 4$

$16 + (-8) + (-3) = 5$

Look at the last row in the table. Can you see the symmetry?
Now:
- Plot the graph using the points (−2, 5) (−1, 0) (0, −3) (1, −4) (2, −3) (3, 0) (4, 5).
- Join the points with a smooth curve.

The graph of $y = x^2 - 2x - 3$:

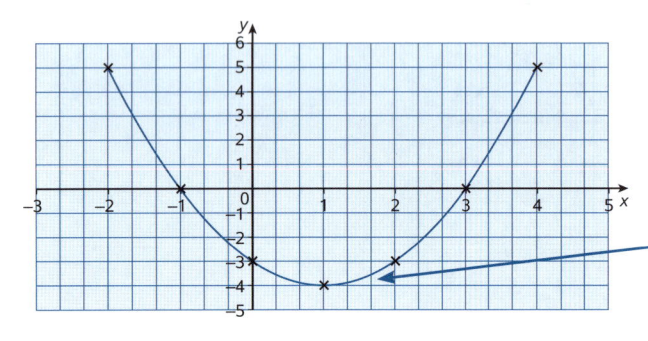

Remember that parabolas are always curved. They have no straight lines!

The lowest point on a parabola is called the vertex. On this graph it is the point (1, −4).

If you do not have a smooth curve, check any point that does not fit the line.

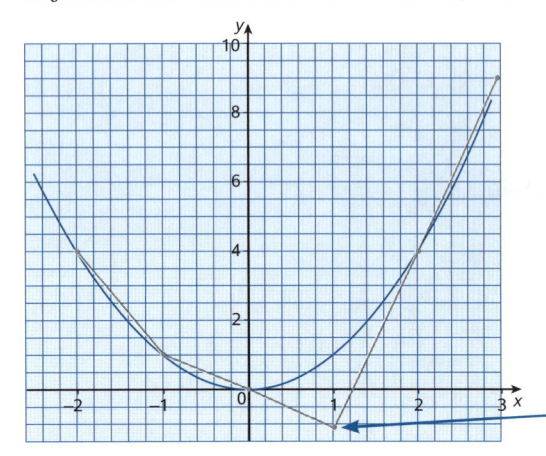

This point does not fit with the curve so you would need to check it for accuracy.

René Descartes (1596–1650)

The curved and linear graphs you have studied show the link between algebra and geometry.

The geometry that you can draw on a piece of paper, or see by throwing a ball, can be changed into the pairs of numbers that are called co-ordinates.

This system of geometry was developed by the French mathematician and philosopher, René Descartes. This is why it is called Cartesian geometry.

When Descartes was at school, he was often ill and he was allowed to stay in bed until 11 o'clock in the morning. He continued this habit all his life because it gave him time to think.

At school he decided that the only subject that was absolutely certain was mathematics. After that all his philosophy was based on mathematics.

After he finished his studies, Descartes travelled across Europe. He finally decided to live in Holland because it suited his character and method of working. When visitors asked him about the mathematical instruments that he used, he showed them

"a pair of compasses with one leg broken, and a folded piece of paper that he used as a ruler"

(John Aubrey)

In the last year of his life Descartes went to work for Queen Christina of Sweden. The Queen liked to work early in the morning, so Descartes could no longer stay in bed until 11 o'clock. He died of pneumonia, which he caught walking to the palace in the cold winter weather to start work.

9 Choose the correct word to complete these sentences.

a René Descartes was born in *France/Holland*.

b He was a mathematician and a *philosopher/psychologist*.

c He preferred to get up and work *early/late* in the morning.

d His mathematics was based on the links between algebra and *geometry/geology*.

e The only subject that he felt was truly *certain/doubtful* was mathematics.

f The instruments that he used were very *simple/complicated*.

g He lived in Holland as it was *right/wrong* for his character and method of working.

h He died in Sweden after catching *pneumonia/paranoia*.

Think about the questions from the start of this chapter. Can you answer them now?

- If a line has the equation $y = 2x - 1$, what is the value of y when $x = 5$?
- When you draw a travel graph, do you plot the time along the x-axis or the y-axis?
- If a graph has the equation $y = x^2 + x - 1$, will the line be straight or curved?
- When you plot the point $(-4, 1)$ is the point in the first or second quadrant?

7 Consolidation: Graphs

Need more practice?
Review and check your understanding here.

Exercise 7.1

1 This is a cooling curve for the chemical naphthalene. It is a liquid at higher temperatures and cools to a solid substance.

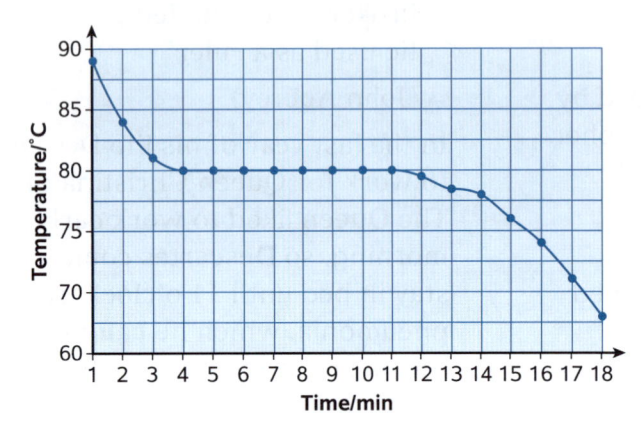

Use the graph to answer these questions:

a What is plotted along the horizontal axis?

b What is plotted along the vertical axis?

c Estimate the temperature when the measurements begin.

d Estimate how fast the liquid cools in the second minute.

e Estimate the temperature when the measurements end.

f Estimate the time when the curve flattens out, and when it starts to drop again.

g Do you know why the curve has a flat section?

2 This data is taken from a physics experiment. A spring is suspended from the ceiling of a laboratory and different loads are attached to the end of the spring.

The stretch, or extension, of the spring is noted.

You can use a graph to illustrate the data.

Load (g)	0	100	200	300	400	500	600	700	800
Ext (mm)	40	44	48	52	56	60	64	72	86

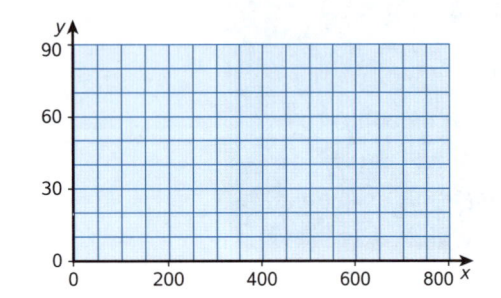

Use graph paper similar to this to draw a graph of this data.

a Before you draw the graph, think about:

  i Which is the independent variable? Draw this on the horizontal axis.

  ii Which is the dependent variable? Draw this on the vertical axis.

  iii Why is it important to give the graph a title and to label both axes?

b Use your graph to:

  i Estimate the extension for a load of 250 g.

  ii Estimate the extension for a load of 450 g.

c Can you estimate the extension for a load of 750 g?

d If the load is 1 kg, can you use this graph? Why/why not?

   Explain your answer.

3 Anna and her parents live in Brussels. Her grandparents live near Cologne, 180 km from Brussels.

They decide to drive towards each other and meet between the two cities.

Anna and her parents leave Brussels at 10 a.m. and drive towards Cologne at a steady speed of 60 km per hour.

Her grandparents leave Cologne at 10 a.m., drive for an hour at a speed of 80 km per hour, and then stop for coffee at 11 a.m. After thirty minutes they continue their journey at 50 km per hour.

This is the graph of Anna's journey with her parents.

Label the axes on this grid, and give the graph a title.

On a copy of this graph, draw the journey for Anna's grandparents and estimate what time they all meet.

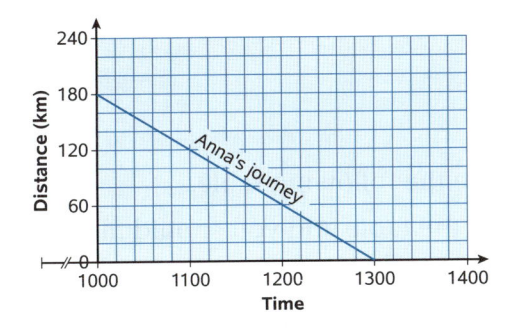

Exercise 7.2

You will need a calculator for some of this exercise. If you have a graphical calculator you can use that.

1 Look at the diagram below:

   a Give the co-ordinates of points A, C ,E, I, and G.

   b Complete the sentence. "The line AB is …… units long and the line CB is …….. units long."

   c The gradient of a line describes its steepness.

   The gradient is defined as: gradient = $\frac{\text{change in } y \text{ co-ordinates}}{\text{change in } x \text{ co-ordinates}}$ or m = $\frac{\text{rise}}{\text{run}}$

   Using your answers to (b), show that the gradient of AC is $\frac{4}{2} = 2$.

d Calculate the gradient of the lines:

　i FG　　**ii** HJ　　**iii** IJ　　**iv** EF

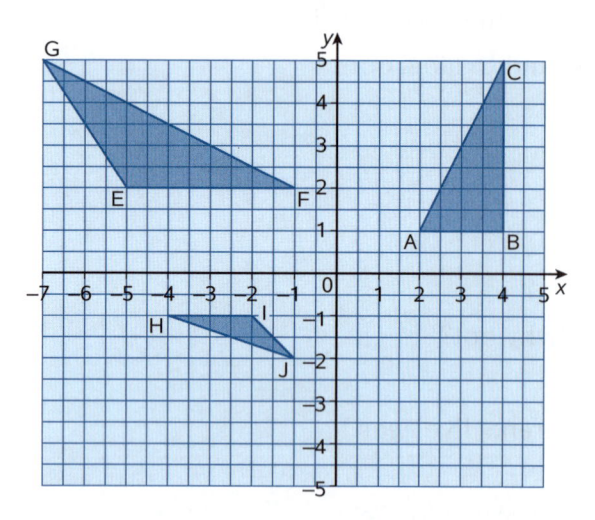

2

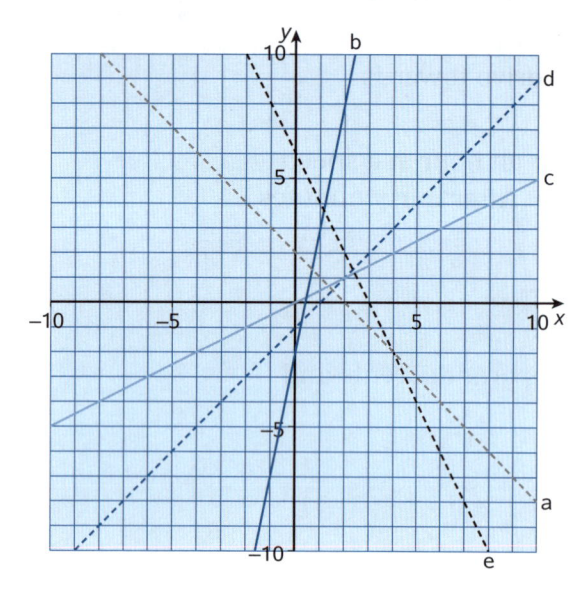

Look at this graph and use it to complete the following table.

The equations of the lines are written in the table and you should fill in the gradient and intercept that match that line.

Line	Equation	Gradient	Intercept
a	$y = 2 - x$	-1	
b	$y = 5x - 2$		
c	$y = \frac{1}{2}x$		0
d	$y = x - 1$		
e	$y = 6 - 2x$		6

a Look at the number before the *x* in the equation. Now look at the gradient on the graph. Can you see a connection?

b Look at the number in each equation. Now look at the intercept, the point where the line crosses the *y*-axis. What is the connection?

c Why is the intercept of the line $y = \frac{1}{2}x$ written as zero?

3 Draw the graphs of the lines

$y = x + 3$ and $y = 2x - 3$ on graph paper.

  a Where do the lines cross?

  b Solve the simultaneous equations

    $-x + y = 3$ and $-2x + y = -3$ using algebra.

  c Look at your result in (a) and compare it with your result in (c). What do you notice?

4 The parabola $y = x^2 - 2x - 3$ is plotted using the co-ordinate points
$(-2, 5)$ $(-1, 0)$ $(0, -3)$ $(1, -4)$ $(2, -3)$ $(3, 0)$ $(4, 5)$.

  a Use this table to calculate the points for the graph of
$y = -x^2 - 2x + 5$.

x	−4	−3	−2	−1	0	1	2
$y = -x^2 - 2x + 5$	−3		5		5		

  b Draw both curves on graph paper, and write down the co-ordinates of the two points where the curves meet.

8 Statistics

> **In this chapter you will answer...**
> - You make a survey of the number of texts sent by pupils in your class in one day.
>   Is this data discrete or continuous?
> - Which average measure would you use to represent football scores in all your school games?
> - If a 120° section of a pie chart represents 27 pupils from that year, how many students are there in total in year 10?
> - What type of correlation would you expect in a scatter graph that showed the age of a bus on one axis, and its value on the other?

8.1 Working with statistics

There are four separate parts to working with statistics.

Part 1 Collecting the data. **Part 3** Analysing the data.
Part 2 Displaying the data. **Part 4** Interpreting and using the data.

In class you will learn about these and practise them separately.

If you are doing a statistics assignment you will need to use all the parts and understand how they fit together.

8.2 Collecting the data

When you are given a statistics assignment, your first decision is how to collect the data.

Primary data is data that you collect yourself.

Methods of collecting primary data include:
- asking your friends
- giving your neighbours a questionnaire
- collecting results from an experiment.

Secondary data is data that someone else has collected.

You can find secondary data in many forms, including:
- in a book
- in newspapers
- on the Internet.

Be careful. When you collect your data you must be sure that you can trust it.

Biased data will give the wrong results.

Example of bias: If you give just some friends a questionnaire about food choices in your school, you will only get their opinion; your friends might have similar food tastes to you, e.g. vegetarian. You will not get the true picture of how the whole school feels.

Quantitative data can be collected using numbers, measurements or masses.

Qualitative data is about preferences, e.g. colour, favourite music, or other opinions.

> **KEY WORDS**
> **Analyse** study in detail
> **Data** factual information that is collected and then organised
> **Questionaire** a set of questions, usually on form

> **KEY WORDS**
> **Bias** prejudice built into a survey. There may be too little data or you may have asked the wrong questions.
> **Survey** a set of questions that is used to collect data.

Statistics 8

Exercise 1 Complete these sentences with the correct word.

> primary   secondary   qualitative   quantitative   biased

a To study the use of water in your town you can use the reports of the local water company. This is …………………… data.

b If you stand beside the road and list the cars going by, and the colour of each one, this is ……………….. data.

c If you stand beside the road and measure the speed of the cars going by, this is …………….. data.

d Data collected from a survey in your class is …………………… data.

e You want to know about the use of sports fields in your town and just ask some of your friends. This is ………………… data.

Exercise 2 For each survey listed, decide whether you would use a questionnaire, an experiment, a book, newspapers, or the Internet to collect the data.

You may use more than one source for any given survey.

Survey	Source of data
a Length of life in different countries.	
b Favourite music or singer.	
c Prices of cameras.	
d The lengths of sentences in a book.	
e The time taken for different students to travel into school.	

8.3 Displaying the data

Displaying the data clearly is very important.

Diagrams can be used to:

- Show the pattern and shape of the data.
- Give a clear understanding of the data more quickly.
- Explain and analyse your results.

This section is going to use two sets of data collected by some high school students. They have been asked to do an assignment about the traffic passing their school.

Zoe is collecting data about the traffic passing the school between 9.00 and 9.15 in the morning. She makes a tally chart to show her results.

KEY WORD

Display organise the data collected into tables and graphs so that the patterns can be seen and analysed.

Remember: Diagrams need a title and an explanation to be effective.

Vehicle	Tally marks	Frequency
Bicycle	⋈ I	6
Motorcycle	III	3
Car	⋈ ⋈ ⋈ I	16
Van	IIII	4
Lorry	⋈	5
Bus	II	2
	Total	36

These are tally marks, ⋈ = 5

Zoe is **counting** the number of vehicles, so her data is **discrete**. She can use a pictogram, a bar chart or a pie chart to display her data.

> **KEY WORD**
> **Discrete data** data that is counted

8.3.1 Pictograms

A pictogram uses symbols or pictures to show the data in a table.

For a pictogram you need:

- Squared paper, as this makes it easier to keep your table neat.
- Simple symbols that are easy to draw.
  You can match the symbols to the survey.
- A key showing what each symbol stands for.
- A title describing why you have drawn the pictogram.

Zoe draws this pictogram:

Vehicles passing the high school on October 8th, 2009 at 0900

Vehicle Name	Numbers of vehicles (🚗 = two vehicles)
Bicycle	🚗 🚗 🚗
Motorcycle	🚗 🚗
Car	🚗 🚗 🚗 🚗 🚗 🚗 🚗 🚗
Van	🚗 🚗
Lorry	🚗 🚗 🚗
Bus	🚗

8.3.2 Bar Charts

Bar charts can use horizontal or vertical bars to show the data on a graph.

For a bar chart you need:

- Squared paper or graph paper.
- An easy scale for the axes, which you should label on the axes.
- A title describing why you have drawn the bar chart.

Zoe draws two bar charts. They show the same information, but one has horizontal bars, and the other has vertical bars.

There are spaces between the bars because they show discrete data.

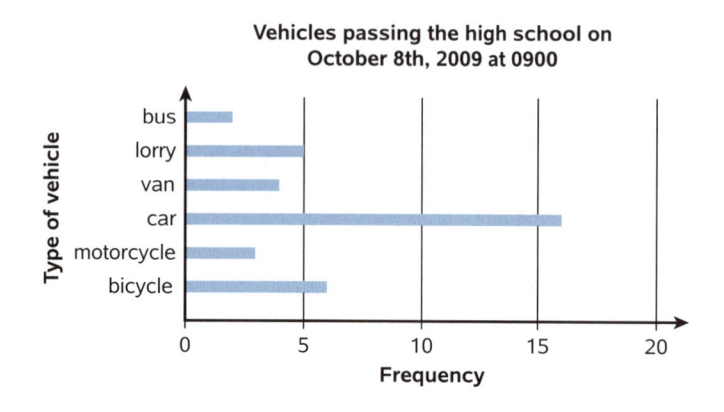

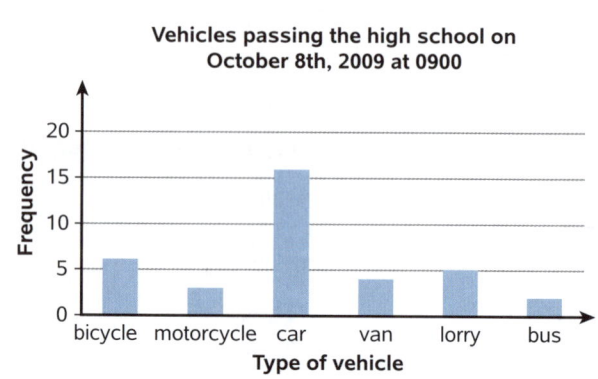

8.3.3 Pie Charts

A pie chart is the best way to show fractions or percentages for a set of data.

For a pie chart you need to:

- know the total number of the data
- calculate the angle for each slice of the pie
- use a drawing compass to draw the circle, and a protractor to measure each angle
- give the chart a title and a key.

It is easier to calculate the angles if you use a table. The total for Zoe's data is 36.

Name of vehicle	Frequency	Fraction	Angle
Bicycle	6	$\frac{6}{36} = \frac{1}{6}$	$\frac{1}{6} \times 360 = 60°$
Motorcycle	3	$\frac{3}{36} = \frac{1}{12}$	$\frac{1}{12} \times 360 = 30°$
Car	16	$\frac{16}{36} = \frac{4}{9}$	$\frac{4}{9} \times 360 = 160°$
Van	4	$\frac{4}{36} = \frac{1}{9}$	$\frac{1}{9} \times 360 = 40°$
Lorry	5	$\frac{5}{36}$	$\frac{5}{36} \times 360 = 50°$
Bus	2	$\frac{2}{36} = \frac{1}{18}$	$\frac{1}{18} \times 360 = 20°$

Why do you think it is called a pie chart?

Zoe can use the table to draw this pie chart:

Vehicles passing the high school on October 8th, 2009 at 0900

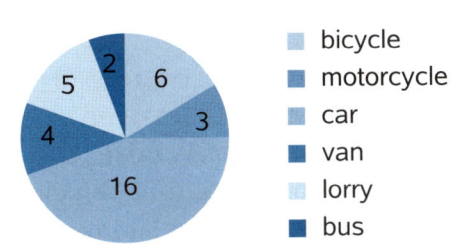

- bicycle
- motorcycle
- car
- van
- lorry
- bus

For Zoe's data, do you think the bar chart or the pie chart is easier to understand?

KEY WORD

Frequency how often something is counted in a survey or experiment

Sam and another friend Joe decide to study the speed of the vehicles as they pass the school.

They use their data to make a frequency table.

Speed (km per hour)	Frequency
0–10	3
11–20	5
21–30	10
31–40	8
41–50	5
51–60	2

- 0 – 10 gives the speeds between 0 and 10 kph.
- Joe and Sam have measured to the nearest whole number.
- Every speed was different so it is quicker to put the values into groups. This is called 'grouped data'.

Joe and Sam are **measuring** the speed of the vehicles, so their data is **continuous**. They can use a histogram or a pie chart to display their data.

A **histogram** is different from a bar chart as the bars are joined together and have no gaps.

A **histogram** is used for **continuous** data and for **grouped continuous** data.

KEY WORD

Continuous data data that is measured

8.3.4 Histograms

For a histogram you need:

◎ squared paper or graph paper

◎ a simple scale for the axes, which you should label on the axes

◎ a title describing why you have drawn the histogram.

Joe and Sam draw this histogram:

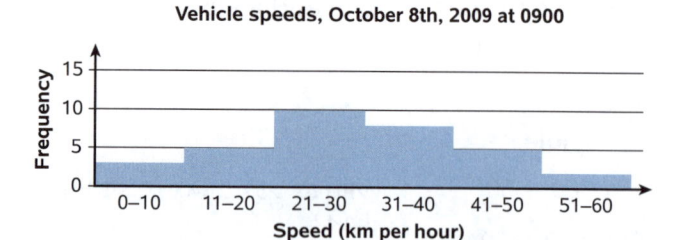

Vehicle speeds, October 8th, 2009 at 0900

Joe and Sam also use their data to draw a pie chart. They calculate the values in the same way as Zoe, but this time the total is 30.

Vehicle speeds on October 8th, 2009 at 0900

> For Joe and Sam's data, do you think the histogram or the bar chart is easier to understand?

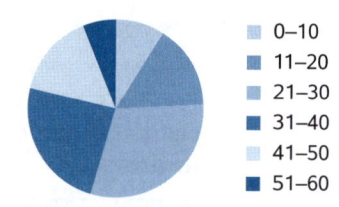

Exercise 3 Use the graphs and tables drawn by Zoe, Joe, and Sam to answer these questions. In each question cross out the word that is false.

a There are *twice/half* as many motorcycles as bicycles.

b A *third/quarter* of the vehicles are travelling between twenty and thirty kilometres per hour.

c There are *more/fewer* lorries than vans.

d Only *three/four* vehicles travel between zero and ten kilometres per hour.

e Zoe is using *discrete/continuous* data.

f Joe and Sam are *measuring/counting* their data.

g The *most/least* common vehicle is the car.

Exercise 4 Here are some answers that you might give your teacher. Write a question for each one.

a Q. What ....?
A. Data that can be counted.

b Q. When ....?
A. Pie charts are used to show the fractions of data.

c Q. Why ....?
A. A key is used to explain the reason behind the graph.

d Q. Where ....?
A. Secondary data can be found in books and magazines or on websites.

Statistics 8

> **Talking points**
>
> Work with a friend to make a study of traffic outside your school.
>
> Draw a pictogram, bar chart, pie chart and histogram of your study. Which do you find easiest to read?
>
> Discuss the differences in comparison to Zoe, Joe and Sam's studies.

> An anagram is when the letters of a word, or words, are put in a different order, e.g. an anagram of 'the eyes' is 'they see'.

Exercise

5 Solve these anagrams to find words about statistics.

The two words at the end will give you the name of a type of diagram that has been explained in this unit.

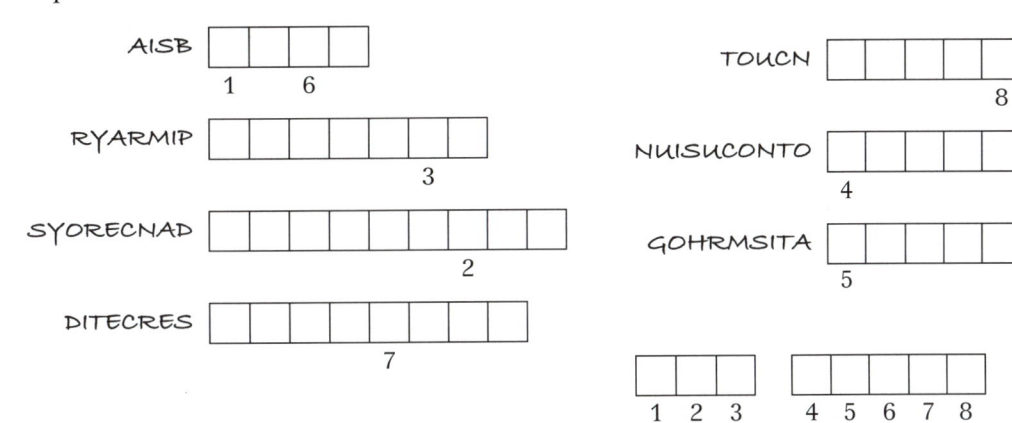

AISB ☐☐☐☐
    1   6

RYARMIP ☐☐☐☐☐☐☐
        3

SYORECNAD ☐☐☐☐☐☐☐☐☐
        2

DITECRES ☐☐☐☐☐☐☐☐
       7

TOUCN ☐☐☐☐☐
        8

NUISUCONTO ☐☐☐☐☐☐☐☐☐☐
        4

GOHRMSITA ☐☐☐☐☐☐☐☐☐
       5

☐☐☐ ☐☐☐☐☐
1 2 3   4 5 6 7 8

8.3.5 Scatter graphs

Some surveys show a link or relationship between two sets of data.

If one quantity is plotted on the horizontal axis and the other quantity is plotted on the vertical axis, there could be:

Positive Correlation

As Maria's age increases, her height increases

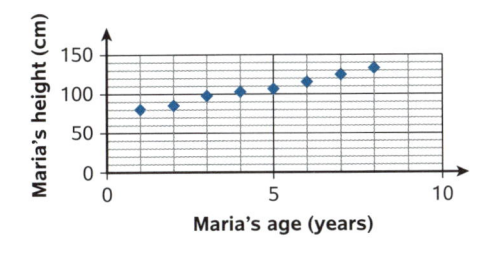

> **KEY WORD**
>
> **Correlation** is a measure of how much two separate things are linked.

Negative Correlation

As the age of the car increases, its value decreases

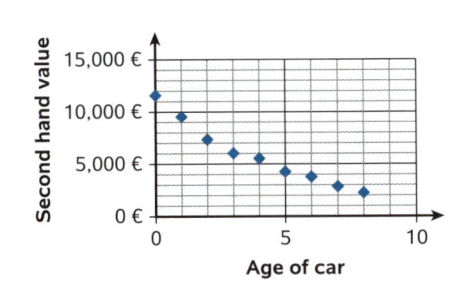

105

No Correlation

There is no connection between a student's age and their average score in hockey

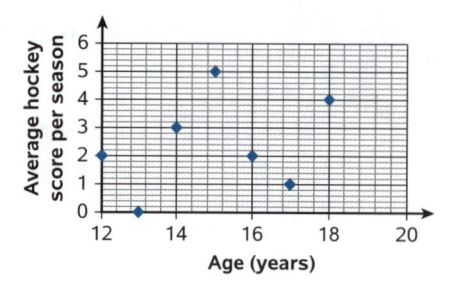

Exercise

6 Here are three different situations.
Complete each sentence with the correct type of correlation.

a Class 10C plotted a scatter graph of their heights against their highest marks in Geography. This graph showed .... correlation.

b When Nina plotted a scatter graph of the millimetres of rain that fell in one month against the hours of sunshine, she expected it to show .... correlation.

c When Zak plotted his class's Maths marks and their Science marks on a scatter graph, the graph showed .... correlation.

Correlation shown in a graph does not always mean that two things are really connected. For a real connection you must be able to say that if one variable is changed, then the other one will change too.

Example

Do you agree with these statements?

◉ "A correlation graph shows that the taller you are the better you can spell."

◉ "There is a positive correlation between the number of stork's nests on the roof of a house, and the number of children that live there."

Newspapers and magazines are good places to look for comments like these. You need to think carefully before you believe them.

8.4 Analysing data

Rie wanted to find the most 'average' person in her class. She collected the data for three charts.

Chart 1 – The heights of all the students to the nearest centimetre.

Chart 2 – The weights of all the students to the nearest kilogram.

Chart 3 – The favourite sport of each student.

Chart 1		Chart 2		Chart 3	
Height (cm)	Frequency	Weight (kg)	Frequency	Sport	Frequency
155	3	36–40	2	Football	8
156	4	41–45	5	Tennis	6
157	8	46–50	8	Hockey	7
158	6	51–55	7	Swimming	4
159	3	56–60	3		
160	1				

Rie looked at the charts and said:

"The average height is 157cm, the average weight is 46–50kg and the average sport is football. Nobody in the class matches this result."

> Why did she choose these answers?

There is more to working with averages than Rie thought.

There are three different 'averages' to think about:

- the **mean** — To find the **mean**, add up all the values, then divide this total by the number of values.
- the **median** — To find the **median**, put the values in order and pick out the central one.
- the **mode** — To find the **mode**, look for the most common value.

Rie looked at her data again and found these results:

Chart 1
Mean = $\frac{3 \times 155 + 4 \times 156 + 8 \times 157 + 6 \times 158 + 3 \times 159 + 1 \times 160}{25} = \frac{3930}{25} = 157.2\,cm$
Median = 157 cm   There are 25 values, the 13th one is the central one
Mode = 157 cm   There are more values of 157 cm than any other

Chart 2
Mean = $\frac{2 \times 38 + 5 \times 43 + 8 \times 48 + 7 \times 53 + 3 \times 58}{25} = \frac{1220}{25} = 48.8\,kg$
Median = 46–50 kg   The 13th value is in this group
Mode = 46–50 kg   This is called the modal class because the data is grouped

Chart 3
Mean is not possible   The data is qualitative
Median is not possible   The data is qualitative
Mode is football

Rie said "I am looking for someone who is 157.2 cm tall, weighs 48.8 kg and whose favourite sport is football. Oh dear, there is nobody in my class who matches these figures and is average"

> In the calculations for Chart 2, Rie used the values 38, 43, 48, 53 and 58. This is because they are the central values in each group within the data.

Why did she have a problem with finding someone like this?

8.4.1 How to choose the 'best average' for a set of data

	Best	But
Mean	If you want to use every piece of data that you have collected.	Very high or very low values will distort the answer.
		The answer may not be one of the values you have collected.
Median	If you want a central value that is not distorted by very high or very low values.	You will have to place the data in order.
		With an even set of data, you will need to add the two central values and divide by two.
Mode	If you want a value that is easy to calculate and understand.	There may be more than one mode – or no mode at all.

7 Class 10C is growing tomato plants and wants to collect some data about the height of the plants and the weight of tomatoes from each one. They grow six plants in the shade and six plants in the sun.

Here are their results. Some of the calculations have been done for you.

Plants in the sun	Height	Number/ plant	Total weight	Plants in the shade	Height	Number/ plant	Total weight
1	12 cm	1	28 g	1	51 cm	6	190 g
2	38 cm	8	250 g	2	56 cm	9	270 g
3	41 cm	9	260 g	3	59 cm	7	235 g
4	44 cm	8	265 g	4	62 cm	8	250 g
5	45 cm	7	252 g	5	62 cm	9	260 g
6	46 cm	6	241 g	6	75 cm	6	210 g
Mean Median Mode	37.7 cm 42.5 cm —	? 7.5 8	216 g ? ?	Mean Median Mode	60.8 cm 60.5 cm 62 cm	? 7.5 ?	236 g ? ?
	a	b	c		d	e	f

Fill in the missing values in the tables.
Use them to decide which 'average' is best in each column.

a I chose the m............. because ....
b I chose the m............. because ....
c I chose the m............. because ....
d I chose the m............. because ....
e I chose the m............. because ....
f I chose the m............. because ....

8.5 Interpreting the data

Many different organisations collect and analyse data.

Example

Governments, schools, businesses, laboratories, and international charities use data to understand the world, make predictions, and set targets for the future, or interpret the past.

For example, the world needs to plan for food, water, and climate change. To do this, it needs to study how the climate changed in the past.

There are some important questions you should ask when you are handling data.

If you are using your own primary data:

- How did you collect your data?
- Was there any bias?
- Was the sample size large enough?
- Are your graphs clear and accurate?
- Have you answered the questions that you asked at the beginning?

If you are using secondary data collected by other people:

- Who collected the data?
- How did they ask the questions? Who did they ask?
- Who paid for the data?
- How big was the sample?

KEY WORD

Sample a small collection of data that is meant to represent a larger group. Usually, the bigger the sample the more accurate the data.

8.6 The weird world of statistics

Consider this example, which shows how statistics can be misleading.

Compare these graphs. Which is the more accurate picture? Look at the vertical axis!

Profits continue to increase sharply.

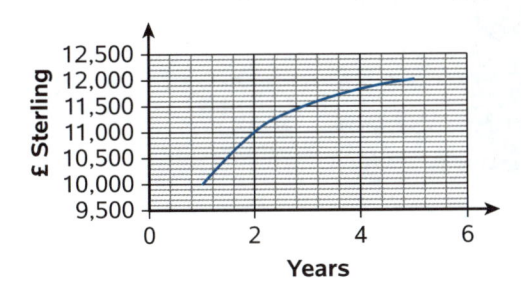

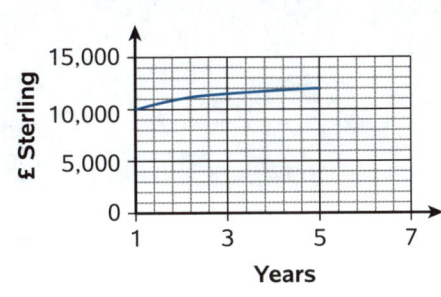

When drawing scatter graphs, think about these examples:

- As **ice cream** sales increase, the rate of deaths by **drowning** increases sharply.

  Therefore, ice cream causes drowning.

- With a decrease in the number of **pirates**, there has been an increase in **global warming** over the same period.

  Therefore, global warming is caused by a shortage of pirates.

- Since the 1950s, both the CO_2 level and **crime** levels have increased sharply.

  Therefore, CO_2 causes crime.

Talking points

Benjamin Disraeli and Mark Twain:
"There are three kinds of lies: lies, damned lies, and statistics."

W.I.E. Gates
"Then there is the man who drowned crossing a stream with an average depth of six inches."

Lawrence Lowell, 1909
"Statistics .....like veal pies, are good if you know the person that made them, and are sure of the ingredients."

Bobby Bragan, 1963:
"Say you were standing with one foot in the oven and one foot in an ice bucket. According to the percentage people, you should be perfectly comfortable."

Louis D. Brandeis
"A man may have six meals one day and none the next, making an average of three meals per day, but that is not a good way to live."

Work with a friend. Look at these examples and discuss why statistics can be "weird". Explain your findings to your class.

Think about the questions from the start of this chapter. Can you answer them now?

- You make a survey of the number of texts sent by pupils in your class in one day. Is this data discrete or continuous?
- Which average measure would you use to represent football scores in all your school games?
- If a 120° section of a pie chart represents 27 pupils from that year, how many students are there in total in year 10?
- What type of correlation would you expect in a scatter graph that showed the age of a bus on one axis, and its value on the other?

8 Consolidation: Statistics

Need more practice?
Review and check your understanding here

Exercise 8.1

You will need a scientific or graphical calculator to answer these questions.

You could also practise using a statistics or spreadsheet package on a computer.

These tables contain weather data from 1954 and 2004. The data was collected in Oxford, UK.

Year	Month	Month	Maximum temperature (C°)	Minimum Temperature (C°)	Rainfall (mm)	Sunshine (hours)
1954	January	1	5.6	0.3	33	75.7
	February	2	6.5	0.2	59.7	79.7
	March	3	10.1	2.9	64.4	107.9
	April	4	12.8	2.8	10.1	202.4
	May	5	15.9	7.2	53.3	145.9
	June	6	17.9	10.3	92.3	157.1
	July	7	18.6	11.3	55.8	157.1
	August	8	19.2	11.3	80.1	123.5
	September	9	17.6	9.4	66.3	168.8
	October	10	15.8	9.3	54.9	94.5
	November	11	10.9	3.8	112.2	60.1
	December	12	9.6	4.4	51.4	54.5

Year	Month	Month	Maximum temperature (C°)	Minimum Temperature (C°)	Rainfall (mm)	Sunshine (hours)
2004	January	1	8.8	2.7	66.1	62.7
	February	2	8.7	2.9	25.5	79.1
	March	3	10.9	3.4	51.8	100.5
	April	4	14.7	6.2	68.8	150.3
	May	5	18.0	8.6	41.1	195.5
	June	6	21.8	12	23.8	223.5
	July	7	22.0	12.2	83.1	169.6
	August	8	23.4	14.2	135	194.1
	September	9	20.1	11.7	28.9	174.3
	October	10	14.7	8.6	131.4	102.3
	November	11	10.9	5.8	34.2	52.5
	December	12	8.6	2.8	37.7	58.3

1 a Use the tables to draw a line graph of the maximum temperatures recorded in Oxford in 1954 and 2004.

   b Use the data in the table to calculate:
      i the mean maximum temperature in 1954
      ii the mean maximum temperature in 2004.

   c Use the data in the table to calculate:
      i the median minimum temperature in 1954
      ii the median minimum temperature in 2004.

   d Using the graph and the figures from (b) and (c) make some statements about the temperatures in 1954 compared with the temperatures in 2004, fifty years later.

> Remember to give the graph a title and label the axes correctly!

2 Look at the rainfall figures in Question 1.

   Copy and complete these two frequency tables, grouping the data.

   Use the data in the tables to draw pie charts for 1954 and 2004.

> Do you remember how to calculate the angles for the pie chart? There is a reminder given in the table.

1954

Rainfall (mm)	Tally	Frequency	Angle
$0 \leq r < 20$			
$20 \leq r < 40$			
$40 \leq r < 60$	IIII	5	$\frac{5}{12} \times 360 = 150°$
$60 \leq r < 80$			
$80 \leq r < 100$			
$100 \leq r < 120$			
$120 \leq r < 140$			

2004

Rainfall (mm)	Tally	Frequency	Angle
$0 \leq r < 20$		0	
$20 \leq r < 40$			
$40 \leq r < 60$			
$60 \leq r < 80$			
$80 \leq r < 100$			
$100 \leq r < 120$			
$120 \leq r < 140$			

> Remember to include a key and a title with your pie charts!

Use your pie charts to compare 1954 and 2004.

Are they the best diagrams to use?

3 Look at the sunshine figures in Question 1.

Use the table to group your data for the sunshine hours in 2004.

Sunshine (hours)	Tally	Frequency
$50 \leq r < 90$		
$90 \leq r < 130$		
$130 \leq r < 170$		
$170 \leq r < 210$		
$210 \leq r < 250$		

Use this table to draw a histogram of the hours of sunshine in 2004.

4 The following data is about the reaction times recorded by a group of girls and a group of boys.

Only the times of the first ten boys and girls have been used.

The time has been rounded to 2 decimal places.

'Reaction time' is the time you take to press a button, or catch a ruler. Compare with the 'thinking time' in the coursework on braking distances. See Chapter 10.

You could try your own experiment and collect your own data.

Girls	Height (cm)	Left hand (secs)	Right hand (secs)
1	158	0.30	0.27
2	158	0.23	0.25
3	160	0.26	0.45
4	165	0.35	0.34
5	163	0.38	0.38
6	174	0.28	0.28
7	164	0.03	0.14
8	154	0.41	0.30
9	160	0.22	0.27
10	166	0.26	0.24

Boys	Height (cm)	Left hand (secs)	Right hand (secs)
1	150	0.30	0.22
2	186	0.26	0.40
3	145	0.17	0.21
4	174	0.23	0.20
5	166	0.22	0.20
6	160	0.23	0.27
7	167	0.38	0.22
8	142	0.24	0.23
9	164	0.22	0.25
10	168	0.22	0.20

a Use the data for the boys to draw a scatter graph for the height of the boys against their left-hand reaction times.

b Is there any correlation between the height of the boys and their reaction times?

c Use the data for the girls to draw a scatter graph for the right-hand reaction times against the left hand reaction times.

d Is there any correlation between the reaction times for different hands?

e Here is some more data on the girls before the times were rounded.

Girls	Height	Left hand	Right hand
1	158	0.297	0.273
2	158	0.2255	0.25
3	160	0.2555	0.4455
4	165	0.3455	0.335
5	163	0.375	0.383
6	174	0.2755	0.275
7	164	0.03	0.14
8	154	0.4055	0.3005
9	160	0.2185	0.273
10	166	0.2605	0.2355
11	165	0.566	3.1095
12	170	0.25	0.2805
13	185	0.3	0.22
14	159	0.32	0.7735
15	163	0.211	0.211
16	151	0.3205	0.1805
17	165	0.2495	0.297
18	163	0.25	0.33
19	163	0.2735	0.2425

Using this data, calculate the mean, median and modal heights of the girls.

f Which measure gives the better average? Why?

9 Probability

In this chapter you will answer...

- What is the probability that you will meet a whale when you go for a walk in a forest?
- If today is Wednesday, May 1st, what is the probability that tomorrow is Thursday, May 2nd?
- The weather forecast gives the chance of rain as 0.4. What is the probability that it will not rain?
- You have eight red socks and 7 blue socks. What is the probability that you will put on a blue sock without first checking its colour?
- What is the probability of there being 2 boys in a family of 2 children?

9.1 Probability questions

All these questions are probability questions. How likely is it that these events will happen?

How can you work out the answers? Match the speech bubbles with those below and try to work out the likelihood of these events.

KEY WORDS

Event single observation in a probability experiment or calculation

Likely probable

Speech bubbles (top row):
- How reliable is my cell phone?
- What is the chance of a thunderstorm next week?
- Will my first serve be in or out?.
- How likely am I to go surfing today?
- What is the probability that a coin will fall heads up?

Speech bubbles (bottom row):
- I listen to the forecast every day
- I always go surfing.
- I can guess!
- I've only had it for 2 months
- I've been practising really hard.

There are more reliable ways to work out some of these answers. You could use experiments, surveys, or theory to give a better answer.

115

9.2 The probability scale

Probability is shown on a scale of 0 to 1. Probabilities are usually written as fractions or decimals. However, some weather forecasts are given as percentages – so the forecaster may say 40% instead of 0.4 or $\frac{2}{5}$.

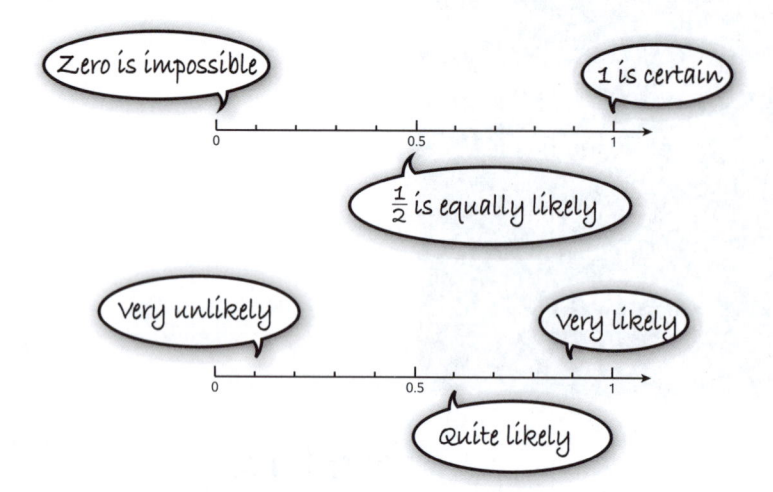

Zero is impossible
1 is certain
$\frac{1}{2}$ is equally likely
Very unlikely
Very likely
Quite likely

KEY WORDS

Impossible an event is impossible if it can never happen

Certain an event is certain if it will definitely happen

Exercise 1

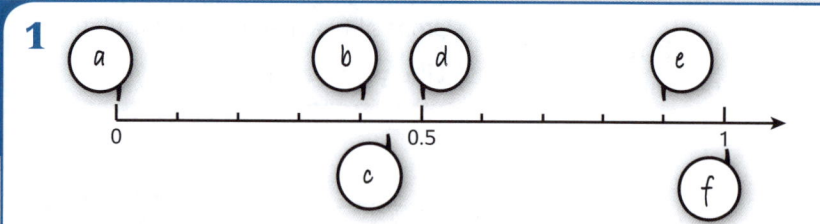

A Match the letters (a–f) on the scale to the statements, 1–6.
1 If you learn a new word you will hear it again before the end of the day.
2 It will get dark tonight.
3 A newborn baby is a boy.
4 Someone in your class has a birthday the same day as you.
5 A cat will live forever.
6 You will play your favourite sport this week.

B Choose the correct word(s) to complete these sentences.

| certain | very likely | impossible |
| equally likely | unlikely | very unlikely |

1 It is .... that you can run 100 m in 15 seconds.
2 It is .... that it will snow in Nairobi in September.
3 It is .... that your friend will text you this evening.
4 It is .... that a random number is odd or even.
5 It is .... that there is ice at the North Pole.
6 It is .... that you can travel faster than the speed of light.

KEY WORD

Chance the likelihood, or probability, of an event happening

116

9.3 The probability that it will not happen

If the weather forecaster tells you that the probability of rain is 0.7, what is the probability that it won't rain?

1 − 0.7 = 0.3, so there is a 30% chance that it won't rain.

In general p(A') = 1 − p(A)

p(A') means the probability that event A does not happen.

p(A) means the probability that event A will happen.

p(A), p(B) etc is a notation that you will find in this chapter to represent probability. There are two kinds of probability, theoretical and experimental.

9.4 Experimental probability

Your teacher asks you to fix a note to your class notice board and gives you some drawing pins.

You drop one – and then step on it – ouch!!

How likely is this?

You can do an experiment to answer the question:

"What is the probability that a drawing pin lands with its point up?"

1. Drop a drawing pin on a table or desk, 100 or 200 times (you can ask a friend to help).
2. Keep a tally chart of how often it lands with the point up.
3. Use your results to calculate the probability.

The calculation is p(point up) = $\frac{\text{number of successful trials}}{\text{number of trials}}$

Sven drops his pin 200 times. It lands with its point up 65 times.

The probability for his pin is p(point up) = $\frac{65}{200}$ = 0.325 or $\frac{13}{40}$.

Will you get the same result every time? Why not?

Exercise

2 A Here is a list of probability questions. Match each question to a method you could use to find out the answer. You may be able to use more than one method.

Methods: survey, experiment, computer simulation, internet search for past data

1. What is the probability that your favourite football team will win its next match?
2. What is the chance that someone in your class is left-handed?
3. What is the probability that all your tomato seeds germinate?
4. If you drop your buttered toast on the floor, how likely is it to land with the butter side down?
5. What is the chance that it will snow in Strasbourg on January 1st?
6. What is the probability that a coin will land with its tail up?

B Lena makes a spinner for a game. She draws a hexagon and divides it into six triangles. She writes the numbers 1–6 on the triangles.

Her friend Max says that her spinner is not a fair one.

They both spin the spinner 48 times and record their results.

	Lena	Max
1	8	7
2	10	9
3	13	11
4	3	2
5	9	10
6	5	9

KEY WORD

Fair a fair coin has no bias and will fall true.

1 What score do you expect for each number?
2 Why are the results different?
3 Can you say that the spinner is fair?
4 Which number is the most likely?
5 Which number is the least likely?
6 Could Lena improve her spinner?

9.5 Theoretical probability

Experimental probability is calculated from experiments or surveys, or the knowledge of past events. For **theoretical** probability calculations you need to think about the number of ways an event might happen.

For theoretical probability, the calculation is:

$$p(A) = \frac{\text{number of possible successful events}}{\text{total number of events}}$$

If you calculate the theoretical probability, will it be the same as the experimental probability? Think about tossing coins or picking letters from a bag when you play Scrabble.

Example

1 If you press the random number key on your calculator 50 times, what is the probability that you will press an eight?

There are 10 different digits, 0 to 9. Only one is an eight.

$p(8) = \frac{1}{10}$

If you press the key 20 times, you will expect

$20 \times \frac{1}{10} = 2$ eights.

If you press the key 100 times, you will expect

$100 \times \frac{1}{10} = 10$ eights.

*Remember! 'Expect an eight' is **not** the same as 'get an eight'. In practice you need to do many trials. The more trials that you do, the more likely it is that your experimental value will be the same as your theoretical value.*

Example

2 Millie put twelve red counters and eight black counters in a bag. She shook the bag, took out a counter, wrote down the colour and replaced the counter in the bag. She repeated this fifty times and recorded the results.

Red	Black
28	22

KEY WORD

Trial a single observation in a probability experiment

a What is the probability that she picked a red counter?
b What is the probability that she picked a black counter?
c Add the answers to (a) and (b).
d How many red counters did she expect? How many did she get?

Answers

a $p(\text{red}) = \frac{12}{20} = \frac{3}{5}$
b $p(\text{black}) = \frac{8}{20} = \frac{2}{5}$
c $\frac{2}{5} + \frac{3}{5} = 1$
d She expected $\frac{3}{5} \times 50 = 30$ red counters. She got 28.

If she did more experiments her actual result would be closer to the one she expected.

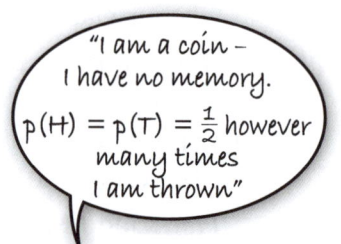

"I am a coin – I have no memory. $p(H) = p(T) = \frac{1}{2}$ however many times I am thrown"

Exercise

3 Match the value of the theoretical probability with the question.

1	What is the probability of being born in March or April?	**a** $\frac{2}{12} = \frac{1}{6}$
2	What is the probability of picking a B from the word PROBABILITY?	**b** $\frac{5}{26}$
3	What is the probability of picking a pink hat from five pink hats and two blue ones?	**c** $\frac{2}{16} = \frac{1}{8}$
4	What is the probability of picking a knight from a set of chess pieces?	**d** $\frac{2}{11}$
5	What is the probability of picking a prime number from the numbers one to ten?	**e** $\frac{8}{16} = \frac{1}{2}$
6	What is the probability of picking a vowel from the letters of the alphabet?	**f** $\frac{5}{7}$
7	What is the probability of picking a pawn from a set of chess pieces?	**g** $\frac{4}{10} = \frac{2}{5}$

9.6 Using diagrams

It is often easier to understand a problem if you use a diagram.

Sample space diagrams or **tree diagrams** are the most useful.

> The English alphabet has 26 letters.
> Five are vowels: a, e, i, o, u
> The rest are consonants.

Example

In a family of two children, what is the probability of there being

a two girls   **b** two boys   **c** a boy and a girl?

A You can use a sample space diagram which lists all the possibilities.
The possibilities are:
two boys, two girls, a boy and a girl or a girl and a boy

$p(boy) = \frac{1}{4}$

$p(girl) = \frac{1}{4}$

$p(a\ girl\ and\ a\ boy)\ \frac{1}{4} + \frac{1}{4} = \frac{1}{2}$

	B	G
B	BB	BG
G	GB	GG

This means that:

◉ a half of all families with two children expect to have a boy and a girl (in either order),

◉ a quarter of all families with two children expect two boys, and a quarter of all families with two children expect two girls.

B You can use a tree diagram which shows the probabilities on its branches.

Read the results in the diagram and you see that - $p(boy) = \frac{1}{4}$ $p(girl) = \frac{1}{4}$ $p(girl\ and\ boy) = \frac{1}{4} + \frac{1}{4} = \frac{1}{2}$	$p(2\ boys) = \frac{1}{2} \times \frac{1}{2} = \frac{1}{4}$ $p(1\ boy,\ 1\ girl) = \frac{1}{2} \times \frac{1}{2} = \frac{1}{4}$ $p(1\ girl,\ 1\ boy) = \frac{1}{2} \times \frac{1}{2} = \frac{1}{4}$ $p(2\ girls) = \frac{1}{2} \times \frac{1}{2} = \frac{1}{4}$

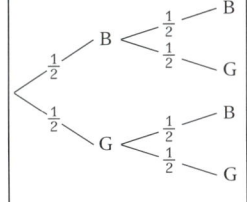

> You multiply the fractions as you move along the 'branches'.

Exercise

4 For each problem, read the question, then complete the diagram and use it to answer the question.

1 The weather forecast gives the chance of rain in the next two days as 0.7 each day.
  a What is the probability of rain on both days?
  b What is the probability that it will not rain on either day?

  a p(rain) = 0.7 × ? =

  b p(no rain) =

```
        0.7 — R
    R <
  0.7    0.3 — R'
 <
  0.3    0.7 — R
    R' <
        0.3 — R'
```

2 A fair coin is thrown twice. What is the probability of
  a throwing two heads
  b throwing 2 tails
  c throwing a head and a tail?
  d Do you recognise these answers from another problem?
    i   p(H) =
    ii p(T) =
    iii p(H and T) =

	Head	Tail
Head		HT
Tail		

3 Alex plays sport every afternoon. He has a choice of football, golf or hockey. The probability that he plays football is $\frac{1}{2}$, the probability that he plays golf is $\frac{1}{3}$ and the probability that he plays hockey is $\frac{1}{6}$.
Some of the probabilities have been put on the tree diagram for you.
Complete Alex's diagram and use it to answer the questions.

  a What is the probability that Alex plays hockey on Monday?
  b What is the probability that Alex plays golf on Monday and Tuesday?
  c What is the probability that Alex does not play football on Monday?
  d What is the probability that Alex plays hockey on Monday, football on Tuesday and golf on Wednesday?

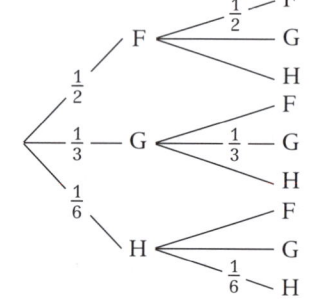

```
              1/2 — F
        F <   — G
      1/2     — H
              — F
 < 1/3 — G <  1/3 — G
              — H
      1/6     — F
        H <   — G
              1/6 — H
```

9.7 Conditional probability

These problems ask you to find out the probability of an event, but you are given an extra piece of information that changes the calculation. We call this extra piece of information "the condition".

Example:

Tom and his mother are at the cinema. They have bought a box of chocolates to eat during the film. There are nine white chocolates and five dark ones left.

If Tom's mother picks a white chocolate and eats it,

what is the probability that the next one she picks is also white?

This is the condition

Here is the tree diagram

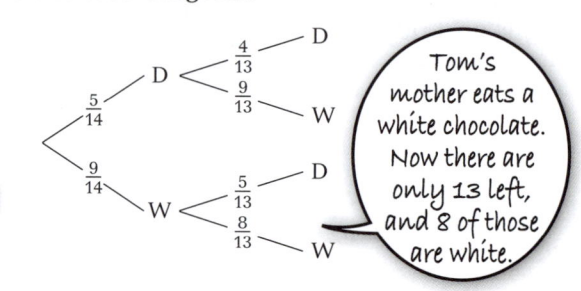

```
              4/13 — D
        D <
  5/14       9/13 — W
 <
  9/14       5/13 — D
        W <
              8/13 — W
```

Tom's mother eats a white chocolate. Now there are only 13 left, and 8 of those are white.

120

a The probability that Tom's mother will eat two white chocolates is
$$p(2W) = \frac{9}{14} \times \frac{8}{13} = \frac{36}{91}$$

b If the first chocolate that Tom's mother eats is a dark one, then p(white) becomes $\frac{9}{13}$.

Exercise 5

1 Deepa put twelve red counters and eight black counters in a bag. She shook the bag, picked a counter, recorded the colour and put the counter on the table. Then she took out another counter.

Complete the tree diagram and use it to find the probability:
  a that she took out two red counters
  b that she took out two different colours
  c that if she took out a black counter first, the second counter was red.

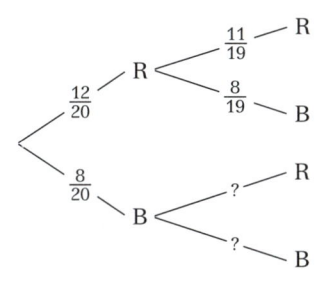

```
            11/19 — R
      R <
 12/20     8/19 — B
     <
  8/20     ? — R
      B <
           ? — B
```

2 The probability that it will rain today is 0.4. If it rains today, the probability that it will rain tomorrow is 0.65. If it does not rain today, the probability of rain tomorrow is 0.5.
Complete the tree diagram and use it to find these probabilities.
  a What is the probability that it will not rain for the next two days?
  b What is the probability that it will rain on one day, and not the other?

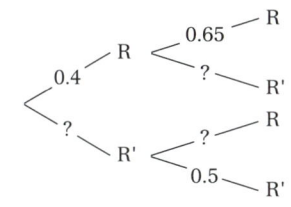

```
            0.65 — R
      R <
  0.4      ? — R'
     <
   ?       ? — R
      R' <
           0.5 — R'
```

Talking points

Play a probability game with your classmate. Look at the questions from the start of the chapter and write 5 similar questions. Read the questions out and ask your classmate to try and work out the answers.

9.8 Words used in the study of probability

Exercise

6 Probability wordsearch.

P	E	L	B	I	S	S	O	P	M	I	I
T	R	Q	S	R	E	U	M	E	I	T	N
N	B	O	I	P	T	Y	L	C	H	C	D
E	E	A	B	C	I	B	R	E	S	E	E
M	F	C	O	A	A	N	O	I	L	R	P
I	K	M	N	I	B	R	N	Q	A	T	E
R	E	G	L	A	E	I	K	E	I	A	N
E	B	E	C	T	H	S	L	Q	R	I	D
P	R	X	I	K	T	C	H	I	T	N	E
X	B	C	E	S	T	I	M	A	T	E	N
E	A	E	L	P	M	A	S	Z	J	Y	T
L	C	O	N	D	I	T	I	O	N	A	L

The word search uses these words:

certain	chance	condition	estimate	experiment
fair	impossible	independent	outcome	probability
reliable	sample	spinner	theoretical	trial

Comprehension

"Probability is the very (a) guide of life"
Marcus Tullius Cicero (106–43 BCE)

Tip: it is not essential to understand every word!

Read this article

Girolamo Cardano was the first person to study the theory of probability. This Italian mathematician was a (b) <u>genius</u>, a (c) <u>rogue</u> and a gambler who wanted to use mathematics to help him win games of dice. He wrote the first book for gamblers. Other mathematicians continued his work and studied such problems as: "How do you divide the prize when your game of chance is (d) <u>interrupted?</u>"

Abraham de Moivre extended Cardano's study by (e) <u>tossing</u> coins and counting the ways he got heads or tails. He discovered that his results made patterns. He translated these patterns into a "bell curve" and then used the information to decide the way insurance rates should be calculated.

Christiaan Huyghens lived in Holland. He was the first mathematician to collect ideas from different areas of study and create a (f) <u>logical</u> theory of probability. He introduced the idea that it is possible to predict results.

Today, the theory of probability is a (g) <u>fundamental</u> idea in modern life. It is (h) <u>vital</u> in many professions and organisations.

Probability ● 9

← It is used by:
- Insurance companies, to calculate rates of insurance.
- Stock markets, to predict the rise and fall of stocks and shares.
- Airline companies, to predict the number of passengers.
- Call centres, to predict the number of operators they will need.
- Engineers, to calculate the safety (i) <u>margins</u> of buildings, bridges, etc.
- Supermarkets, to order products and minimise (j) <u>waste</u>.
- Doctors, to monitor the spread of diseases and the effects of drugs.
- Governments, to predict population growth and plan new schools and hospitals.
- Physicists, to study the structure of atoms.

Can you think of some more examples?

7 Look at the words labelled (a)–(j) and choose the best meaning.
   a Guide: set of instructions/set of problems
   b Genius: happy person/clever person
   c Rogue: dishonest person/hard-working person
   d Interrupted: started/stopped
   e Tossing: throwing/finding
   f Logical: interesting/reasonable
   g Fundamental: basic/funny
   h Vital: important/expensive
   i Margins: rules/limits
   j Waste: surplus/confusion

Think about the questions from the start of this chapter.
Can you answer them now?
- What is the probability that you will meet a whale when you go for a walk in a forest?
- If today is Wednesday, May 1st, what is the probability that tomorrow is Thursday, May 2nd?
- The weather forecast gives the chance of rain as 0.4. What is the probability that it will not rain?
- You have eight red socks and 7 blue socks. What is the probability that you will put on a blue sock without first checking its colour?
- What is the probability of there being 2 boys in a family of 2 children?

123

9 Consolidation: Probability

Need more practice?
Review and check your understanding here.

Exercise 9.1

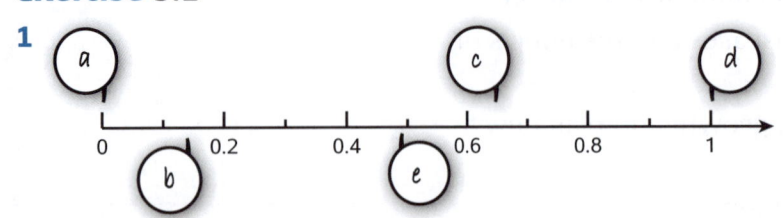

1

Probability scale showing positions: a near 0, b near 0.2, c near 0.6, e near 0.6, d near 0.9.

Fit these words into the probability scale above.

impossible   unlikely   equally likely   probable   certain

2 Twelve numbers were generated by a random number programme on a computer and written on cards.

1, 17, 17, 14, 10, 15, 6, 16, 17, 20, 9, 3

The cards were put in a bag and taken out one by one. Each card was recorded and then replaced in the bag.

What is the probability that

a N = 17
b N ≤ 10
c N = 20
d N is a prime number
e N is a multiple of 3

3 This table lists some results of football matches from the Australian Premier League.

Use the table to calculate:

a The probability that a team has scored forty or more points.
b The probability that a team has scored fewer than thirty-two points.
c The probability that a team has a mean score of 1.11 goals.
d The probability that a team has a mean score of more than 1.60 goals.

	Team	Matches Played	Points	Mean Goals
1	Sydney FC	27	48	1.78
2	Melbourne Victory	27	47	1.74
3	Gold Coast United	27	44	1.63
4	Wellington Phoenix	27	40	1.48
5	Perth Glory	27	39	1.44
6	Newcastle United	27	34	1.26
7	North Queensland Fury	27	32	1.19
8	Central Coast Mariners	27	30	1.11
9	Brisbane Roar	27	30	1.11
10	Adelaide United	27	29	1.07

4 A seed company advertises that its seeds have a 75% chance of germinating.
Here are the results from an experiment using five packets of maize seeds.
Complete the percentage rate of germination.

Packet	1	2	3	4	5
Number of seeds	36	35	34	35	37
Number of seedlings	26	28	24	29	30
Percentage	$\frac{26}{36} \times 100 = 72\%$	?	?	?	?

Use the table to calculate:

a The probability that there are at least 35 seeds in the packet.

b The probability that 75% or more of the seeds germinate.

c Do you agree with the seed company?

Extension

5 Buffon's needle.

A French mathematician, le Comte de Buffon, investigated a link between probability and the value of π.

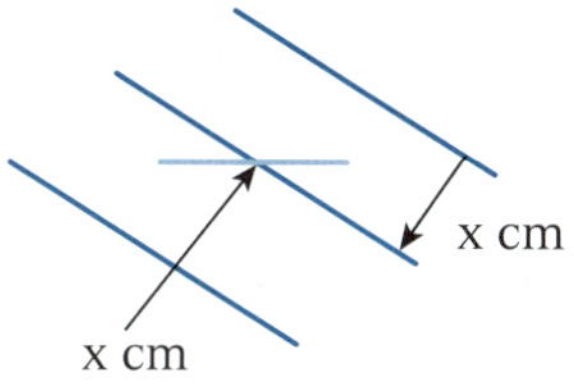

To copy his experiment,

◉ Find a needle x cm long

◉ Draw a set of parallel lines. The lines must be x cm apart

◉ Drop the needle onto the parallel lines fifty times

◉ Count the number of times that the needle crosses a line.

Buffon's theory predicts that

p(crossing a line) = $\dfrac{\text{the number of times that the needle crosses a line on the grid}}{\text{the number of times that the needle is dropped}} = \dfrac{2}{\pi}$

How close is your answer to the correct value of π?
Does your estimate improve if you do more trials with a friend?

Exercise 9.2

Think about each half of the tile!

1 The game of dominoes has 28 tiles.
Use the pictures to calculate the probability of the following:

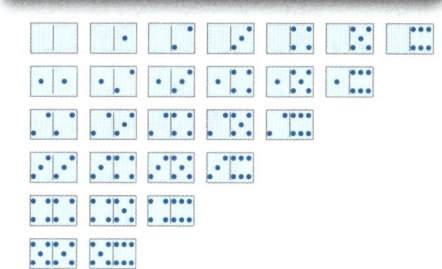

a p(double tile)

b p(blank tile)

c p(spots add to 7)

d p(spots subtract to 1)

e p(at least one 6)

2 Marc makes a spinner. He cuts out a pentagon. He colours two sections dark blue, two white, and one is light blue.

Calculate these probabilities:

a p(dark blue)

b p(white)

c p(light blue)

d p(black)

3 There is a village in Wales called
Llanfairpwllgwyngyllgogerychwyrndrobwllllantysiliogogogoch

> Try this question with some other long place names.

Look at the word and calculate:

a p(B)   b p(L)   c p(G)   d p(Y)

4 Peta has a bag of sweets. There are 20 orange ones, 15 green ones, and 10 yellow ones. She puts her hand in the bag and picks one without looking.

a Calculate:

i p(orange)   ii p(green)   iii p(yellow)

b Peta wants to do an experiment. She calculates the number of each colour she should expect if she picks sixty sweets.

How many of each colour does she expect?

Peta picks a sweet, records the colour, and then puts the sweet back in the bag. She does this sixty times.

Here are Peta's results:

orange	green	yellow
28	22	10

c Can you say why her results are not the same as her calculations?

5 Jude is playing darts. He knows that the probability that he will hit the centre is 64%. He throws two darts.

Calculate:

a p(he does not hit the centre the first time)

b p(he hits the centre twice)

c p(he hits the centre once in two throws)

d p(he does not hit the centre)

> For questions 5 to 8 you will need to draw either a tree diagram or a sample space diagram.

6 Edek goes to school by bus, but if the bus is late his mother takes him in her car.

The probability that the bus is late is 10%. The probability that Edek is late if his mother takes the car is 25%.

Use the tree diagram below to calculate the probability that:

a the bus and the car are both late.

b the bus is late, but the car is not.

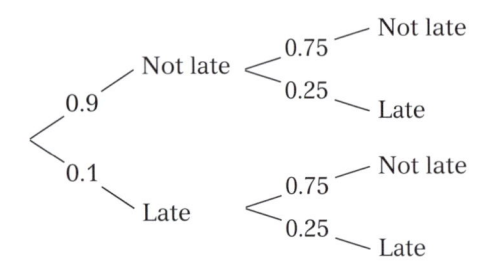

```
                    0.75 — Not late
         Not late <
       /            0.25 — Late
   0.9
  <
   0.1
       \            0.75 — Not late
         Late    <
                    0.25 — Late
```

7 Anu, Bren and Charlie like to sit in a row at the back of the class.

Make a list of all the different orders that they could sit in – ABC etc…

Use your list to calculate the probability:
  a that they all sit in alphabetical order
  b that Anu and Charlie sit together
  c that Charlie sits between Anu and Bren.

> **Extension**
>
> **8** If you toss three coins, how many different ways can they fall?
>   **a** Draw a sample space diagram and list all the different combinations.
>   Use your diagram to calculate the following. Give your answers as fractions.
>   **i** p(3 Heads)   **ii** p(2 heads, 1 tail)   **iii** p(1 head, 2 tails)   **iv** p(3 tails)
>
>   **b** Extend your diagram to show all the ways that four coins can fall.
>   **c** Calculate the probabilities of getting all heads, or all tails for four coins.
>   **d** Repeat for five coins.
>   **e** Can you build a pattern in your results?
>   **f** Can you see this pattern in other questions that you have answered in another chapter?

Exercise 9.3

1 Nico is baking a cake and needs to use two eggs.

He has a box of twelve eggs; four with brown shells and the rest with white shells. He is in a hurry and does not look when he takes an egg from the box. He breaks one egg and puts it in a bowl, then breaks another.

What is the probability that he uses:

  a two brown eggs
  b two white eggs
  c one brown egg and one white one?

Draw a tree diagram for each question.

2 Bobbie and her father are playing a word game. They have a bag of letters. There are eleven letters left in the bag, five vowels and six consonants.

Bobbie takes a letter from the bag, puts it on the table and takes another one.

What is the probability that she gets:

  a two vowels
  b two consonants
  c one vowel and one consonant?

3 Class 10C are choosing a committee to raise money for earthquake victims. They need three people for the committee. There are seven boys and nine girls in class 10C.

What is the probability that the committee will have:

  a three girls?
  b three boys
  c at least two boys
  d two girls and one boy?

10 Assessment

In this chapter you will answer...
- Have you revised for your test tomorrow?
- Do you have any results in your coursework?
- Do you know the time of your exam next week?
- Did you understand the corrections on the board?

10.1 Different assessments

Your teachers and schools expect to give you regular tests and examinations. These help them to know how well you and your class are doing, and how well you have understood all the new things that you are learning.

- **Tests** are short groups of questions, set by your teacher and given in class
- **Examinations** are longer groups of questions, usually on several ideas that you have learnt. They will be set by your school to check on the progress of the pupils over a term or a year
- **External examinations** (such as the IGCSE) are set by organisations outside your school called examination boards. Examinations give qualifications that will allow you to go on to training or university
- **Coursework** is an extended piece of work that you are expected to do on your own. You will work on it for several days or in a series of lessons. The marks may be added to your marks for a written examination.

Remember: when you are doing a test or examination, you will be working on your own. Your teacher wants to know how well you have understood the work.

KEY WORDS

Test a set of questions to check your understanding

Examination a longer set of questions

Coursework an extended piece of work, often on statistics or mathematical modelling

10.1.1 Mental arithmetic tests

These are short tests. Your teacher reads out the questions and you listen, work out the answer in your head and write down the answer.

To help you should:

- listen carefully
- ask your teacher to repeat each question
- ask your teacher for tests that have been given before, so that you can practise
- learn any new words.

Assessment 10

Exercise 1 Here are some possible questions.
Read each one aloud, and then match the calculation and the answer.

Question	Calculation	Answer
If one pencil costs 65 cents, how much do three pencils cost?	$\sqrt{16} + 5^2$	52
Write down the product of six and eight.	$2(x + 3) = 22$	29
A cup of tea costs 8 dirhams and a cake costs 12 dirhams. What is the cost of two cups of tea and three cakes?	65×3	8
Add the square root of sixteen to the square of five.	6×8	195
I think of a number, add three, and multiply the result by two. If the answer is twenty-two, which number did I think of?	$2 \times 8 + 3 \times 12$	48

10.1.2 Written class tests

These tests are a set of written questions that you answer on paper.
The questions are usually on ideas that you have just learnt.
You must write down all your calculations to show that you have understood each question.
You may be allowed to put your hand up and ask for help.

Before you do a class test:

- revise the work that you are being tested on
- make sure that you have learnt the words that you use in the topic.

During a class test:

- read each question carefully and make sure that you understand it
- answer the question and write down your working
- draw diagrams clearly, marking every detail.

After a class test:

- listen while your teacher explains the solutions
- repeat any questions that you got wrong: "do the corrections"
- if you still do not understand, ask for help.

Exercise 2 Complete the sentences with the words *before, during, while* or *after*.

a Everybody is nervous .... a test.

b .... a test you can do your corrections.

c You cannot talk to your friends .... you are doing a test.

d It is a good idea to revise your work .... doing a test.

e .... a test you should read each question carefully.

10.1.3 School examinations

These are longer and more formal than class tests.
You will work in silence and need to have all the right equipment.
You may be allowed to put your hand up and ask questions if you do not understand a word or phrase.
These examinations are normally taken at the end of a school term or the end of a school year.
They will be set on all the work done in that term, or year.
You will need to revise carefully for them.

KEY WORDS

Revision going back over work that you have already studied and making sure that you understand it.

Exercise

3 Here are some pictures of the equipment that you need in a school examination. Match the correct word to the picture.

> drawing compass/pair of compasses pencil pencil sharpener
> protractor ruler eraser/rubber calculator pen

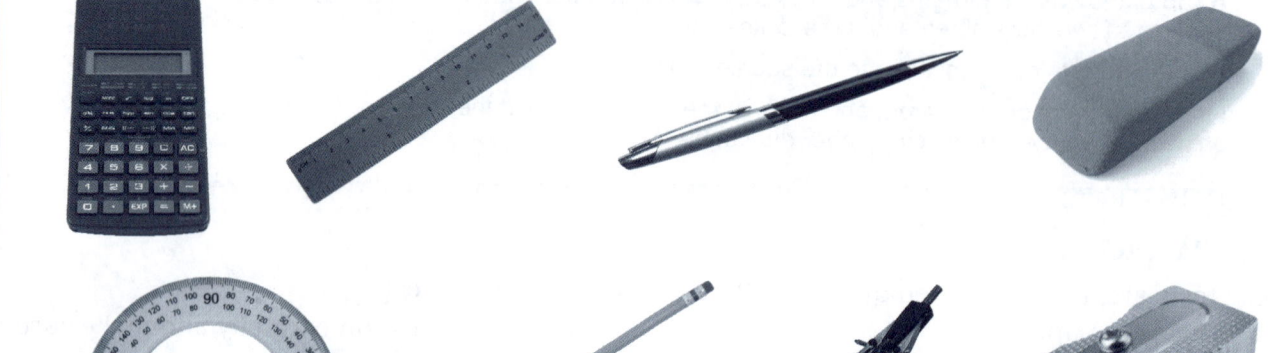

4 Why do you need this equipment?
Complete these sentences with the correct word(s) from the box.

   a I need a .... so that I can measure lines and draw accurate diagrams.
   b I need a .... to work through complicated problems.
   c I need a .... so that I can measure the size of different angles.
   d I need a/n .... to correct any mistakes in my diagrams.
   e I need a .... to draw circles or construct triangles.

10.2 Revising for tests and examinations

You need to revise carefully for mathematics tests and examinations.

Revising for mathematics is not the same as revising for history or geography.

Here is advice for making your revision simple and effective:

- Ask your teacher for a list of the topics that you need to revise.
- Make a revision timetable, and give yourself plenty of time.
- Revise regularly. A short time every day is the best.
- Don't just read your books. You need to <u>do</u> Mathematics to learn it.
- Work questions on paper. Study examples in your textbook or notes, put a piece of paper over the solution and work it again. Is the answer the same?
- Learn from your mistakes. Why did you get the question wrong the first time?
- Try plenty of different questions.
- Work with a friend, a "study buddy", and explain ideas to each other.
- Work somewhere that you feel comfortable. Some people find it useful to listen to music while they revise, other people like to work in silence.
- Take regular breaks. Promise yourself a treat approximately every forty minutes.
- Use a revision book for your course and do the practice questions.
- Find a revision website. A good one will explain why an answer is wrong.

Remember:
- Don't just read, you need to practise.
- Don't leave it until the last minute.
- Don't do too much. If you get stuck or bored, change to another subject.
- Don't use your calculator for every simple calculation.
  Try some questions without it!

> **Exercise**
>
> **5** Read these sentences and decide if each one is true (T) or false (F).
>
> a If I revise at the last minute I will gain a better mark.
> b It is a good idea to work with a friend.
> c I must use my calculator for every solution.
> d Regular breaks are a good idea.
> e The best way to revise is just to read my textbook.
> f Making mistakes can help you to learn.

10.3 External examinations

External examinations are set by governments or organisations outside your school.
They may be used as qualifications to give you a place at another school, college, university, or further training.
External examinations are formal and there are strict rules and regulations to ensure that everyone works alone and there is no cheating.
You will not be able to talk or ask questions and will be asked to enter and leave the room in silence.

Before the examination:
- Make sure that you know the syllabus.
- Revise carefully.
- Ask for some practice papers and work through them until you are confident.
- Make sure that you have the correct equipment and that it is in good working condition.
- Check the batteries in your calculator.
- Make sure you know which papers will need a calculator and which papers do not allow one.

During the examination:
- Sit down, make sure you are comfortable and take some deep breaths to help you relax.
- Don't rush. You should have plenty of time.
- Read the instructions on the front of the paper carefully. You should read them two or three times.
- Follow the instructions!
- Find the page with formulae written on it so that you can refer to them easily.
- Write clearly and include all your calculations. You will gain marks for them.
- Do the easy questions first!
- Write each answer clearly on the line given.
- Remember to include any units. E.g. cm^2, grams, $, €, etc.
- Look at the clock regularly. Do not spend too much time on one question.
- If you are stuck, try another question.
- If you have a practical problem you may put up your hand and ask a supervisor for help.

After the examination:
- It will be several weeks before you receive your marks.
- It is possible to ask for your marks to be checked again if you think they are too low.

10.3.1 Command terms

External examinations use special words and phrases in their instructions. It is important that you learn these words and follow the instructions or you will lose marks.

Here are some of the most common phrases:

Command term	Meaning
Calculate	Write the calculations that you do, and the answer.
Complete	Finish a diagram or calculation that has already been started. E.g. Complete the pie chart or tree diagram.
Construct	Use a ruler and drawing compass to draw an accurate diagram.
Draw	Use a pencil and ruler, drawing compass or protractor to draw an accurate diagram. Label the diagram carefully.
Expand	Remove the brackets (algebra questions). E.g. Expand $4(3t + 1)$ gives $12t + 4$
Explain	'Explain' questions give you the answer, but ask you to write down a sentence explaining why you think the answer is correct.
Find	Write the calculations that you do, and the answer.
Give a reason for your answer	'Give a reason for your answer' questions give you the answer, but ask you to write down a sentence explaining why you think the answer is correct.
Give your answer….	The answer must be written according to the instruction. E.g. Give your answer in the simplest form, means $15 : 5 = 3 : 1$ $x + x + 3 + x + x + 5 = 4x + 8$
Measure	Use the diagram given on the paper, and measure the length of a line, or the size of an angle. Examination papers will always tell you whether the diagram is accurate. If they do not tell you, it is not an accurate diagram and is only drawn to help you understand the question.
Show that	'Show that' questions give you the answer, but ask you to write down all the calculations and show that you have understood the question.
Simplify	Means the same as 'give your answer in its simplest form'.
Solve	Find the solution(s), to an equation(s). E.g. $5(x - 3) = 35$ $x - 3 = 7$ $x = 10$
Trial and error or trial and improvement	You use approximate values until you find the correct value. Used to solve equations.
Work out	Write the calculations that you do, and the answer.
Write down	Write the answer. You do not need to write any calculations.
Write your answer…	'Write your answer to the nearest whole number' or 'write your answer as a percentage'. E.g. 56.218 is written as 56 (to the nearest whole number) 0.95 is written as 95%

There are three special command terms that are used for **drawing line graphs**:

Plot	Mark the place of each point on the graph in exactly the right place.
Draw	Mark all the points on the graph and connect them with a smooth line. Label the axes, the scale and the important points.
Sketch	A sketch is less accurate than a drawing, but should still give a clear idea of the shape of the graph and any points where the line(s) cross the axes. Label the axes and give some scale marks.

6 Here is an examination question. The question has been answered by two different students, Ali and Jana. Look at the answers and decide which student will gain the most marks for each part of the question.

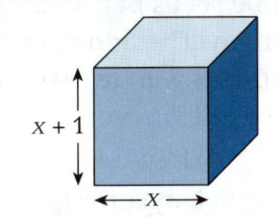

A cuboid has a square base of side x cm.
The height of the cuboid is 1 cm more than the length of the base, x cm
The volume of the cuboid is 225 cm³

a Show that $x^3 + x^2 = 225$

Ali's answer	Jana's answer
$x \times x \times (x+1) = x^3 + x^2 = 225$	Height of cuboid $= x + 1$
	Volume of cuboid $= x \times x \times (x+1)$
	$= x^2(x+1)$
	$= x^3 + x^2$
	$= 225$

b The equation $x^3 + x^2 = 225$ has a solution between $x = 5$ and $x = 6$.
Use a **trial and improvement** method to find this solution.
Give your answer to 1 decimal place

Ali's answer	Jana's answer		
$x = 5.8$	$x = 5.5$	$5.5^3 + 5.5^2 = 196.625$	Too small
	$x = 6.0$	$6^3 + 6^2 = 252$	Too large
	$x = 5.9$	$5.9^3 + 5.9^2 = 240.2$	Too large
	$x = 5.8$	$5.8^3 + 5.8^2 = 229.9$	Too large
	$x = 5.7$	$5.7^3 + 5.7^2 = 217.7$	Too small
	The closest answer to 1 d.p is 5.8		

10.4 Coursework

Coursework tasks are longer assignments that allow you to work alone and try your own mathematical ideas.

- You are given several lessons and homework times to work on an assignment, and a deadline or date when you have to complete it.
- You may be allowed to use a computer, but some parts of an assignment are often easier to do if they are hand-written. Writing out the results of an assignment uses more new words. However, remember that you are using mathematics, and can explain your results using tables, graphs, and diagrams as well as words.
- You will be asked to write a plan at the beginning and a conclusion at the end, so you will need to write clear English sentences for these.

Coursework may be set as part of an external examination. The marks you gain will be added to those you are given for the other paper(s). This will be easier if you have done some practice coursework before you start.

There are three main types of coursework:

- Investigations which look for general rules and patterns.
- Statistics assignments that set you a question to answer, ask you to collect data and then analyse that data to answer the question.
- Modelling assignments that ask you to look at a practical situation and find equations and graphs to help you analyse it.

You will find assignments easier if you keep to a plan. This flowchart on the right gives you an outline, but you do not need every step for each type of investigation.

KEY WORDS

Coursework an extended piece of work on statistics or mathematical modelling
Investigation an extended mathematical puzzle

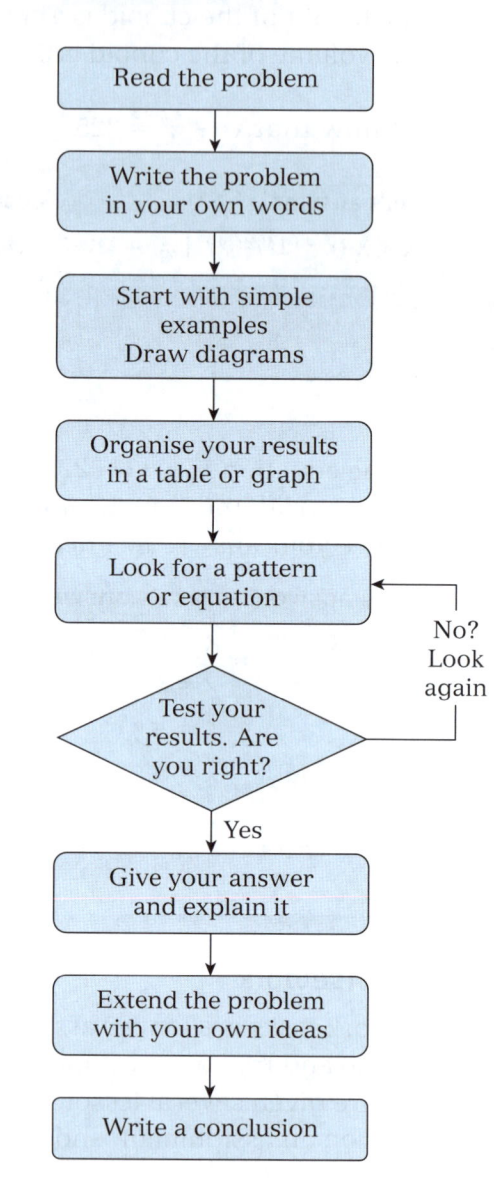

Read the problem

Write the problem in your own words

Start with simple examples
Draw diagrams

Organise your results in a table or graph

Look for a pattern or equation

Test your results. Are you right? — No? Look again

Yes

Give your answer and explain it

Extend the problem with your own ideas

Write a conclusion

7 Match each word with its meaning. The first pair has been done for you.

make clear	finish	mistaken	question
complete	correct	task	thought
ending	begin		

a start	begin
b assignment	
c right	
d finish	
e explain	
f conclusion	
g wrong	
h problem	
i idea	

Here are examples of two short assignments.
- Assignment One is an investigation called "How many squares are there on a chessboard?"
- Assignment Two is a modelling task about the braking speeds of cars.

You can study them and think about how you would do a similar task. Look at the notes beside the working out and try to match the notes to the this flowchart.

10.5 Assignment examples

10.5.1 Assignment one: How many squares are there on a chessboard?

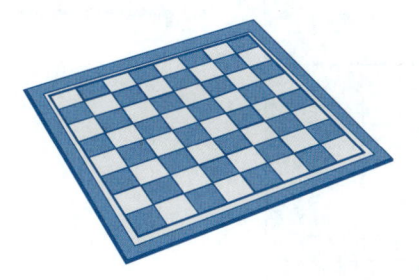

If you look at a chessboard you can see 8 φ 8 = 64 small squares. But if the squares can be any size, how many can you see?

Here is one solution. There are many other ways of solving this problem

A If I draw squares on a chessboard, how many squares can I draw?

Squares can be different sizes.

Look at this:

> Write the problem in your own words.

Here is one square.

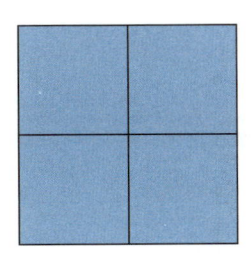

> Start at the beginning, with the simplest form of the question. Draw diagrams to show your working.

Here are four small squares and one big one. The total is 5.

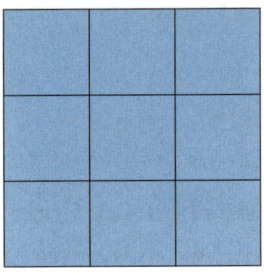

1 3 × 3 square, **4** 2 × 2 squares, and **9** 1 × 1 squares

B

Diagram	1 × 1 squares	2 × 2 squares	3 × 3 squares	4 × 4 squares	5 × 5 squares
1	1				
2	4	1			
3	9	4	1		
4*	16	9	4	1	
5*	25	16	9	4	1

> Use the pattern to look for the next result. Draw a diagram to check your prediction.
> Put your results in a table. Look for patterns.

*These results are from the pattern, not from diagrams.

Looking at this table I can see a pattern. It uses the square numbers.

C I think the answer for a 4 × 4 square will give **16** 1 × 1, **9** 2 × 2, **4** 3 × 3, **1** 4 × 4.

I can check this by drawing:

> For square numbers, see Chapter 3.

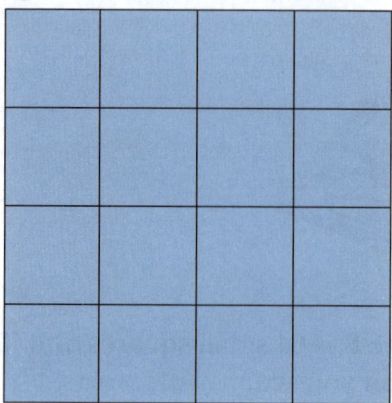

D Using this pattern, it is clear that the number of squares on a chessboard is

$8^2 + 7^2 + 6^2 + 5^2 + 4^2 + 3^2 + 2^2 + 1^2 = 64 + 49 + 36 + 25 + 16 + 9 + 4 + 1 = \underline{204}$

There are 204 squares on a chessboard.

> Give your solution.

E If a chessboard could have any number of squares, an **n × n** board would have a total of

$1^2 + 2^2 + 3^2 + 4^2 + 5^2 + \ldots\ldots\ldots n^2$ squares

To extend the problem, think how many squares there are on a board that only has dots.

> Extend your result.

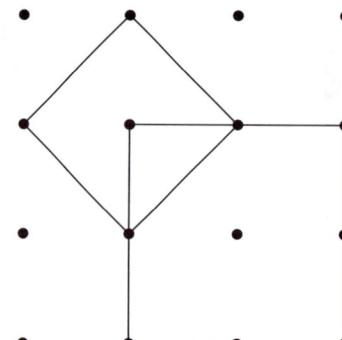

10.5.2 Assignment two: Braking distances

This diagram is published by the UK government in the Highway Code

When a driver stops a car, s/he must think first, then brake so that the vehicle stops.

In this assignment you are asked to find equations that will model the link between the speed, and the thinking and braking distances.

Typical Stopping Distances

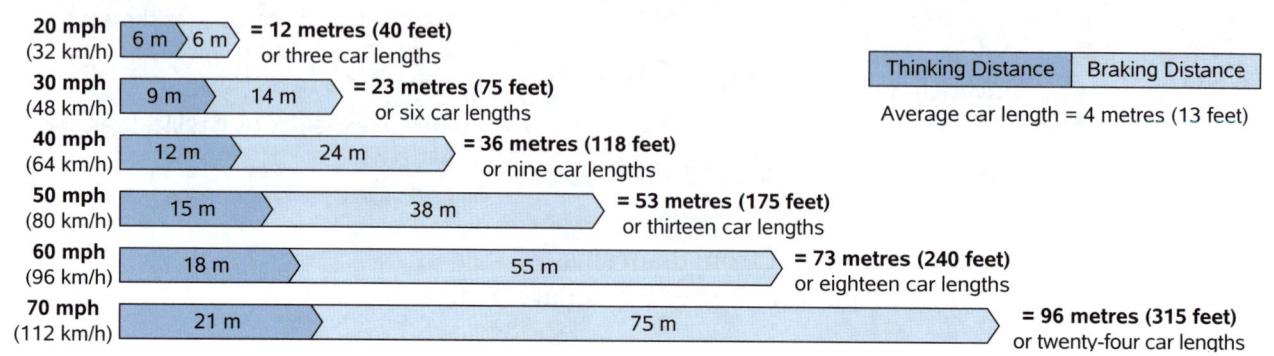

20 mph (32 km/h) | 6 m | 6 m | = 12 metres (40 feet) or three car lengths
30 mph (48 km/h) | 9 m | 14 m | = 23 metres (75 feet) or six car lengths
40 mph (64 km/h) | 12 m | 24 m | = 36 metres (118 feet) or nine car lengths
50 mph (80 km/h) | 15 m | 38 m | = 53 metres (175 feet) or thirteen car lengths
60 mph (96 km/h) | 18 m | 55 m | = 73 metres (240 feet) or eighteen car lengths
70 mph (112 km/h) | 21 m | 75 m | = 96 metres (315 feet) or twenty-four car lengths

| Thinking Distance | Braking Distance |

Average car length = 4 metres (13 feet)

Assessment 10

A Start by writing the problem in your own words. This can also be a simple plan of the way that you intend to do the assignment.

"The diagram with this assignment shows the different thinking and breaking distances for a car travelling at different speeds. the question asks me to find the equations that link the speed, and the thinking and braking distances together. I will do this by looking at each case separately, by drawing graphs, and then by using the graphs to find the separate equations."

B The connection between the speed and the thinking distance.

Speed (kph)	Thinking distance
32	6 m
48	9 m
64	12 m
80	15 m
96	18 m
112	21 m

Look at the simple case first.

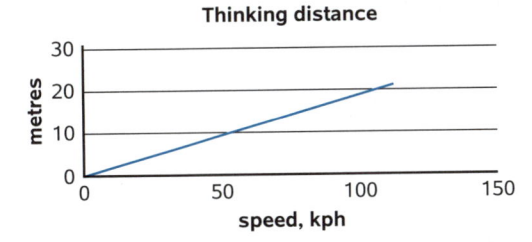

Draw a diagram.

The graph is a straight line, so

thinking distance $= k \times$ speed or TD $= k \times s$

If TD = 6 m, then the speed = 32 kph

$6 = k \times 32$

$k = \frac{6}{32}$

The formula is **TD $= \frac{6}{32} \times$ speed**.

C The connection between the speed and the braking distance is

Speed (kph)	Thinking distance
32	6 m
48	14 m
64	24 m
80	38 m
96	55 m
112	75 m

Draw another diagram and look for a clear shape in the line.

If you look at the figures, you will see that there is no clear straight line.

The graph shows that the connection is a curve.

137

The best way of finding the equation is to use a spreadsheet, as you can see below.

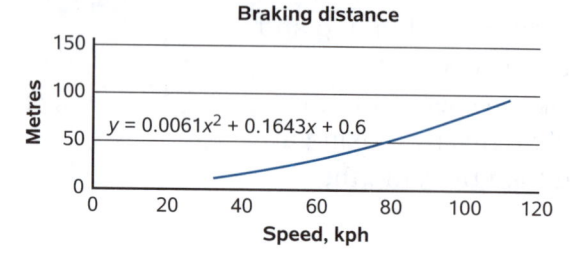

Braking distance

$y = 0.0061x^2 + 0.1643x + 0.6$

(Metres vs Speed, kph)

The formula is:
Braking Distance = $0.0061 \times$ **speed**^{2} $- 0.0232 \times$ **speed** $+ 0.6$

D The connection between the speed and the braking distance.

Look for a pattern or a formula.

Using a spreadsheet it is also possible to give the formula that connects the speed and the overall stopping distance.
Stopping distance = $0.0061 \times$ **speed**^{2} $+ 0.1643 \times$ **speed** $+ 0.6$

E Discuss your findings. See if you can find other figures that agree or disagree with these figures and compare the data.

F The distances given in the Highway Code assume that the road is dry and the vehicle is in good condition.

To extend the problem you could ask:

- Does the weight or the length of the vehicle make any difference?
- Does the age or experience of the driver change the figures?

Extend the problem.

G Write a summary of your findings at the end of the assignment.

Write a conclusion.

Think about the questions from the start of this chapter. Do you know how to answer them now?
- Have you revised for your test tomorrow?
- Do you have any results in your coursework?
- Do you know the time of your exam next week?
- Did you understand the corrections on the board?

Glossary

Translate these key words into your first language.
Listen to the glossary pronunciation at www.oxfordsecondary.co.uk/oclssupport

Accurate (adj) Exactly correct

Acute angle (n) An angle between 0° and 90°

Adjacent side (n) The side next to the given angle in a right-angled triangle

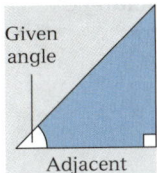

Algebra (n) Mathematics that uses letters AND numbers

Alphabet (n) A set of letters used in a language.
Mathematics uses Latin and Greek letters
a, b, c….
α, β, γ…..

Alternate angles (n, pl) Two angles are equal if they are on opposite sides of a line crossing two parallel lines. May be called Z angles

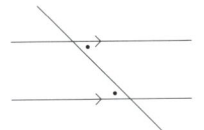

Analysis (n) Using the data collected in statistics to explain and predict

Angle of depression (n) The angle formed when you look down at something from the horizontal

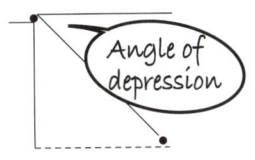

Angle of elevation (n) The angle formed when you look up at something from the horizontal

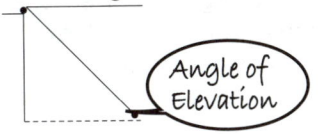

Approximate (adj) Almost exact or correct
$\frac{22}{7}$ is an approximate value for π

Arc (n) Part of the circumference of a circle

Area (n) The size of a surface, measured in square units cm², m² ….

Arithmetic (n) The mathematics of numbers; adding, subtracting, multiplying, and dividing

Assignment (n) An exercise or task set for students that is usually completed outside the classroom

Average (n) A typical value for a group of numerical data
See also: mean, median, and mode

Axis, axes (pl) (n) A line from which co-ordinates are measured
x-axis and y-axis

Bar chart (n) A graph used in statistics that uses bars to show data

Base (n) The bottom of a solid shape. The surface in contact with the support

Bias (n) The change in a statistical result caused by poor data

BIDMAS The order of working through an arithmetical sum
Brackets, **I**ndices, **D**ivision, **M**ultiplication, **A**ddition **S**ubtraction
See chapter 3

Border (n) The edge of a flat shape

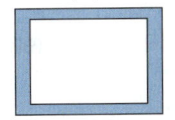

Brackets (n, pl) Symbols that tell you to do the sum inside them first ( ), [ ],

Calculate (v) Find an answer by using numbers

Calculator (n) A small electronic machine used for making calculations

Calculator key (n) The button on a calculator that is pressed to give numbers or operations

Capacity (n) The amount that something can hold. See volume. Measured in cubic units mm³, cm³ …

Centimetre (n) Metric measurement of length 100 centimetres = 1 metre

Centre (n) The middle of a circle. The point where the pin of a drawing compass is put.
A is the centre of this circle

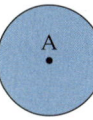

Chance (n) The likelihood of an event taking place. Another word for probability.

Check (v) Go through your work and make sure that it is correct

Chord (n) A straight line joining two points on the circumference of a circle

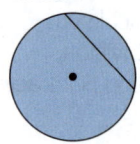

Circumference (n) The perimeter of a circle

Conclusion (n) The summing up at the end of a piece of mathematics, where the mathematics is used to come to a decision

Congruent (adj) Congruent triangles are exactly the same size and shape

Constant (n) The number that does not change in an algebra expression
$A \varphi \pi r^2$, π is the constant

Construct (v) Use a ruler and drawing compass to draw an accurate diagram

Continuous data (n) Data that is measured
Height, mass, speed…

Conversion graph (n) A graph used to change one quantity to another e.g. °F to °C

Conversion line (n) The line on a conversion graph that shows how to read off the answer

Convert (v) Change from one set of units to another
2 km = 2000 m

Co-ordinates (n, pl) Pairs of co-ordinates are used to fix the position of a point on a graph (3, 4)

Correct (adj) True, accurate, right

Corrections (n, pl) When a sum is done wrong, the corrections are done to show where the mistakes occurred

Correlation (n) The relationship or connection between two variables. Correlation may be positive, negative or neither. Height and weight can show positive correlation

Corresponding angles (n, pl) Two angles are equal when a straight line crosses two parallel lines.
May be called F angles

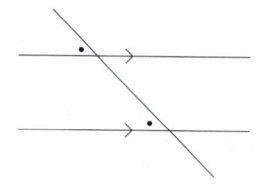

Cosine (n) Trigonometry ratio
$$\text{cosine} = \frac{\text{adjacent side}}{\text{hypotenuse}}$$

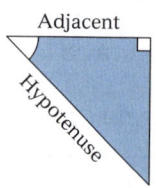

Counting numbers (n, pl) The numbers in order, starting at 1
1, 2, 3, 4, 5….

Course (n) A set of lessons. May be a set of topics leading to an examination

Coursework (n) An extended piece of work that may be assessed as part of an external examination

Cube (n) A solid with six square faces and twelve edges that are all the same length

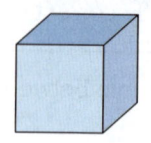

Cuboid (n) A solid with six faces. The faces are rectangles.

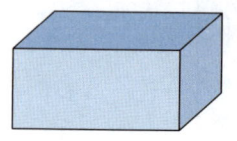

Cylinder (n) A solid prism with a circular base

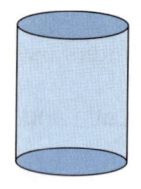

Data (n) Facts and figures collected for later study

Decimal (n) Number written using a decimal point 0.36, 0.051

Decimal places (n, pl) The number of figures after the decimal point
π = 3.142 to 3 decimal places

Decrease (v) Make smaller

Degree (n) (a) The unit used to measure the size of an angle, a full turn is 360°
(b) The unit used to measure temperature

Denominator (n) The bottom number of a fraction
$\frac{5}{8}$, 8 is the denominator

Glossary

Diagram (n) A picture drawn to make a problem clear

Diameter (n) A straight line that goes through the centre of a circle. The circle is divided into two halves

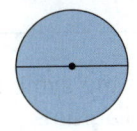

Dictionary (n) A book which explains the meaning of words. A mathematical dictionary gives the meaning of words used in mathematics

Dimension (n) A measurement of length, height or width. A line has one dimension, a flat figure has two dimensions and a solid has three dimensions

Direct variation (n) When two variables have a constant ratio $y = \mathbf{k}x$, $\mathbf{k}$ is a constant

Discrete data (n) Data that is counted
e.g. the number of children in a family

Display (n) The figures on the screen of a calculator

Double (v) Multiply by two
6 is double 3

Draw a diagram (v) Use a pencil and ruler, compasses or protractor to draw the picture of a problem or show a practical situation

Drawing compass (n) An instrument used for drawing circles

Eliminate (v) Remove a variable from an equation. Used as a method when solving simultaneous equations

Equal (adj) The same as. In mathematics the same size or number

Equation (n) A statement in algebra. The two sides of an equation are equal
$5x + 2 = 12$
$x^2 - x + 2 = 0$ ....

Equilateral triangle (n) A three-sided figure. All the sides are the same length and all the angles are 60°

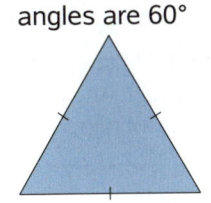

Equipment (n) The things that you need for study, a hobby, a job....

Erase (v) Rub out, remove marks from paper

Eraser (n) A piece of rubber for removing pencil marks

Event (n) A single observation in a probability experiment or calculation

Examination (n) A written test, set on several topics that have been studied

Example (n) A written solution that shows a general rule

Exercise (n) A set of questions for you to practise a mathematical rule

Exercise book (n) A book in which you write answers to exercises or problems set by your teacher

Expand (v) Multiply out an expression in algebra
$5(x - 2) = 5x - 10$

Exponent (n) The small number to the right of another number or letter that tells you how often you must multiply
$7^3 = 7 \times 7 \times 7$
$y^2 = y \times y$

Expression (n) A mathematical phrase that is written in letters and numbers. There is no = (equals) sign so it is not an equation

External assessment (n) Examinations and coursework set by organisations, and not by your school

Factor (n) A number that divides exactly into another number
The factors of 28 are 1, 2, 4, 7, 14 and 28

Flow chart (n) A diagram that shows the order in which to work

Folder (n) A cover in which to keep loose papers

Formula (n), **Formulae** (pl) Symbols and numbers that give a mathematical rule
The formula for the perimeter of a rectangle is $P = 2(l + w)$

Fraction (n) A number written as one number divided by another
$\frac{5}{8}, \frac{1}{2}, \frac{2}{3}$ ......

Frequency (n) Used in statistics. The number of times an event occurs

Function (n) The relationship between two different variables
$f(x) = 2x - 3$
$f(5) = 2 \times 5 - 3 = 7$

Gradient (n) The slope of a line

Gram (n) Metric measurement of mass or weight
1000 grams = 1 kilogram

Graph (n) A diagram using axes, that shows the relationship between two different variables or quantities

Graph paper (n) Paper used for drawing graphs. It is ruled into regular squares

Grouped data (n) Data that is put into sections so that the calculations are easier
5 – 9 kg
10 – 14 kg.....

Hinge (n) A moving joint. There is one at the top of a drawing compass

Horizontal (adj) At 90° to the vertical.
A horizontal line is parallel to the top of the page

Hypotenuse (n) The longest side of a right-angled triangle. The hypotenuse is the side opposite the right angle

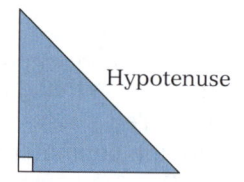

Hypotenuse

Improper fraction (n) A fraction where the numerator is a larger number than the denominator
$\frac{12}{5}$

Incorrect (adj) Not true, inaccurate, not right, wrong

Increase (v) Make larger

Independent variable (n) The variable that does not need another for its values. The independent variable is normally plotted along the x-axis. Time is an independent variable

Index (n), **Indices** (pl) The small number to the right of another number or letter that tells you how often you must multiply
$7^3 = 7 \times 7 \times 7$
$y^2 = y \times y$

Inequality (n) A statement in algebra. The two sides of an inequality are not equal. One side is less than the other
$5x + 2 > 12 \quad x > 2$
x takes the values 3, 4,5.....

Infinity, ∞ (n) A quantity larger than any defined quantity. Any number divided by zero is infinite

Instrument (n) Piece of equipment, tool

Integer (n) A whole number. The number may be positive or negative. Zero is an integer
... –2, –1, 0, 1, 2, 3...

Intercept (n) The point where a line or curve crosses either the x- or y-axis

Internal assessment (n) Examinations and coursework set by your teacher or school

Intersection (n) The point where two lines or curves cross on a graph

Interval (n) Used in statistics for the difference between the lowest and highest values in a group.
The interval for adult height is 120–210 cm

Inverse function (n) The opposite operation. Multiplying and dividing are inverse operations. The inverse function of tan x is tan^{-1} y etc

Investigation (n) An extended mathematical puzzle, often given as a piece of coursework

Isosceles triangle (n) A three-sided figure with two sides that are the same length. The two angles between the sides and the base are equal

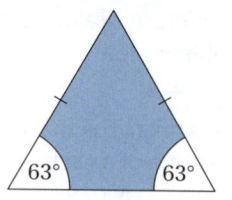

Key (n) A key explains the symbols used in graphs or diagrams

Kilogram (n) Metric measurement of mass or weight
1 kilogram = 1000 grams

Kilometre (n) Metric measurement of length
1 kilometre = 1000 metres

Like terms (n, pl) Terms in algebra can only be added or subtracted if they are alike. xy is not like x or y
$3xy + x - xy = 2xy + x$

Linear equation (n) An equation with two variables that gives a straight line when, plotted on a graph
$y = 2x - 1$

Linear function (n) A function with two variables that gives a straight line when, plotted on a graph
$f(x) = 2x - 1$

Line of symmetry (n) A line that cuts a shape exactly in half so that one side reflects the other

Litre (n) Metric measurement of volume
1 litre = 1000 ml = 1000 cm³

Margin (n) A space at the edge of a page, used for writing the number of a question when you are doing an exercise

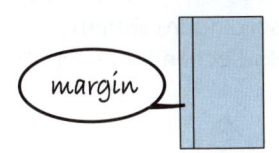

Glossary

margin

Mirror image

Mass (n) The quantity of matter in a body. Weight varies with gravity, mass is always the same

Mean (n) An average.
The sum of quantities divided by the number of quantities
The mean of 6, 8, 9, and 11 is $(6 + 8 + 9 + 11)/ 4 = 8.5$

Measure (v) Find out the size of something. You can measure lengths, angles, volume, mass, time….

Median (n) An average.
The middle number in a set of numbers, that are in order
The median of 5, 8, 9, 11, 13 is 9

Mensuration (n) The mathematics of measuring length, area and volume

Mental arithmetic (n) Calculations done in your head. Only the answer is written down

Metre (n) Metric measurement of length
1000 metres = 1 kilometre

Metric measure (n) Measuring system based on the metre

Milligram (n) Metric measurement of mass or weight
1000 milligrams = 1 gram

Millimetre (n) Metric measurement of length
1000 millimetres = 1 metre

Mirror image (n) An exact reflection in a straight line

Mirror line (n) A line that cuts a shape exactly in half so that one side reflects the other

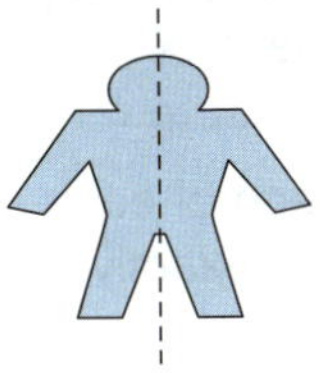

Mistake (n) A part of a sum that is not correct. An answer that is wrong

Mixed number (n) A number made up of both a whole number and a fraction
$6\frac{2}{3}, 9\frac{5}{8}$….

Mode (n) An average.
The most frequent value in a given group 5, 6, 6, 7, 9, 11, 15
The mode is 6

Modelling (n) Fitting a mathematical analysis to a practical situation

Multiple (n) Any number that is a product of another number
Multiples of 7 are
7, 14, 21, 28, 35….

Natural numbers (n, pl) The set of numbers used for counting. Zero is not a natural number
1, 2, 3, 4, …..

Negative (adj) A negative number has a value that is less than zero.
The opposite of positive

Number pattern (n) A sequence of numbers that follows a rule
The rule, × 2 and add 3 gives
5, 7, 9, 11……

Numerator (n) The top number of a fraction
$\frac{5}{8}$ – 5 is the numerator

Numerical (adj) Using numbers

Obtuse angle (n) An angle between 90° and 180°

Operation (n) A rule that allows you to create new numbers by combining others.
Adding, subtracting, multiplying and dividing are all operations

Operator (n) The symbol used for an operation +, ÷, −, × ….

Opposite side (n) The side facing the given angle in a right-angled triangle

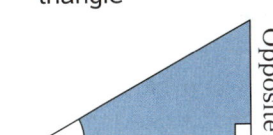

Origin (n) (0, 0) the point where the x-axis crosses the y-axis

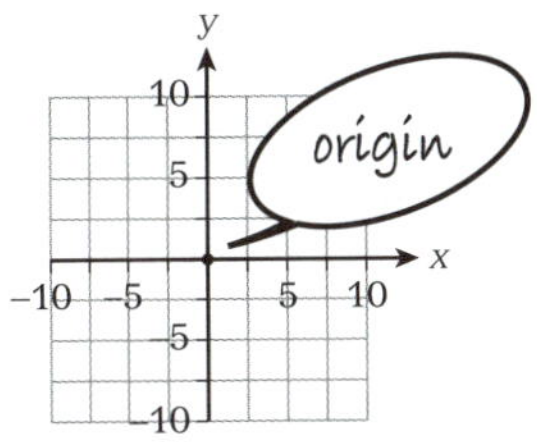

origin

Pair of compasses (Drawing compass) (n) An instrument used for drawing circles

Parabola (n) A curved line with the general equation $ax^2 + bx + c$
The path of a ball that has been thrown

143

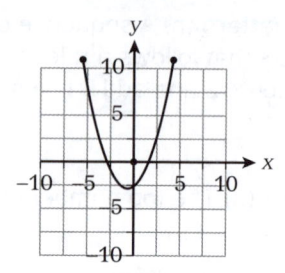

Parallel lines (n, pl) Two lines that are always exactly the same distance apart. Parallel lines never meet and are shown by arrows

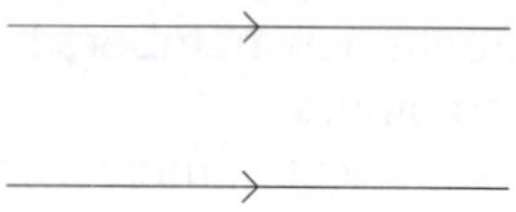

Pencil (n) An instrument for drawing or writing. The mark can be erased

Pencil case (n) Container for pens, pencils, erasers etc

Pencil sharpener (n) An instrument that is used to give pencils a sharp point

Percentage (n) A fraction with the denominator 100
$45\% = \frac{45}{100}$

Perimeter (n) The edge, or outline, of a closed figure
$P(\text{rectangle}) = 2(l + w)$

Perpendicular (adj) Perpendicular lines cross at an angle of 90°

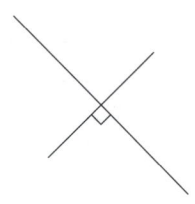

Pictogram (n) A graph used in statistics. Pictures or symbols are used to represent data

Pie chart (n) A graph used in statistics. A circle is divided into slices, and the slices represent the frequency of the data

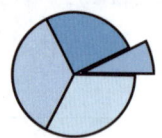

Planner (n) A diary used to note lessons and homework

Plot (v) Mark the place of each point on the graph exactly

Polygon (n) A flat figure with three or more straight sides. If all the sides and angles are the same size it is called a regular polygon

Positive (adj) A positive number has a value that is more than zero. The opposite of negative

Power (n) The small number to the right of another number or letter that tells you how often you must multiply
$7^3 = 7 \times 7 \times 7$
$y^2 = y \times y$

Practice (n) An exercise that is repeated and helps you to improve

Practise (v) Improve a skill by repetition

Preparation (n) Work done before a lesson

Primary data (n) Statistical data that you collect yourself

Prime factor (n) Any factor of another number that is also a prime number
$28 = 2 \times 2 \times 7$
The prime factors are 2 and 7

Prime number (n) A number that can only be divided by itself or by one
2, 3, 5, 7, 11, 13.....

Prism (n) A solid figure with the same cross-section for its whole length

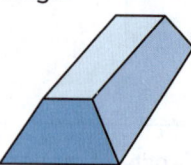

Probability (n) The likelihood, or chance, that an event will occur

Proof (n) A set of steps that establishes the truth of an idea
The proof of Pythagoras Theorem in Chapter 5

Proportion (n) The relationship between different parts of something

Protractor (n) Instrument used to measure angles

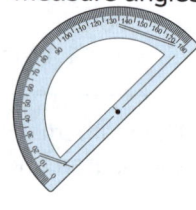

Pyramid (n) A solid figure with a square or rectangular base and four triangular sides that meet at a point

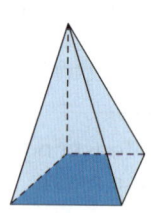

Quadrant (n) One quarter of a graph. In the first quadrant both x and y are positive

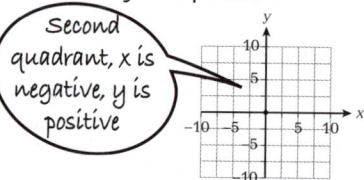

Second quadrant, x is negative, y is positive

Glossary

Quadratic function (n) A function with the general equation
f(x) = ax² + bx + c

Quadrilateral (n) A flat figure with four straight sides

Qualitative data (n) Data that is not measured or counted
Colour of eyes, favourite game….

Quantitative data (n) Data that can be measured or counted
Height, number of cars….

Questionnaire (n) A set of questions that is used to collect information

Radius (n) A straight line from the centre of a circle to the circumference

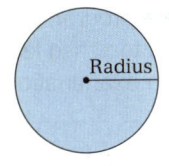

Random number (n) Numbers selected by chance from a given range. Computers and scientific calculators have programmes to create a sequence of random numbers

Ratio (n) A comparison between two numbers. Usually written in the simplest numbers possible
150:30 = 5:1

Rational number (n) A number that can be written as a fraction

Real numbers (n, pl) All the numbers that can be placed on a number line

Reflex angle (n) An angle between 180° and 360°

Regular polygon (n) In a regular polygon all the sides are the same length and all the angles are the same size

Revise (v) Go back over work that you have already studied and make sure that you understand it

Right angle (n) An angle of exactly 90°

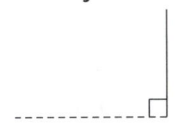

Rotation (n) Turning round a fixed point called the centre of rotation. A rotation of 180° is a half turn

Rotational symmetry (n) An exact correspondence of points around a central position

rotational symmetry of order 6

Ruler (n) A straight edge used to draw accurate lines and measure length

Sample (n) A small collection of data that represents a larger group

Sample space diagram (n) A table used for listing the outcomes when calculating theoretical probability

| ABC | ACB | BCA |
| BAC | CAB | CBA |

Scale (n) The relationship between a map or a model and the thing it represents
A model scale of 1:50 means that every 1 cm on the model represents 50 cm on the ground

Scalene triangle (n) A three-sided figure with unequal sides and angles

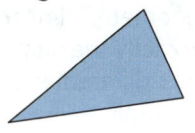

Scatter graph (n) A graph used for finding out whether there is a connection, or correlation, between two variables

Secondary data (n) Statistical data that is not collected by you

Sector (n) A slice of a circle

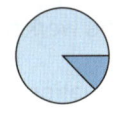

Semicircle (n) Half a circle

Sequence (n) A set of numbers arranged in a pattern that is given by a rule
−2, 1, 4, 7, 10……
The rule is 'add 3'

Set square (n) A triangular piece of plastic or metal that is used to draw right angles or other set angles

Share (v) Divide into parts
$35 shared by 5 people is $7 each

Show that (v) In an examination 'Show that' questions give you the answer, but ask you to write down all the calculations and show that you have understood the question

145

Significant figures (n, pl) A number is rounded to *y* significant figures when it contains *y* figures with a meaning
50.5621 = 50.6 (3 s.f.)

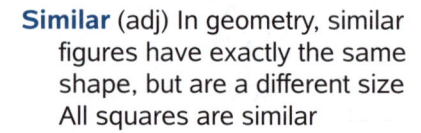

Similar (adj) In geometry, similar figures have exactly the same shape, but are a different size
All squares are similar

Simplify (v) Fractions: divide again until both numerator and denominator are as low as possible $\frac{45}{80} = \frac{9}{16}$
Algebra: collect like terms until the expression is as short as possible.
$2(a + b) - 3b = 2a - b$

Simultaneous equations (n, pl) Equations that must be worked at the same time.
Two simultaneous equations will have two unknown values, etc
$2x + y = 5$
$x - y = 1$
$x = 2, y = 1$

Sine (n) Trigonometry ratio
$\text{sine} = \frac{\text{opposite side}}{\text{hypotenuse}}$

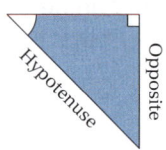

Sketch (n) A drawing that gives a clear idea of the shape of the graph and any points where the line(s) meet or cross the axes

Smooth curve (n) A curve with no breaks or sharp changes of direction

Square (n) A quadrilateral with four equal sides and four equal angles

Square root (n) A number that, when multiplied by itself, gives a square number
$\sqrt{49} = 7$
7 is the square root of 49

Solid (n) A shape with three dimensions
Cube, cylinder, sphere….

Solution (n) The answer to a problem or the answer to an equation that makes that equation true

Solve (v) Find the solution(s), to (an) equation(s)
$5(x - 3) = 35$
$x - 3 = 7$
$x = 10$

Speed (n) The rate at which something moves.
Measured in m/sec, km/hr….
The speed of light is 2.998×10^8 m/sec

Sphere (n) A perfectly round solid. All the points on the surface are the same distance from the centre.

Spreadsheet (n) A computer programme that helps you to study number patterns, create graphs and analyse statistics

Standard form (n) A way of writing large or small numbers in the form $a \times 10^n$ where *a* is a number between 0 and 10
5.79×10^3

Statistics (n, pl) The mathematics of collecting and analysing data

Straight line (n) A line that does not bend or curve

Study (v) Learn

Subject (n) The term of an equation that is on its own
$v = u + at$
v is the subject

Substitute (v) Replace the letter in a formula with an exact value.
If $P = 2(l + w)$
$L = 5, w = 1.5$
$P = 2(5 + 1.5) = 13$

Survey (n) A way to collect data for statistics by asking questions

Syllabus (n) A series of topics that creates a complete programme of study. The list of topics to learn before you take an examination

Symbol (n) A sign that represents a word or a sentence.
The symbol for addition is +

Table (n) A diagram that is used to list information, making it easier to use. The information can be in words, numbers or both together

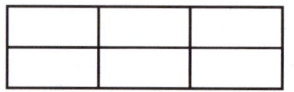

Tally marks (n, pl) Groups of lines that give the frequency in a statistics table
|||| is 4
卌 is 5

Tangent (1) (n) A line that touches a curve at one point.
The tangent of a circle is at 90° to the radius

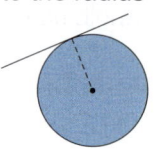

146

Glossary

Tangent (2) (n) Trigonometry ratio
$$\text{tangent} = \frac{\text{opposite side}}{\text{adjacent side}}$$

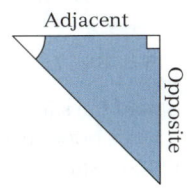

Term (n) One piece of an algebra expression
$3x + 5xy - y^2$ has three terms

Test (n) A short examination

Tetrahedron (n) A solid with four triangular faces

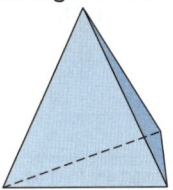

Textbook (n) A printed book for study. A mathematics text book has explanations, examples and exercises

Theorem (n) A mathematical statement that can be proved by logical steps and reasoning
Pythagoras' theorem

Timetable (n) A list of the times and days when lessons take place

Tree diagram (n) A branched diagram used when calculating probabilities

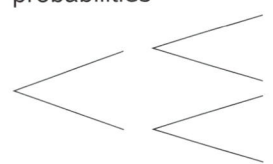

Trial (n) In probability, each observation or experiment is called a trial

Trial and error (n) Making several calculations and using the errors to move closer to an accurate solution

Trial and improvement (n) Using several calculations to improve a solution and make it more accurate

Triangle (n) A flat figure, with three straight sides and three angles. The sum of the angles is 180°

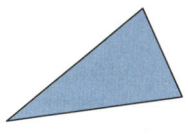

Triangular prism (n) A prism with a constant cross section. The cross section is a triangle

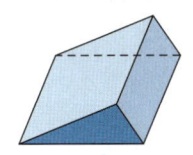

Trigonometry (n) The study of the relationships between lines and angles in triangular shapes

Underline (v) Draw a line underneath a word. Used to show the final answer to a sum or problem
$y = 7.34$

Unequal (adj) Not equal. Not the same size or number

Variable (n) A changing quantity. In an (*x*, *y*) graph, *x* is the independent variable and *y* is the dependent variable

Variation (n) A connection between two variables. May be direct or inverse

Vertex, vertices (pl) (n) The point(s) on a solid or a flat figure where lines or planes meet
A cube has 8 vertices
A triangle has three vertices

Vertical (adj) At 90° to the horizontal. A vertical line is at right angles to the bottom of the page

Vertically opposite angles (n, pl) When two straight lines intersect, the opposite angles are equal

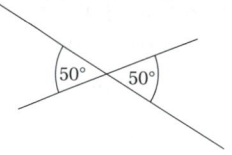

Volume (n) The amount of space occupied by a three-dimensional solid. Measured in cubic units, cm^3, m^3, etc

Weight (n) The force of gravity on an object. Weight changes as gravity changes.
Mass does not change with gravity

Whole number (n) An integer, starting from zero. 0, 1, 2, 3, ….

Working (out) (n) The written calculations needed when solving a problem. Clear working (out) is important in examinations

Zero (n) Also called nought or null. The origin of the number line
$x - x = 0$

Answers

Chapter 1 Starting the course

1. **a)** ruler, pencil. **b)** drawing compass. **c)** ruler. **d)** pencil, eraser. **e)** protractor. **f)** ruler. **g)** set square, protractor.
2. **a)** F, **b)** T, **c)** F, **d)** T, **e)** F
3. 1 d, 2 f, 3 b, 4 e, 5 c, 6 a

Chapter 3 Number

1. 1 c, 2 a, 3 d, 4 b
2. **a)** F, the answer is 58, **b)** T, **c)** F, the number is 18, **d)** T
3. 1 **c)** 18 2) **b)** 8 3) **a)** −32 4) **c)** 5832
4. 1 **a)** 120, 90, 270 2 **a)** 2, 5, 31 **b)** 9,18,120 **c)** 1,2, 5, 120, 3) **c)** 13, 4) **a)** The answer to 35 ÷ 7 is a prime number **b)** One hundred and twenty one is a square number **c)** Forty five is a multiple of nine **d)** 11 is one of the prime factors of 132 **e)** The factors of 28 are 1, 2, 4, 7, 14, and 28
5. 1 **a)** $4\frac{5}{7}, 2\frac{7}{8}$, **b)** $\frac{13}{4}, \frac{580}{579}$, **c)** $\frac{15}{30}, \frac{13}{52}$
   2 **a)** $\frac{2}{3}$, or **c)** $\frac{120}{180}$ 3 **a)** $\frac{15}{8}$, or **c)** 1.875
6. 1 **b)** 31.8km, 2 **a)** 49.68, 3 **a)** 24%, 4 **a)** $3.85
7. **Comprehension**
   a) Water covers about 66% of the Earth's surface, but most of it is too salty for our use. **b)** Of what is left, about 20 % is in remote areas, and much of that arrives at the wrong time and in the wrong place, as monsoons and floods. **c)** Humans can use less than 0.08% of all the Earth's water. **d)** We use about 70% of the water we have in farming. **e)** The World Water Council believes that by 2020 we shall need 17% more water than is available if we are to feed the world. **f)** Only 2.5% of the world's water is not salty, and two thirds of that is frozen.
8. 1 **a)** $\frac{3}{4}$ can, 2 **b)** 9 litres, 3 **d)** 17.5 cm, 4 **a)** 125 litres
9. 1 d, 2 a, 3 d, 4 a
10. 1 b, 2 b, 3 d, 4 a, 5 b, 6 c

Chapter 2 Studying mathematics

1. **b)** begun **c)** test **d)** examination **e)** wrong **f)** inaccurate **g)** teacher **h)** misunderstand **i)** end **j)** different
2. **a)** work out, **b)** work on, **c)** work out, **d)** working

11. **Comprehension**
    a) heavier/lighter **b)** Uranus/ Pluto **c)** largest/smallest **d)** Venus/ Mercury **e)** Mercury/Jupiter **f)** Earth/Neptune.

12. **a)** 21 people stay **b)** She takes 59.9 seconds **c)** It will be worth £115.76 **d)** The recipe needs 80 grams of flour **e)** 727 cans can be filled **f)** The ratio is 5:2 **g)** The difference is 1.9×10^{27} **h)** The diameter is 8×10^{-7}

13. **Comprehension**
    a) cubic/square **b)** divided/ multiplied **c)** is not/is **d)** irregular /regular pattern **e)** factors/ multiples **f)** even/odd This is only true if you do not use 2, the only even prime number. **g)** He was born in Madras (Chennai) in India. **h)** At a London hospital. **i)** He called it a very uninteresting number. **j)** The theory of prime numbers.

Consolidation: Number

Exercise 3.1

1. **a)** 5431 **b)** 1345 **c)** 1354, 1534, 3154, 3514, 5314, or 3134 **d)** 1345, 1435, 3415, 3145, 4315 or 4135 **e)** 1435, 1345, 1543, 1435, 1453 or 1345 Difference = 5431 − 1345 = 4086
2. −58, −3, 0, $3\frac{1}{4}$, 8.75, 23, 37
3. **a)** (i) 7 °C (ii) 12 °C (iii) +1 °C **b)** (i) 7 °C (ii) 11 °C (iii) 24 °C
4. **a)** 24, **b)** 30, **c)** 15, **d)** 12
5. **a)** 18 − 5 = 13 **b)** 2 + 2 = 4 **c)** 6 + 7 = 13 **d)** 18 + 4 = 22 **e)** 81 − 27 = 54
6. **a)** (8 + 4) ÷ 2 + 7 = 13 **b)** 8 + (4 ÷ 2) + 7 = 17 **c)** (8 + 4) ÷ (2 + 1) = 4
7. **a)** 389 **b)** 187 **c)** 294 **d)** 450
8. **a)** Yes **b)** Yes **c)** No **d)** Yes

3. 1 c, 2 g, 3 a, 4 b, 5 d, 6 e, 7 f
4. You may need to read the same page of a mathematics book several times before you understand it
5. **a)** It was set on Tuesday, **b)** Jane Austen, **c)** Page 125, **d)** History, **e)** S/he has an ICT lesson on Tuesday

9. **a)** $64 = 2^6$ **b)** $315 = 3^2 \times 5 \times 7$ **c)** $210 = 2 \times 3 \times 5 \times 7$ **d)** $1764 = 2^2 \times 3^2 \times 7^2$
10. The answer is always 1089

Exercise 3.2

1.

Improper fraction	Mixed number	Fraction less than 1
$\frac{9}{8}, \frac{19}{12}$	$2\frac{2}{3}, 1\frac{7}{8}, 9\frac{1}{8}$	$\frac{25}{26}, \frac{3}{4}, \frac{4}{5}$

2.

Mixed number	Improper fraction
$5\frac{1}{3}$	$\frac{16}{3}$
$1\frac{5}{8}$	$\frac{13}{8}$
$14\frac{2}{7}$	$\frac{100}{7}$
$2\frac{3}{5}$	$\frac{13}{5}$
$8\frac{4}{7}$	$\frac{60}{7}$
$5\frac{1}{4}$	$\frac{21}{4}$

3. **a)** $\frac{3}{5} = \frac{9}{15} = \frac{60}{100}$, **b)** $\frac{15}{4} = \frac{30}{8} = \frac{90}{24}$, **c)** $\frac{5}{7} = \frac{10}{14} = \frac{25}{35}$, **d)** $\frac{3}{4} = \frac{12}{16} = \frac{75}{100}$
4. **a)** 126€ **b)** 80 kg **c)** 200° **d)** 36 km **e)** 60 tonnes
5. **a)** $\frac{15}{14} > \frac{14}{15}$ **b)** $3\frac{3}{8} = \frac{27}{8}$ **c)** $\frac{1}{81} < \frac{1}{80}$ **d)** $\frac{3}{7} < \frac{5}{8}$ **e)** $\frac{4}{7} = \frac{32}{56}$ **f)** $\frac{2}{3} > \frac{66}{100}$
6.

Fraction	Decimal fraction	Percentage
a) $\frac{3}{8}$	0.375	37.5%
b) $\frac{14}{25}$	0.56	56%
c) $\frac{33}{100}$	0.33	33%
d) $\frac{9}{20}$	0.45	45%
e) $\frac{11}{20}$	0.55	55%
f) $\frac{16}{10}$	1.6	160%

148

Answers

7 **a)** Spanish: $62\frac{1}{2}$% Maths: 76%. Henry's maths mark is better
b) i) 47% are boys, **ii)** 46% are girls
c) 25 apples

8 **a)** 26% **b)** $\frac{11}{25}$ **c)** 4500

9 **a)** 1:4 **b)** 1:3 **c)** 3:7 **d)** 4:15 **e)** 1:4

10 **a)** 70 g butter **b)** 16 girls
c) 6.4 kg sugar

11 **a)** 5:3 **b)** Hue: 450 HKD and Hana: 750 HKD **c)** 7:5 **d)** Hue: 500 HKD and Hana 700HKD

12 **a)** 25% **b)** 10% **c)** 12.5%

13 **a)** 170% **b)** 39.2% **c)** $626.24

14 **a)** 1.41 **b)** 1.42 **c)** almost the same **e)** 2.01, **f)** $\sqrt{2}$, $\sqrt{2}$, 2

Exercise 3.3

1

Calculation	Whole number	One decimal place	Four significant figures
a $15 \div 7 =$	2	2.1	2.143
b $\sqrt{(4+13)} - 1 =$	3	3.1	3.123
c $2\pi + \sqrt{5} =$	9	8.5	8.519
d $(\sqrt{5}+\sqrt{7})^2 =$	24	23.8	23.83
e $\frac{1+\sqrt{5}}{2} =$	2	1.6	1.618
f $7\pi =$	22	22.0	21.99

2 **b)** and **c)** are not written in Standard Form

3 4.5×10^{-6}, 3.8×10^{-2}, 5×10^{0}, 3.2×10^2, 5.75×10^5, 5.7×10^6

4 **a)** 2.31×10^9 **b)** 1.375×10^{-1}
c) 7.211×10^{-2} **d)** 8.522×10^3
e) 7.644×10^{16}

5 **a)** 193 seconds = 3 minutes 13 seconds **b)** 19700 seconds = 5 hours 28 minutes 20 seconds
c) 5 hours 25 minutes 7 seconds

6 **a) i)** 400 **ii)** 9 **iii)** 64 **iv)** 20
v) 100 000 **vi)** 1 **b)** $9 > 8$, so $3^2 > 2^3$
c) $(5^3 \div 5^4) < (5^4 \div 5^3)$ **d)** $6^3 \div 6^3$ and $(7^3)^0$

7 **a)** 3×10^5 **b)** 1.4×10^6 **c)** 4.4×10^6
d) 3600 drops **e)** $180\,cm^3$ or 0.18 litres

8 **a)** 1×10^7 **b)** 1×10^{21}

Chapter 4 Algebra

1 **1** c **2** f **3** a **4** b **5** g **6** d **7** e

2 **1 b)** $13a - 3b$ **2 a)** $5x^2 + 2xy - y^2$
3 c) $12x^2y$ **4 b)** $\frac{8n^2}{m}$ **5 b)** $12x - 8y$
6 c) $-4f + 16g$

3 **1** f **2** c **3** d **4** e **5** b **6** a

4 **a)** True, **b)** False $P = 2(x - 4) + 2x$,
c) False $A = \frac{y}{2}(y - 2)$, **d)** True,
e) True, **f)** False $A = z(z + 5)$

5 **1 c)** $x = 7$, **2 a)** $x = 6$, **3 b)** $x = 10$,
4 b) $x = 1$

6 **a)** $2(n + 2) - 6 = 42$ $n = 22$
b) $2(n + 3) + 2n = 42$ $n = 9$
c) $2n + 42 = 180$ $n = 69$
d) $3n + 6 = 42$ $n = 12$

7 • Label the equations (1) and (2).
• Multiply one or both equations by the correct number so that the numbers in front of the terms to be eliminated are the same.
• Eliminate by adding or subtracting the equations.
• Substitute your first answer in equation (1) or (2) to find the second answer.
• Check your answers using the equations that you started with.

8 **1** Use **f)** $3x + 4y = 40$ and **b)** $x + y = 13$ $x = 12, y = 1$
2 Use **a)** $4x + 3y = 45$ and **d)** $x + 2y = 20$ $x = 6, y = 7$
3 Use **c)** $x + y = 13$ and **e)** $3x - 4y = 11$ $x = 9, y = 4$

9 **a** Five is *greater* than zero
b Twenty is *greater* than two
c If $2x + 3 \geq 15$ then x is *greater than or equal to* six **d** If $5 - 3x \leq 2$ then x is *greater than or equal to* one

10 **a** x is more than or equal to 4
4, 5, 6, 7, ...
b x is more than -1
0, 1, 2, ...
c x is less than or equal to 2
... -1, 0, 1, 2
d x is less than 0
... $-3, -2, -1$

11 1

• Counting numbers	Add one each time
• Odd numbers	Add two each time
• Prime numbers	No known rule
• Fibonacci numbers	Add the first two numbers to give the third .....
• Triangle numbers	$\frac{n}{2}(n + 1)$
• Powers of 2	2^n

2 The prime number sequence
3 a) He added the first two numbers to give the third, the second and third to give the fourth.. **b)** The sixth number is 11 **c)** 2 is both even and prime **d)** $123 = 3 \times 41$ **e)** $200 - 1 = 199$ **f)** They are built in the same way, but the first two numbers are different
4 This is the Conway sequence which starts with '3'. '3' can be spoken as 'one three', and written as '13'. This becomes 'one one, one three' or '1113'. And so on ...

12 Comprehension
a) He worked in the Library of Alexandria in Egypt
b) al-Khwārizmī, is also called 'the father of algebra' **c)** He wrote thirteen books **d)** The solutions are only in whole numbers, or integers
e) Diophantus worked on algebra about 500 years before al-Khwārizmī, **f) Youth** also means adolescence or the years that he was a teenager
A **sage** is a wise man who is older as well as wiser
Fate is another word for destiny
g) He was married for five years before his son was born **h)** $\frac{1}{6}$ is larger than $\frac{1}{12}$ **i)** You can write $\frac{1}{2}$ as 0.5 **j)** He was 84 years old

Consolidation: Algebra

Exercise 4.1

1 **a)** $7 - \frac{n}{2}$ **b)** $2\dot{n} + 3$ **c)** $\sqrt{n}$ **d)** $2(n + 3)$
e) $(n + 7)^2$ **f)** $\frac{1}{2}(3n + 7)$

2 **a)** $2x + y$ **b)** $2m + 9n$ **c)** $9ab + 2a - 3b$
d) $5x^2 - y^2$ **e)** $3x^2 + 3xy + y^2$
f) $13m^2 - 5m$ **g)** no change

3 **a)** $15x^2$ **b)** $48mn^2$ **c)** $36x^3y^2$
d) $7x^2 \times 7x^2 = 49x^4$ **e)** $27a^3b^3$
f) $\frac{11xy^2}{2}$ **g)** $5m^2n^2$

149

4 a) $4x + 12$ b) $3x^2 - 3x$ c) $7y^2 - 14y$
   d) $15a + 20$
5 a) $10x - 8$ b) $3y + 18$ c) $a + 17$ d) $3b$
6 a) 5 b) 0 c) 13 d) 0 e) 8 f) 21 g) 9 h) 1
7 a) 75.4 m b) 4.46 cm
8 a) 6 km per hr b) 280 km
   c) 45 seconds
9 a) 2410 cm³ b) 1330 cm³ c) 1050 cm³
10 a) $P = 4w + 8$ b) $P = 40$ cm
   c) $A = w(w + 4)$ d) 117 cm²
11 a) $5x + 100 = 180°$ b) $x = 16°$
12 a) $V = x(x + 5)(x - 2)$ b) $V = 420$ cm³

Exercise 4.2
1 a) $x = 3$ b) $y = 4$ c) $a = -1$ d) $x = 12$
   e) $a = -4$ f) $x = 23$ g) $b = 8$
2 a) $y = \frac{10}{3} = 3\frac{1}{3}$ b) $b = \frac{4}{5}$ c) $m = 10$
   d) $x = \frac{19}{4} = 4\frac{3}{4}$
3 a) $x = 4$ b) $m = 2$ c) $z = 1\frac{1}{4}$ d) $c = -7$
4 a) $x = \frac{1}{2}$ b) $y = -4$ c) $x = \frac{8}{3}$ d) $z = 2$
5 a) $P = 2(x + 6) + 2x = 4x + 12$
   b) $x = 9$
6 a) $\theta + (\theta + 45) + (\theta - 30) = 180$,
      $3\theta + 15 = 180$ b) $\theta = 55°$
7 a) $7N + 5 = 19$ b) $N = 2$
8 a) $a = 13, b = 5$ b) $m = 1, n = 3$
   c) $x = 3, y = -1$ d) $f = 2, g = 3$
9 a) $x + y = 13$ and $4x + 2y = 38$,
      so $x = 6, y = 7$ b) $x - y = 6$ and
      $2(x + y) = 32$, so $x = 11, y = 5$
   c) $2c + p = 5$ and $3c + 2p = 9.25$,
      so $c = \$0.75, p = \$3.50$
10 a) $x \le 3$ b) $y > -2$ c) $\pi \ne 3$ d) $z \ge 0$
   e) $g < 17$
11 a) x is less than 10, b) one third is
   not equal to 0.33, c) y is greater
   than or equal to 3, d) k is greater
   than negative five, e) d is less than
   or equal to zero
12
a) $x > 1$

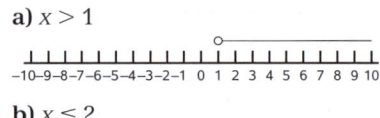

   ─┼┼┼┼┼┼┼┼┼┼┼○┼┼┼┼┼┼┼┼┼┼─
   –10-9-8-7-6-5-4-3-2-1 0 1 2 3 4 5 6 7 8 9 10

b) $x \le 2$

   ─┼┼┼┼┼┼┼┼┼┼┼┼┼●┼┼┼┼┼┼┼┼─
   –10-9-8-7-6-5-4-3-2-1 0 1 2 3 4 5 6 7 8 9 10

c) $x \ge 2$

   ─┼┼┼┼┼┼┼┼┼┼┼┼┼●┼┼┼┼┼┼┼┼─
   –10-9-8-7-6-5-4-3-2-1 0 1 2 3 4 5 6 7 8 9 10

d) $x > \frac{8}{3}$

   ─┼┼┼┼┼┼┼┼┼┼┼┼┼┼○┼┼┼┼┼┼┼─
   –10-9-8-7-6-5-4-3-2-1 0 1 2 3 4 5 6 7 8 9 10

e) $x < 2$

   ─┼┼┼┼┼┼┼┼┼┼┼┼┼○┼┼┼┼┼┼┼┼─
   –10-9-8-7-6-5-4-3-2-1 0 1 2 3 4 5 6 7 8 9 10

13 a) 3, 5, 7, 9, 11, ...
   b) 49, 44, 39, 34, 29, ...
   c) 2, 8, 32, 128, 512, ...
   d) 729, 243, 81, 27, 9 ...
   e) 2, 4, 16, 256, 65536, ...
14 a) Start with twelve, subtract five
      each time
   b) Start with 1.5, multiply by two
      each time
   c) Start with sixty four, divide by
      two each time
   d) Start with seven, add three
      each time
   e) Start with fourteen, subtract
      one half each time
15 a) 3, 9, 15, 21, 27, ...
   b) 2, 5, 10, 17, 26, ...
   c) 46, 42, 38, 34, 30.... 1, $\frac{1}{2}, \frac{1}{3}, \frac{1}{4}, \frac{1}{5}$

Chapter 5 Geometry
1 a) Obtuse angle 120° Reflex angle 240°
   b) Acute angle 75° Reflex angle 285°
   c) Reflex angle 225° Obtuse angle 135°
   d) Straight line 180°
   e) Obtuse angle 135° Reflex angle 225°
2 a) M has three <u>acute</u> angles, b) T
   has two <u>right</u> angles,
   c) M, H and E have <u>parallel</u> lines,
   d) A has two <u>obtuse</u> angles, e) The
   right angles in E add up to <u>360°</u>, f) I
   is a straight line with an angle of
   <u>180°</u>, g) V has one <u>acute</u> angle and
   one <u>reflex</u> angle, h) O contains a <u>full
   turn</u> with an angle of <u>360°</u>
3 a) I am <u>an isosceles</u> triangle.
   b) I am <u>an equilateral</u> triangle.
   c) I am a <u>scalene</u> triangle.
   d) I am a <u>right-angled</u> triangle.
   e) I am a <u>right-angled isosceles</u>
      triangle.
5

	Shape of faces	Number of faces (F)	Number of edges (E)	Number of vertices (V)	F + V − E
a) Cube	Squares	6	12	8	6 + 8 − 12 = 2
b) Cuboid	Rectangles	6	12	8	6 + 8 − 12 = 2
c) Square based pyramid	One square Four triangles	5	8	5	5 + 5 − 8 = 2
d) Triangular prism	Two triangles Three rectangles	5	9	6	5 + 6 − 9 = 2
e) Tetrahedron	Four triangles	4	6	4	4 + 4 − 6 = 2

6 a) kilometres, b) millilitres,
   c) kilograms, d) centimetres,
   e) grams, f) litres, g) millimetres
7 a) metres b) kilograms c) centimetres
   d) millilitres, grams e) 45 litres
8

Formula	Answer	Units
a $C = 2\pi r$,	195	cm
b $A = \frac{(a + b)}{2} h$	39	cm²
c $V = $ base area $\times$ height	4.5	m³
d $A = s^2$	49	cm²,
e $V = \pi r^2 h$	503	m³
f $A = bh$,	405	mm²

9 a) A, T, B, C, D, E, K, M, U, V, W, Y
   b) H, I, X
   c) N, H, I, S, Z
   d) X
   e) O
   f) F, G J, L, P, Q, R
   g) H, I
10

Name	Number of lines of symmetry	Order of rotational symmetry
a) Rectangle	2	2
b) Square	4	4
c) Parallelogram	0	2
d) Isosceles trapezium	1	0
e) Rhombus	2	2
f) Arrowhead	1	0

Consolidation: Geometry
Exercise 5.1
1 a) 143° b) 128° c) 46° d) 48°
2 a) every acute angle is 64°, every
      obtuse angle is 116° b) every
      acute angle is 39°, every obtuse
      angle is 141° c) every acute angle
      is 67°, every obtuse angle is 113°

Answers

d)

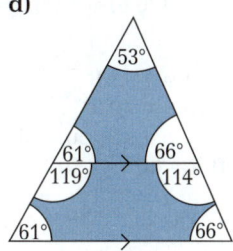

3 a) equilateral, three, length
   b) isosceles, length, two c) right-angled d) scalene, different, angles e) 180°

4

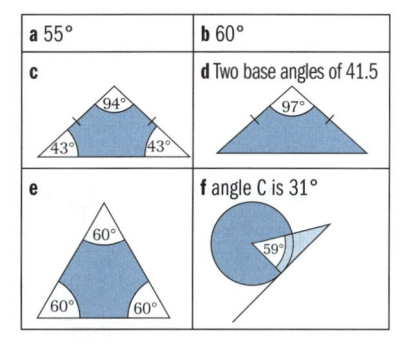

a 55°	b 60°
c	d Two base angles of 41.5
e	f angle C is 31°

5 a) DI, EI, and FI b) isosceles triangle
   c) 360 ÷ 5 = 72° d) interior angles = 180° − 72° = 108° e) exterior angles = 360° ÷ 5 = 72° f) 360°

6 a) equilateral b) All the sides are the same length c) 60° each d) 60° e) 360° f) Yes

7

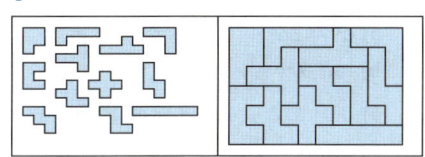

Exercise 5.2

1 $C = 2\pi r = 75.4\,cm$
   $A = \pi r^2 = 452\,cm^2$ (3 s.f)

2 $C = \pi d = 25.1\,m$
   $A = \pi r^2 = 50.3\,m^2$

3 a) $r = C \div 2\pi = 7.00\,cm$
   b) $d = 2r = 14.0\,cm$

4 $A = 2.5^2 \times \pi = 19.6\,m^2$

5 $P = 80 + \frac{1}{2} \times 2\pi \times 80 = 206\,mm$

6 (a) Area of square = $14^2 = 196\,cm^2$
   (b) Area of circles = $4 \times \pi \times 3.5^2$ = $154\,cm^2$ (c) $196 − 154 = 42\,cm^2$

7
   $A = bh$
   $A = 7 \times 12$
   $A = \underline{84\,cm^2}$

8
   $A = \frac{1}{2}bh$
   $A = \frac{1}{2} \times 2.5 \times 1.5$
   $A = \underline{1.875\,m^2}$

9
   $V = \pi r^2 h$
   $V = \pi \times 5^2 \times 12$
   $V = \underline{942\,mm^2}$

10
   $A = h\left(\frac{a+b}{2}\right)$
   $A = 5 \times \left(\frac{7+9}{2}\right)$
   $A = \underline{40\,cm^2}$

11
   $V = lbh$
   $V = 14 \times 10 \times 8$
   $V = \underline{1120\,cm^3}$

12
   $V = \frac{1}{3}Ah$
   $V = \frac{1}{3} \times 8^2 \times 5.5$
   $V = \underline{117\,cm^3}$

13
   $A = lb$
   $A = 3\frac{1}{4} \times 2\frac{1}{3}$
   $A = 7\frac{7}{12}\,m^2$

14 a) $9\,cm^2$ b) $81\,cm^2$ c) $9:81 = 1:9$

15 a) $64\,cm^3$ b) $512\,cm^3$ c) $64:512 = 1:8$

16

Ratio of length	Ratio of area	Ratio of volume
1 : 2	1 : 4	1 : 8
1 : 3	1 : 9	1 : 27
1 : 5	1 : 25	1 : 125
1 : a	1 : a^2	1 : a^3

17 $V(cone) = \frac{1}{3} \times 3.5^2 \times \pi \times 10 = 128.2817\,cm^3$
    $V(cylinder) = 3.5^2 \times \pi \times 30 = 1154.5353\,cm^3$
    $V(Total) = \underline{1280\,cm^3}$ (3 s.f)

18 $A = \frac{1}{2} \times 30 \times 14 + \frac{1}{2} \times 30 \times 36$
    $A = \underline{750\,cm^2}$

Extension

a) Tetrahedron: 4 triangular faces, 6 edges, 4 vertices, b) Cube: 6 square faces, 12 edges, 8 vertices, c) Octohedron: 8 triangular faces, 12 edges, 6 vertices, d) Dodecahedron: 12 pentagonal faces, 30 edges, 20 vertices. e) Icosahedron: 20 triangular faces, 30 edges, 12 vertices

Chapter 6 Pythagoras' theorem and trigonometry

1 a) *longest*, b) *90°*, c) *do not*, d) *must*, e) *largest*, f) *all*, g) *more than*, h) *Greece*, i) *will not* j) *17 cm*, k) *square root key*, l) *two*

3 a) *hypotenuse*, b) *opposite*, c) *adjacent*, d) *cosine*, e) *sine*, f) *tangent*, g) $\frac{e}{d}$ h) $\frac{f}{d}$

4 1 c, 2 b, 3 c, 4 a, 5 b, 6c

5

Problem	Diagram	Answer
A ladder rests against a wall, making an angle of 70° with the ground. If the ladder is six metres long, how far up the wall does it reach?		5.64 m
Miki is lying on top of a cliff, looking down at a boat. The cliff is 65 m high and Miki's angle of depression is 22°. How far away is the boat?		161 m
A rectangular field is 210 m long and 130 m wide. What angle does the diagonal make with the longer side?		31.8°

151

The base angles of an isosceles triangle are 65°. The base measures 8.6 cm. How long are the equal sides? **10.2 cm**

The shadow of a tree is 130 m long. The sun is shining at angle of 22°. How tall is the tree? **52.5 m**

6

Angle	sin	cos	tan
30°	$\frac{1}{2}$	$\frac{\sqrt{3}}{2}$	$\frac{1}{\sqrt{3}}$
60°	$\frac{\sqrt{3}}{2}$	$\frac{1}{2}$	$\sqrt{3}$
45°	$\frac{1}{\sqrt{2}}$	$\frac{1}{\sqrt{2}}$	1

7 Comprehension
a) A triangle is stronger than a quadrilateral. b) Similar triangles are the same shape. c) Congruent triangles are the same size and the same shape d) In English, the third century starts in 201 C.E. The 3rd century is the period from 201 to 300 in accordance with the Julian calendar in the Roman Empire. e) Yes, he was. f) No, it can be a triangle of any shape.
g) You need at least two, but three will give greater accuracy.

Consolidation: Pythagoras

Exercise 6.1

1 a) $y = \sqrt{5^2 + 7^2} = 8.60$ cm
   b) $y = \sqrt{6^2 - 3.5^2} = 4.87$ cm

2 a) has a right angle because $29.9^2 = 11.5^2 + 27.6^2$ **b)** does not have a right angle because $14.4^2 \neq 8.4^2 + 11.2^2$

3 a) $BC = \sqrt{6^2 + 4^2} = 7.21$ cm
   b) $BD = \sqrt{9.4^2 - 7^2} = 6.27$ cm
   c) $FG = \sqrt{8.4^2 - 5.5^2} = 6.35$ cm

4
diagonal length = $\sqrt{7^2 + 9^2}$ = **11.4 m**

5
diagonal length $\sqrt{\frac{1}{2}(7.5^2)}$ = **5.30 cm**

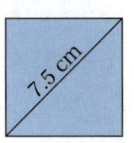

6
a) height = $\sqrt{90^2 - 45^2}$ = **77.9 mm**
b) area = $\frac{1}{2} \times 90 \times 77.9$ = **3510 mm²**

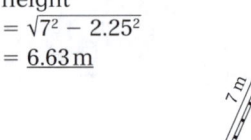

7
height = $\sqrt{7^2 - 2.25^2}$ = **6.63 m**

8 a) A(−2, 0) B(4,6) C(5,3)
b) (i) $AB^2 = 6^2 + 6^2$, $AB = \sqrt{72} = 8.49$
(ii) $BC^2 = 3^2 + 1^2$, $BC = \sqrt{10} = 3.16$
(iii) $AC^2 = 7^2 + 3^2$, $AC = \sqrt{58} = 7.62$
c) The triangle does not contain a right angle because $8.49^2 \neq 3.16^2 + 7.62^2$

Extension

a A really clever spider would imagine the net of the room.

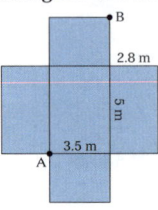

He can then choose different routes.
(i) Along the edges of the room. $5 + 3.5 + 2.8 =$ **11.3 m**
(ii) Across the floor and up the end wall. $\sqrt{5^2 + 3.5^2} + 2.8 =$ **8.90 m**
(iii) Across the side wall and along the edge of the ceiling. $\sqrt{5^2 + 2.8^2} + 3.5 =$ **9.23 m**
(iv) Directly from A to B. $\sqrt{3.5^2 + (5 + 2.8)^2} =$ **8.55 m**
(v) Across the end wall and along the edge of the ceiling. $\sqrt{3.5^2 + 2.8^2} + 5 =$ **9.48 m**
b) The fly can go directly, so $AB = \sqrt{5^2 + 2.8^2 + 3.5^2} =$ **6.71 m**

Exercise 6.2

1 a) tan 55° = 1.4281, **b)** cos 15° = 0.9659, **c)** tan 85° = 11.43,
d) sin 20° = 0.3420 **e)** cos 90° = 0
f) sin 62° = 0.8829

2 a) $\theta = 76.0°$ **b)** $\varphi = 11.8°$
c) $\alpha = 44.6°$ **d)** $\theta = 70.3°$
e) β does not exist, the sine of an angle ≤ 1 **f)** $\beta = 30°$

3 a) $\cos 38° = \frac{y}{6.8}$, $y = 5.4$
b) $\sin 70° = \frac{4.35}{y}$, $y = 4.6$
c) $\tan 56° = \frac{7.9}{y}$, $y = 5.3$
d) $\cos 53° = \frac{4.8}{y}$, $y = 8.0$

4 a) $\cos^{-1} \frac{4.8}{(5.9)} = 35.6°$
b) $\tan^{-1} \frac{6.78}{(8.95)} = 37.1°$
c) $\sin^{-1} \frac{3.8}{(4.3)} = 62.1°$
d) $\cos^{-1} \frac{8.5}{(12)} = 44.9°$

5 a) A 20°, B 15°, C 90°
b) $\tan 20° = \frac{35}{CB}$, $CB = 96.2$ m
$\tan 15° = \frac{35}{CA}$ $CA = 130.6$ m
c) $CA - CB = 34.4$ m

6 a) $\sin 32° = \frac{h}{12}$, $h = 6.36$ m
b) Area = $\frac{1}{2} \times 15 \times 6.36 = 47.7$ m²

7 $\tan 30° = \frac{h}{10}$, $h = 10 \times \frac{1}{\sqrt{3}} =$ 5.77 cm², $A = 57.7$ cm²

Extension
The height of the gnomon is $15 \times \tan 52 = 19.2$ cm

Exercise 6.3

1 a) $d^2 = 25^2 + 14^2$, $d = 28.7$ cm
b) $\tan \theta = \frac{14}{25}$, $\tau = 29.2°$

2 a) $d^2 = 28^2 + 40^2$, $d = 48.8$ km
b) $\tan \theta = \frac{40}{28}$, $\theta = 55.0°$

This figure is known as the bearing, the angle between the path of the ship and the north

3 a) angle of elevation = $\tan^{-1} \frac{324}{(900)}$ = **19.8°**
b) angle of elevation = $\tan^{-1} \frac{322}{(900)}$ = **19.7°**
With lengths as large as these there is very little difference between the answers to **(a)** and **(b)** If you are using smaller numbers, you will need to measure the height of the person and the tree or building.

Answers

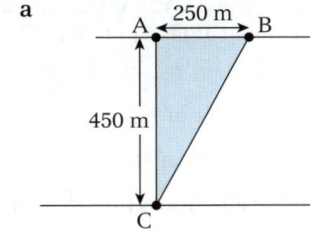

4 a) $\sin 30° = \frac{CD}{15}$, CD = <u>7.5 cm</u>
b) $\cos 30° = \frac{AD}{15}$, AD = <u>13.0 cm</u>
c) BD = AD − 11 = <u>2.0 cm</u>
d) $CB^2 = BD^2 + CD^2$, CB = <u>7.76 cm</u>
e) Area = $\frac{1}{2} × 11 × 7.5$ = <u>41.25 cm²</u>

5 a)

Felix is at C. A is the first tree, B is the second tree.

b) $CB^2 = 450^2 + 250^2$
CB = <u>515 m</u>
c) Angle = $\cos^{-1} \frac{450}{(515)}$
Angle = 29.1°

Extension
The lengths of the hypotenuses give a series:
$\sqrt{2}$, 2, $\sqrt{8}$ ($2\sqrt{2}$), 4, $\sqrt{32}$ ($4\sqrt{2}$) The rule for this series is "multiply by $\sqrt{2}$ each time"

Chapter 7 Graphs

1 a) *freezing*, b) *10 °C*, c) *horizontal*, d) *is not*, e) *colder*, f) *negative*

2 a) She weighed approximately 6.9 kilograms, b) She was between $5\frac{1}{2}$ months and 6 months old, c) (i) possibly (ii) No, d) The data is not valid after 12 months, so the graph cannot be extended accurately. e) "A <u>smooth curve</u> can be <u>drawn</u> as the <u>baby's growth</u> is <u>continuous</u>"

3 a) Roshan cycles faster on his way home.
b) On his way to visit his grandparents, Roshan is travelling at 15 km per hour.
c) From 1100 until 1130, the graph is flat because Roshan is resting.
d) Roshan has travelled 72 kms in one day.
e) Average speed = $\frac{\text{Total distance}}{\text{Total time}}$.
Roshan's average speed is 18 km per hour.

4 a) Jasmina walked steadily for an hour, then rested before continuing.
b) Javed walked steadily for an hour, but did not rest.
c) Javed walked faster than Jasmina.
d) Jasmina rested for half an hour.
e) Javed walked at a steady speed of 3 km per hour.
f) Jasmina walked at an average speed of 1.0 km per hour.

5 Shape A is a trapezium.
Shape B is a square.

6

x	y = 5 − x	
x = −1	y = 5 − (−1) = 6	(−1, 6)
x = 1	y = 5 − 1 = 4	(1, 4)
x = 2	y = 5 − 2 = 3	(2, 3)

a) The gradient of this graph is −1.
b) The y-intercept is 5.

7

a) Which graph(s) slope(s) up from left to right?	$y = 9x$, $y = \frac{1}{2}x + 5$, $y = x + 11$
b) Which graph is drawn through the origin?	$y = 9x$
c) Which graph is the steepest?	$y = 9x$
d) Which graph is the flattest?	$y = 4$ because it is horizontal
e) Which graph(s) slope(s) backwards?	$y = −2x + 3$, $y = 4 − 2x$, $y = 6 − x$
e) Which graph is horizontal?	$y = 4$

8

NIOIRG	ORIGIN	(0,0)
NEPCTETIR	INTERCEPT	[graph showing intercept]
ENUCSQEE	SEQUENCE	(1,1) (2,2) (3,3)...
IOARNCTDEOS	COORDINATES	(2, 10) (5,6)
DNIAGTRE	GRADIENT	Gradient = $\frac{\text{rise}}{\text{run}}$ [graph]
XEAS	AXES	[graph]
AUQONEIT	EQUATION	$y = 4x − 3$
ALIRNE ONUFINCT	LINEAR FUNCTION	$y = mx + c$
SEPET	STEEP	$m = 12$

9 a) René Descartes was born in *France*.
b) He was a mathematician and a *philosopher*.
c) He preferred to get up and work *late* in the morning.
d) His mathematics was based on the links between algebra and *geometry*.
e) The only subject that he felt was truly *certain* was Mathematics.
f) The instruments that he used were very *simple*.

153

g) He lived in Holland as it was *right* for his character and method of working.
h) He died in Sweden after catching *pneumonia*.

Consolidation: Graphs

Exercise 7.1

1 a) Time, b) Temperature, c) 88–89 °C, d) 5–6 °C, e) 68 °C f) 4 min – 11 min, g) as the liquid solidifies

2 a)

Graph to show extensions given by different loads on a spring

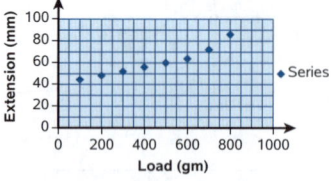

b) (i) 50 mm, (ii) 58 mm,
c) approximately 80 mm, d) No. After 600–700 g the spring begins to stretch and the graph is not directly proportional.

3 Journeys of Anna and her parents and grandparents

They will meet about 1135.

Exercise 7.2

1 a) A (2,1) C (4,5) E (−5, +2) I(−2, −1) and G (−7, 5)

b) "The line AB is 2 units long and the line CB is 4 units long"
c) gradient, $m = \frac{CB}{AB} = \frac{4}{2} = 2$
d) (i) gradient of FG $= \frac{-3}{6} = -\frac{1}{2}$
   (ii) gradient of HJ $= \frac{-1}{3} = -\frac{1}{3}$
   (iii) gradient of IJ $= \frac{-1}{1} = -1$
   (iv) gradient of EF $= \frac{0}{4} = 0$

2

Line	Equation	Gradient	Intercept
a	$y = 2 - x$	−1	2
b	$y = 5x - 2$	5	−2
c	$y = \frac{1}{2}x$	$\frac{1}{2}$	0
d	$y = x - 1$	1	−1
e	$y = 6 - 2x$	−2	6

a) The number before the 'x' gives the gradient
b) The number without 'x' is the intercept where the line crosses the y-axis
c) The line $y = \frac{1}{2}x$ goes through the origin (0,0)

3

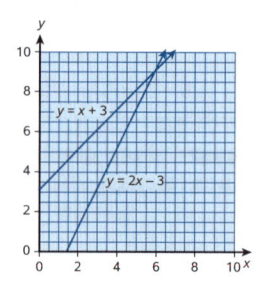

a) The lines cross at the point (6, 9)
b)
$-x + y = 3$ (1)
$-2x + y = -3$ (2)
Subtract (1) − (2) $x = 6$
Using (1) $-6 + y = 3$
          $y = 9$
c) Simultaneous equations can be solved using algebra or using a graph

4 a)

x	−4	−3	−2	−1	0	1	2
$y = -x^2 - 2x + 5$	−3	2	5	6	5	2	−3

b) The parabolas intersect at (−2, 5) and (2, −3)

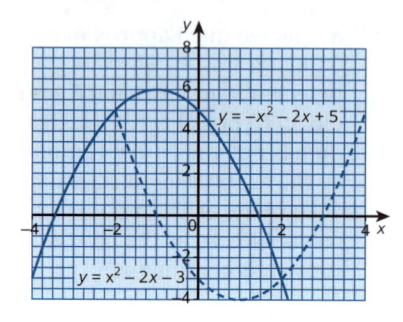

Chapter 8 Statistics

1 a) secondary, b) qualitative, c) quantitative, d) primary, e) biased

2

Survey	Source of data
a) Length of life in different countries	The Internet, newspapers, or books
b) Favourite music or singer	A questionnaire, the Internet
c) Prices of cameras	The Internet, newspapers
d) The lengths of sentences in a book	An experiment, a book
e) The time taken for different students to travel into school	Questionnaire

3 a) *half*, b) *third*, c) *more*, d) *three*, e) *discrete*, f) *measuring*, g) *most*

4 a) What is discrete data?
b) When do you use a pie chart and not a bar chart?
c) Why is it important to remember the key to your graphs?
d) Where do you find secondary data?

5 BIAS, PRIMARY, SECONDARY, DISCRETE, COUNT, CONTINUOUS, HISTOGRAM, BAR CHART

6 a) no, b) negative, c) positive

7

Plants in the sun	Height	Number/plant	Total weight
Mean	37.7 cm	6.5 cm	216 g
Median	42.5 cm	7.5	251 g
Mode		8	–
	a	b	c

Plants in the shade	Height	Number/plant	Total weight
Mean	60.8 cm	7.5	236 g
Median	60.5 cm	7.5	242.5 g
Mode	62 cm	9	
	d	e	f

a) I chose the median because it was not affected by the low value of 12 cm.
b) I chose the mode because it is an easy measure when you are counting.
c) I chose the median because it is not affected by the low value of 28 g.

Answers

d) I chose the mean because the values are not widely spread.
e) I chose the median because it is easy to calculate. I could choose the mean too, because the data is consistent.
f) I chose the median because it is not affected by the low value of 190 g.

Consolidation: Statistics

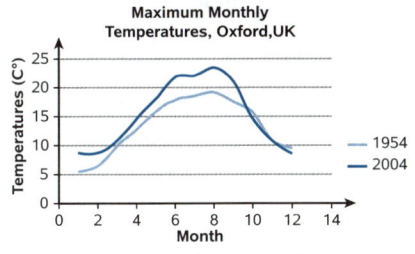

1 a) Maximum Monthly Temperatures, Oxford, UK

b) (i) 13.4 °C **(ii)** 15.2 °C
c) (i) 5.8 °C **(ii)** 7.4 °C
d) The graph shows that the general trend of temperatures was lower in 1954 than in 2004. In 1954, the last three months were warmer than those in 2004. In 2004, the mean maximum temperature was higher than that in 1954.
In 2004, the median minimum temperature was higher than that in 1954.

> Be Careful!! These figures are only true for one place and for two different years. You should not use them to make any general conclusions.

2

1954			
Rainfall (mm)	Tally	Frequency	Angle
$0 \leq r < 20$	I	1	$\frac{1}{12} \times 360 = 30°$
$20 \leq r < 40$	I	1	$\frac{1}{12} \times 360 = 30°$
$40 \leq r < 60$	IIII	5	$\frac{5}{12} \times 360 = 150°$
$60 \leq r < 80$	II	2	$\frac{2}{12} \times 360 = 60°$
$80 \leq r < 100$	II	2	$\frac{2}{12} \times 360 = 60°$
$100 \leq r < 120$	I	1	$\frac{1}{12} \times 360 = 30°$
$120 \leq r < 140$			

Rainfall, Oxford, 1954 (mm)

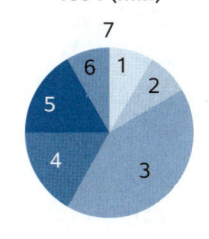

Key
1. $0 \leq r < 20$
2. $20 \leq r < 40$
3. $40 \leq r < 60$
4. $60 \leq r < 80$
5. $80 \leq r < 100$
6. $100 \leq r < 120$
7. $120 \leq r < 140$

2004			
Rainfall (mm)	Tally	Frequency	Angle
$0 \leq r < 20$			
$20 \leq r < 40$	IIII	5	$\frac{5}{12} \times 360 = 150°$
$40 \leq r < 60$	II	2	$\frac{2}{12} \times 360 = 60°$
$60 \leq r < 80$	II	2	$\frac{2}{12} \times 360 = 60°$
$80 \leq r < 100$	I	1	$\frac{1}{12} \times 360 = 30°$
$100 \leq r < 120$			
$120 \leq r < 140$	II	2	$\frac{2}{12} \times 360 = 60°$

Rainfall, Oxford, 2004 (mm)

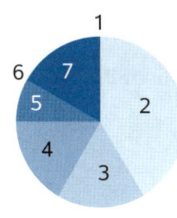

Key
1. $0 \leq r < 20$
2. $20 \leq r < 40$
3. $40 \leq r < 60$
4. $60 \leq r < 80$
5. $80 \leq r < 100$
6. $100 \leq r < 120$
7. $120 \leq r < 140$

These pie charts can be useful when you are making comparisons, but you need clear titles and a good key to explain them.

3

Sunshine (hours)	Tally	Frequency
$50 \leq r < 90$	IIII	4
$90 \leq r < 130$	II	2
$130 \leq r < 170$	II	2
$170 \leq r < 210$	III	3
$210 \leq r < 250$	I	1

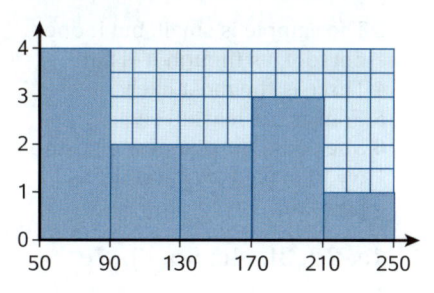

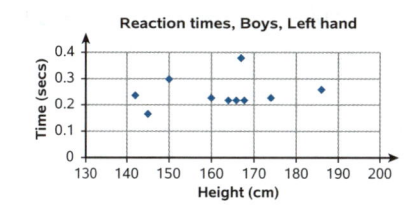

4 a) Reaction times, Boys, Left hand

b) There is no correlation between the boys' height and their reaction times when they are using their left hands.

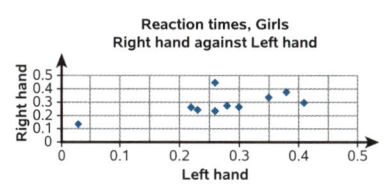

c) Reaction times, Girls Right hand against Left hand

d) There is moderate correlation between the reaction times for different hands. One point (0.03, 0.14) does not fit in with all the other data. It is an 'outlier' and the original measurement may have been wrong.
e) The mean of the girls' heights is 163.5 cm. The median of the girls' heights is 163 cm, and the mode for the girls' heights is 163 cm. The range of the heights is 185 cm − 151 cm = 34 cm
f) The data has a small range, with no outliers, so all three measures of average give answers that agree, and so all are valid.

Chapter 9 Probability

1
A 1 c, 2 f, 3 d, 4 b, 5 a, 6 e
B 1 unlikely, 2 very unlikely, 3 very likely, 4 equally likely, 5 certain 6 impossible

2
A 1 Internet search for past data
2 Survey or experiment
3 Experiment, internet search for past data
4 Experiment
5 Internet search for past data
6 Computer simulation or experiment

B 1 Each number should be equally likely, and 48 ÷ 6 = 8 so the expected score for each number is 8.
2 This is an experiment so it is not likely that all the trials will give exact answers. Lena made her own spinner and it is probably not accurate enough.

3 The sample is small, but it does not look as though it is fair.
4 Three is the most likely
5 Four is the least likely
6 She could make a new one, and try to make it as carefully as possible.

3 1a, 2d, 3f, 4c, 5g, 6b, 7e

4 1 a) p(rain) = 0.7 × 0.7 = 0.49
b) p(no rain) = 0.3 × 0.3 = 0.09

2)

a) $p(2H) = \frac{1}{4}$		Head	Tail
b) $p(2T) = \frac{1}{4}$	Head	HH	HT
c) $p(H \text{ and } T) = \frac{1}{4} + \frac{1}{4} = \frac{1}{2}$	Tail	TH	TT
d) the probabilities are the same as the boy/girl ones in the family of two children.			

3) a) p(Hockey, Monday) = $\frac{1}{6}$
b) p(G, M and T) = $\frac{1}{3} \times \frac{1}{3} = \frac{1}{9}$
c) p(F') = $\frac{1}{2}$
d) p(H, F, G) = $\frac{1}{6} \times \frac{1}{2} \times \frac{1}{3} = \frac{1}{36}$

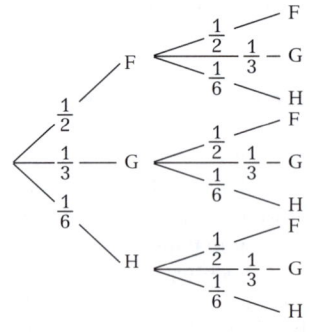

5 1 a) p(2Red) = $\frac{12}{20} \times \frac{11}{19} = \frac{33}{95}$
b) p(R, B) = $\frac{12}{20} \times \frac{8}{19} + \frac{8}{20} \times \frac{12}{19} = \frac{48}{95}$
c) p(R if B first) = $\frac{12}{19}$

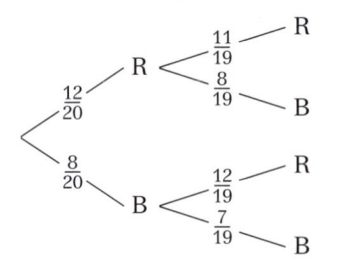

2) a) p(R') = 0.6 × 0.5 = 0.3
b) p(R, R') = 0.4 × 0.35 + 0.6 × 0.5 = 0.44

7 a) set of instructions
b) clever person
c) dishonest person
d) stopped
e) throwing
f) reasonable
g) basic
h) important
i) limits
j) surplus

Consolidation
Exercise 9.1

1 Impossible (a), unlikely (b), equally likely (e), probable (c), certain (d)

2 a) p(N = 17) = $\frac{3}{12} = \frac{1}{4}$
b) p(N ≤ 10) = $\frac{5}{12}$
c) p(N = 20) = $\frac{1}{12}$
d) p(N is a prime number) = $\frac{4}{12} = \frac{1}{3}$
e) p(N is a multiple of 3) = $\frac{4}{12} = \frac{1}{3}$

3 a) p(S ≥ 40) = $\frac{4}{10} = \frac{2}{5}$
b) p(S < 32) = $\frac{3}{10}$
c) p(M = 1.11) = $\frac{2}{10} = \frac{1}{5}$
d) p(M > 1.60) = $\frac{3}{10}$

4

Packet	1	2	3	4	5
Percentage	$\frac{26}{36} \times 100$ = 72%	80%	71%	83%	81%

a) p(S ≥ 35) = $\frac{4}{5}$ = 80%
b) p(G ≥ 75) = $\frac{3}{5}$
c) On this survey the seed company only has a 60% chance that their statement is true. You need to do some more experiments.

5 Buffon's needle. There are results on the internet. The best result was achieved in 1901 when a needle was dropped 3408 times!

Exercise 9.2

1 a) p(double tile) = $\frac{7}{28} = \frac{1}{4}$
b) p(blank tile) = $\frac{8}{28} = \frac{2}{7}$
c) p(spots add to 7) = $\frac{3}{28}$

d) p(spots subtract to 1) = $\frac{6}{28} = \frac{3}{14}$
e) p(at least one 6) = $\frac{7}{28} = \frac{1}{4}$

2 a) p(dark blue) = $\frac{2}{5}$
b) p(white) = $\frac{2}{5}$
c) p(light blue) = $\frac{1}{5}$
d) p(black) = 0

3 a) p(B) = $\frac{1}{58}$ b) p(L) = $\frac{11}{58}$
c) p(G) = $\frac{7}{58}$ d) p(Y) = $\frac{5}{58}$

4 a) i) p(orange) = $\frac{20}{45} = \frac{4}{9}$ ii) p(green) = $\frac{15}{45} = \frac{1}{3}$ iii) p(yellow) $\frac{10}{45} = \frac{2}{9}$

	orange	green	yellow
Peta's results	28	22	10
Peta expects to get	27	20	13

c) Her results are not the same as her calculations because they are experimental. Her calculations predict what she should expect. The more trials she does, the closer her experimental results will be to her predicted results.

5 a) p(he does not hit the centre the first time) = 1 − 0.64 = 0.36
b) p(he hits the centre twice) = 0.64 × 0.64 = 0.4096
c) p(he hits the centre once in two throws) = 0.64 × 0.36 + 0.36 × 0.64 = 0.4608
d) p(he does not hit the centre) = 0.36 × 0.36 = 0.1296

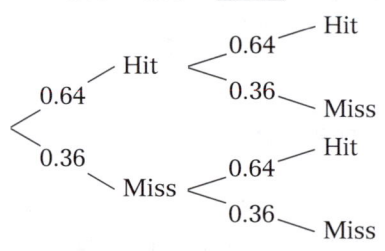

6 a) p(the bus and the car are both late) = 0.1 × 0.25 = 0.025
b) p(the bus is late, but the car is not) = 0.1 × 0.75 = 0.075

7 a) p(alphabetical order) = $\frac{1}{6}$
b) p(Anu and Charlie sit together) = $\frac{4}{6} = \frac{2}{3}$
c) p(Charlie sits between Anu and Bren) = $\frac{2}{6} = \frac{1}{3}$

ABC	BAC	CAB
ACB	BCA	CBA

Answers

8 Extension

a)

3 coins	HHH			(i) $p(3H) = \frac{1}{8}$
	HHT	HTH	THH	(ii) $p(2H,1T) = \frac{3}{8}$
	HTT	THT	TTH	(iii) $p(1H,2T) = \frac{3}{8}$
	TTT			(iv) $p(3T) = \frac{1}{8}$

b)

4 coins	HHHH						$p(4H) = \frac{1}{16}$
	HHHT	HHTH	HTHH	THHH			$p(3H,1T) = \frac{4}{16} = \frac{1}{4}$
	HHTT	HTHT	HTTH	THTH	THHT	TTHH	$p(2H,2T) = \frac{6}{16} = \frac{3}{8}$
	HTTT	THTT	TTHT	TTTH			$p(1H,2T) = \frac{4}{16}$
	TTTT						$p(4T) = \frac{1}{16} = \frac{1}{4}$

c) $p(4H) = p(4T) = \frac{1}{16}$

d) $p(5H) = p(5T) = \frac{1}{32}$

e) There is a pattern in the denominator of the fractions — $\frac{1}{2}, \frac{1}{4}, \frac{1}{8}, \frac{1}{16}, \frac{1}{32}, \frac{1}{64}$ ......the powers of 2

f) There is a pattern in the numerator of the fractions. Can you find Pascal's triangle? There are symmetries too. This was the basis of de Moivre's research.

Exercise 9.3

1 $p(2B) = \frac{4}{12} \times \frac{3}{11} = \frac{12}{132}$

$p(2W) = \frac{8}{12} \times \frac{7}{11} = \frac{56}{132} = \frac{14}{33}$

$p(1W, 1B) = \frac{8}{12} \times \frac{4}{11} + \frac{4}{12} \times \frac{8}{11}$
$= \frac{64}{132} = \frac{16}{33}$

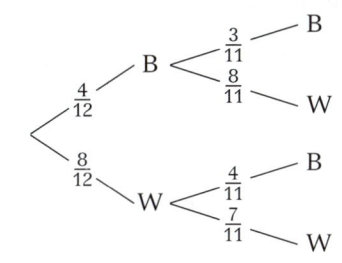

[tree diagram with branches B (3/11), W (8/11) from B (4/12); and B (4/11), W (7/11) from W (8/12)]

2 $p(2V) = \frac{5}{11} \times \frac{4}{10} = \frac{20}{110}$

$p(2C) = \frac{6}{11} \times \frac{5}{10} = \frac{30}{110}$

$p(1C, 1V) = \frac{6}{11} \times \frac{5}{10} + \frac{5}{11} \times \frac{6}{10} = \frac{60}{110}$

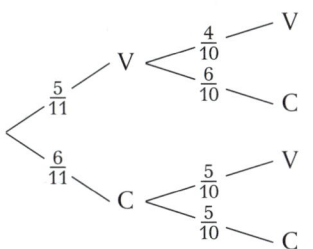

[tree diagram with V (5/11) branching to V (4/10), C (6/10); and C (6/11) branching to V (5/10), C (5/10)]

3 a) $p(3G) = \frac{9}{16} \times \frac{8}{15} \times \frac{7}{14} = \frac{504}{3360} = \frac{3}{20}$

b) $p(3B) = \frac{7}{16} \times \frac{6}{15} \times \frac{5}{14} = \frac{210}{3360} = \frac{1}{16}$

c) $p(2B*) + p(3B) = (\frac{9}{16} \times \frac{7}{15} \times \frac{6}{14})$
$+ (\frac{7}{16} \times \frac{9}{15} \times \frac{6}{14}) + (\frac{7}{16} \times \frac{6}{15} \times \frac{9}{14})$
$+ \frac{1}{16} = \frac{27}{80} + \frac{1}{16} = \frac{2}{5}$

d) $p(2G, 1B) = (\frac{9}{16} \times \frac{8}{15} \times \frac{7}{14}) + (\frac{7}{16} \times \frac{9}{15} \times \frac{8}{14}) + (\frac{7}{16} \times \frac{9}{15} \times \frac{8}{14}) = \frac{9}{20}$

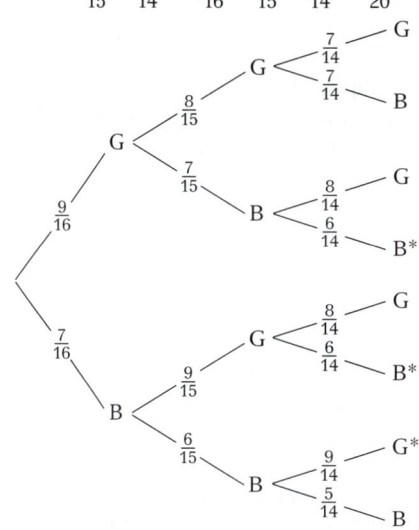

[large tree diagram showing G/B branches with probabilities]

Chapter 10 Assessment

1

Question	Calculation	Answer
If one pencil costs 65 cents, how much do three pencils cost?	65×3	195
Write down the product of six and eight	6×8	48
If a cup of tea costs 8 dirhams and a cake costs 12 dirhams, what is the cost of two cups of tea and three cakes?	$2 \times 8 + 3 \times 12$	52
Add the square root of sixteen to the square of five	$\sqrt{16} + 5^2$	29
If you think of a number, add on three, and multiply the result by two, and obtain the answer twenty two, which number did you think of?	$2(x + 3) = 22$	8

2 a) before **b)** after **c)** while **d)** before **e)** during

3 Equipment in order (top-left to bottom-right) – calculator, ruler, pen, rubber, protractor, pencil, drawing compass, pencil sharpener.

4 a) ruler **b)** calculator **c)** protractor **d)** eraser/rubber **e)** drawing compass/pair of compasses

5 a) False **b)** True
c) False **d)** True
e) False **f)** True

6 Jana will gain the most marks.

7

a) start	begin
b) assignment	task
c) right	correct d)
d) finish	complete
e) explain	make clear
f) conclusion	ending
g) wrong	mistaken
h) problem	question
i) idea	thought

Index

accuracy 25
   decimal places 25
   significant figures 25
   standard form 26–7
al-Khwarizhmi 46
Alexandria, Egypt 46
algebra 35
   consolidation exercises 48–52
   Diophantus 46–7
   equations and word problems 41
   finding a formula 39
   inequalities 43–4
   linear equations 40–1
   sequences 44–6
   simplifying algebraic expressions 36
   simultaneous equations 41–3
   substitution 37
   using formulae 37–8
angles 53–4
   acute angles 53, 56
   angle of depression 78
   angle of elevation 78
   angles between straight lines 54
   angles in parallel lines 54–5
   obtuse angles 53
   reflex angles 53, 56
   right angles 53, 59
answers 148–57
area formulae 62
assessment 128
   assignment examples 135–8
   coursework 133–4
   external examinations 131–3
   mental arithmetic tests 128
   revising for tests and examinations 130–1
   school examinations 129–30
   written class tests 129
assignments 135–8
   braking distances 136–8
   chessboard squares 135–6

bar charts 102
braking distances 136–8
Buffon's needle 125

calculators 9, 77–8
capacity 58
Cardano, Girolamo 122
chance 116
chessboard squares 135–6
Christina of Sweden 95
Cicero, Marcus Tullius (106–43 BCE) 122
circles 59–60
   chord 59
   circumference 59
   diameter 59

   important formulae 60
   radius 59
   tangent 59
compasses 7
co-ordinates 90–1
correlation 105–6
counting numbers 17
coursework 128, 133–4
cubes 58
cuboids 58
cylinders 58, 59

data 100–1
   analysing 106–8
   best average 107–8
   biased data 100
   continuous data 103
   discrete data 102
   displaying 101–6
   interpreting 108
   primary data 100
   qualitative data 100
   quantitative data 100
   secondary data 100
decimal places 25
Descartes, René (1596–1650) 95
Diophantus 46–7
direct proportion/variation 23

Einstein, Albert 34
equations 43
   equations and word problems 41
   linear equations 40–1
   simultaneous equations 41–3
equipment 5–6, 10, 130
   books and paper 8
   calculators 9, 77–8
   drawing compasses 7
   folders and dividers 9
   protractors 7
Euler's Formula 59
examinations 128
   external examinations 131–3
   revising 130–1
   school examinations 129–30

factors 19
Fibonacci numbers 45
folders 9
formulae 35, 37–8, 39
   circles 60
   Euler's Formula 59
   remembering 76
   volume formulae 62–3
fractions 20
Frisius, Gemma 80

geometry 53
   angles 53–4

angles between straight lines 54
angles in parallel lines 54–5
Cartesian geometry 95
circles 59–60
consolidation exercises 67
mensuration 61–4
metric measures 60–1
pi (π) 60
polygons with more than four sides 57–8
quadrilaterals 57
solids 58–9
symmetry 64–6
triangles 55–6
glossary 139–47
Golden Ratio 33
gradients 92
graphs 86
   co-ordinates 90–1
   consolidation exercises 96–9
   conversion graphs 86–7
   curved graphs 94–5
   distance-time graphs 88–90
   real life graphs 87–8
   scatter graphs 105–6
   straight line graphs 91–3

Hardy, G. H. 28
histograms 103, 104–5
Howitt, Mary 82
Huyghens, Christiaan 122
hypotenuse 73–4

indices 24–5
integers 17
intercepts 92
investigations 134

Leonardo da Vinci 33
Liu Hui 80

mensuration 61
   area formulae 62
   volume formulae 62–3
mental arithmetic tests 128
metric measures 60–1
mirror image 64
mirror line 64
de Moivre, Abraham 122
multiples 19

nanometres 34
numbers 17
   1729 28
   accuracy 25–7
   consolidation exercises 29–34
   fractions 20
   number sets 17
   operations 17–18

Index

order of operations 18
percentages 21–2
powers and indices 24–5
prime numbers, factors and multiples 19
problem solving 27–8
ratio and proportion 23–4

operations 17–18

parabolas 94
Parthenon, Athens 33
Pascal, Blaise (1623–1662) 52
Pascal's Triangle 52
pentominos 69
percentages 21–2
pi (π) 60
pictograms 102
pie charts 103
planets 27
Plato 33
Platonic solids 71
polygons 55
    polygons with more than four sides 57–8
polyhedrons 59
powers 24–5
prime numbers 19
prisms 59
probability 115
    conditional probability 120–1
    consolidation exercises 124–7
    experimental probability 117–18
    probability questions 115
    probability scale 116
    probability that it will not happen 117
    theoretical probability 118–19
    using diagrams 119–20
    words used in the study of probability 122–3
problem solving 27–8
proportions 23–4
protractors 7
pyramids 58, 59
Pythagoras 33
Pythagoras' theorem 72
    consolidation exercises 81–5
    Pythagoras' triples 73
    using 73–4

quadratic functions 94
quadrilaterals 57, 66

Ramanujan, Srinivasa 28
rational numbers 17
ratios 23
revision 129, 130–1

samples 108
significant figures 25
solids 58–9, 71
standard form 26–7
statistics 100
    analysing data 106–8
    collecting the data 100–1
    consolidation exercises 111–14
    displaying the data 101–6
    interpreting the data 108
    weird world of statistics 109–10
    working with statistics 100

study 11, 15–16
    basics 11
    organisation 14
    studying in class 12–13
    studying on your own 13
    using a maths textbook 14
sundials 84
symmetry 64–6
    line symmetry 64
    rotational symmetry 65

tests 128, 129
    revising 130–1
tetrahedrons 59
Thales 75
trials 118
triangles 55–6
    equilateral triangles 55
    isosceles triangles 56
    right-angled triangles 56
    scalene triangles 55
triangulation 80
trigonometry 72, 75
    consolidation exercises 81–5
    exact values 79–80
    problems in words 78–9
    remembering formulae 75
    triangulation 80
    using your calculator 77–8

varying directly 23
volume 58, 62–3